BE RESTORED

"Reading this book took longer than expected, for I wasn't merely reading a book, I was encountering the Lord anew in my heart."

From the afterword by Fr. Mark Toups
Vicar general of the Diocese of Houma-Thibodaux

"This is an exceptionally powerful book. I honestly can't think of anyone I know who will not benefit immensely from this—myself very much included! I don't think I have ever come across a book on healing sexual wounds that is quite as raw and direct as this, and that is precisely why it has such a powerful impact. I especially appreciated the exercises at the end of each chapter. All too often this essential step is neglected, leaving the reader with no immediate, prayerful application. Finally, as a victim of childhood sexual abuse, I found particularly helpful the chapters dedicated to understanding and healing that trauma."

Fr. John Riccardo
Founder of Acts XXIX

"Reading this book felt like finding a gemstone in the midst of a wasteland. Numerous authors write about sexual brokenness, but none address the subject with a complete understanding of the causes that Bob Schuchts has in this book. He offers not only insightful perspectives on the core problems but also his expertise on what is needed to destroy disordered desires to find the freedom to reclaim God's plan for sexual wholeness. We speak from personal experience when we say the message of this book can save your soul and marriage. We plan to order this book by the case and distribute it to the many people we meet who need to glean Schuchts's wisdom."

Bruce and Jeannie Hannemann
Directors of RECLAIM Sexual Health

"A gifted healer and writer, Bob Schuchts dives into areas of deep shame and brokenness and surfaces the truth that Jesus can restore us. His sound understanding of Catholic anthropology, psychology, and spirituality—culled from more than forty years of clinical and pastoral experience—makes this a must-read for all who seek to restore and be restored."

Andrew Comiskey
Founding director of Desert Stream Ministries

"When I invited Bob Schuchts to teach a course for the Theology of the Body Institute on sexual healing and redemption in 2009, little did I know what an impact it would have on my own life. Wounds I didn't even know I had came to light, and thus began a much deeper journey of healing. Schuchts's insights in this book—gained through decades of experience as a therapist, teacher, and retreat leader, but even more through taking his own healing journey seriously—serve as a gentle and luminous invitation into the open side of Christ, the source of all our healing."

Christopher West
President of the Theology of the Body Institute

"The reality of the oversexualized culture can be daunting. When we experience its effects through woundedness and sin we are often left devastated and hopeless. Although the path is not easy, there is a path to restoration. Through vulnerable stories, practical tools, and decades of experience, Bob Schuchts invites readers to be honest about their sexual history so the light of Christ can shine through and heal. Too often authors write about sexual issues from afar or circle around them, but Schuchts, with the confidence of Jesus, guides us through our sexual stories into restoration and healing."

Jake Khym
Executive director of Life Restoration Ministries

"With personal stories and biblical truth, Bob Schuchts courageously treads into the darkness of wounds and trauma to bring them into the healing light of Christ's love. His masterful articulation of how a person's sexuality is impacted by the wounds in their history allows the reader to enter new levels of self-awareness and understanding of both their past and present struggles. This knowledge, along with the practical tools offered, are stepping stones to freedom in Jesus. *Be Restored* is a must-read for anyone desiring freedom, hope, and healing in their sexuality."

Heather Khym
Cohost of *Abiding Together* Podcast

"*Be Healed* wonderfully broke open the healing conversation for all of us, and *Be Restored* stands right beside it as its continuation and well-developed completion. Bob Schuchts gently yet courageously walks with the reader into the painful depths of sexual brokenness and offers a beautiful pathway from darkness to light in Christ Jesus. Insightful, piercing, and practical, this book will bless all who read it."

Fr. John Burns
Author of *Lift Up Your Heart*

"Our world, our Church, and our families are experiencing an unprecedented amount of brokenness. All too often, individuals who carry deep sexual wounds enter their vocations or ministries seeking to offer the wholeness to others that they have yet to receive in their own lives. For this reason, the work of Bob Schuchts and the John Paul II Healing Center helping others find healing and peace from sexual brokenness is foundational to the new evangelization."

Jason Evert
Founder of Chastity Project

"This book will challenge you, comfort you, convict you, and call you to a deeper love than you ever knew was possible but always ached to experience."

From the foreword by Sr. Miriam James Heidland, S.O.L.T.
Author of *Loved As I Am*

"Bob Schuchts shows us that mercy is not a quick fix. Mercy is power. It leaves us stronger for our wounds that have been healed. This is a biblical principle too often forgotten. 'When I am weak, then I am strong,' said St. Paul. And 'when sin abounded, grace abounded all the more.' Jesus himself tells us: those who have been forgiven much, love more. The world needs this book now more than ever!"

Scott Hahn
Catholic theologian and author

"This is a desperately needed book. *Be Restored* gets to the heart of our sexual brokenness and offers lasting healing and restoration. It doesn't provide a Band-Aid approach; it's more like open-heart surgery with Jesus, Our Divine Physician. I have benefitted tremendously from the conference that inspired this book and I am confident *Be Restored* will bless many people."

Matt Fradd
Author of *The Porn Myth*

"It's hard to imagine anyone in our culture today who doesn't need to read this book. It gets to the source of so many of our struggles and helps remove the obstacles to our faith, our identity, and our efforts to live a whole and abundant life in Christ. A must-read!"

Carrie Gress
Author of *The Marian Option*

BE RESTORED

Healing Our Sexual Wounds through Jesus' Merciful Love

BOB SCHUCHTS

AVE MARIA PRESS AVE Notre Dame, Indiana

Nihil Obstat: Héctor R.G. Pérez, S.T.D., C.S.L.J.
        Censor Librorum

Imprimatur: +William A. Wack, C.S.C.
        Bishop of Pensacola-Tallahassee
        Given at Pensacola, FL on 25 May 2021

The *Nihil Obstat* and *Imprimatur* are official declarations that a book or pamphlet is free of doctrinal or moral error. No implication is contained therein that those who have granted the *Nihil Obstat* or *Imprimatur* agree with its contents, opinions, or statements expressed.

Founded in 1865, Ave Maria Press is a ministry of the United States Province of Holy Cross.

www.avemariapress.com

Paperback: ISBN-13 978-1-64680-023-0

E-book: ISBN-13 978-1-64680-024-7

Cover image © EXTREME-PHOTOGRAPHER / GettyImages.com.

Cover design by Ave Maria Press. Text design by Andy Wagoner.

Printed and bound in the United States of America.

Library of Congress Cataloging-in-Publication Data
Names: Schuchts, Bob, author.
Title: Be restored : healing our sexual wounds through Jesus' merciful love
    / Bob Schuchts.
Description: Notre Dame, Indiana : Ave Maria Press, [2021] | Includes
    bibliographical references. | Summary: "This book is an essential guide
    to healing sexual wounds. It highlights paths to freedom from sexual
    sin, shame, and identity confusion. Readers will discover the reasons
    behind the emotional pain linked with sexual wounds"-- Provided by
    publisher.
Identifiers: LCCN 2021018963 | ISBN 9781646800230 (paperback) | ISBN
    9781646800247 (ebook)
Subjects: LCSH: Sex--Religious aspects--Catholic Church. | Psychic
    trauma--Religious aspects--Catholic Church. | Counseling--Religious
    aspects--Catholic Church. | BISAC: RELIGION / Christianity / Catholic |
    RELIGION / Christian Ministry / Counseling & Recovery
Classification: LCC BX1795.S48 S44 2021 | DDC 241/.664--dc23

The Spirit of the Sovereign Lord *is on me,*
because the Lord *has anointed me*
to proclaim good news to the poor.
He has sent me to bind up the brokenhearted,
to proclaim freedom for the captives
and release from darkness for the prisoners,
to proclaim the year of the Lord's *favor*
and the day of vengeance of our God,
to comfort all who mourn,
and provide for those who grieve in Zion—
to bestow on them a crown of beauty
instead of ashes,
the oil of joy
instead of mourning,
and a garment of praise
instead of a spirit of despair.
They will be called oaks of righteousness,
a planting of the Lord
for the display of his splendor.

Isaiah 61:1–3

CONTENTS

FOREWORD

Every now and then a deeply anointed book comes along that is a particular sign of and answer to the heartbreak of our times. The book you are about to read is that precious treasure.

Within our hearts and within our society and world, we see deep pain and brokenness in our masculinity and femininity, within how we live as men and women, as sons and daughters of God. We see the brokenness of our failure to love and how we have all been pierced to the core of our being by the rupture of sin and the entrance of suffering. All of us have moments in our lives that we do not wish to speak of and memories we would rather forget. For many of us, these sorrowful mysteries remain unspoken, plunged to the outposts of our hearts and minds, exiled within a deep sea of misery, shame, and confusion. For others, we try to "get over it," often telling ourselves and others just to be holier and wondering why we still have areas of hardness of heart, why the pain and self-condemnation still come back, and why we feel we have to try so hard to be good and accepted and loved just as we are.

These are deep mysteries, my dear friends, and they are sacred parts of our stories to be tenderly encountered and brought into communion. The restoration of the masterpiece that is you is a lifelong work, and Jesus is the exquisite artist who makes all things new. There is nothing that has ever happened to you or that you have done that is beyond the power of God to heal. And he wants to do so. Jesus did not come to condemn us. He came to save us. He came to save you in every single place you have ever found yourself. He came to save you in your most glorious moment and in your most shameful secret. And he comes to you again right now. He gently leads you and guides you.

People often ask me if the ongoing journey of recovery, the revealing of wounds and the restoration of the heart, is worth it. I can tell you with resounding clarity, *Yes!* In the past fifteen years of journeying through my story that contains addiction, sexual trauma, and other types of trauma, there is nothing more agonizingly beautiful than the continual paschal mystery of every moment of my life united to Jesus in his suffering, death, and resurrection. I am convinced that the only way is through. And amen to it. For even now we begin to taste and experience the glorious freedom of the children of God.

This book will challenge you, comfort you, convict you, and call you to a deeper love than you ever knew was possible but always ached to experience. Whether you yourself have suffered sexual trauma, have inflicted it on others, or are only now beginning to see the effects of wounding in your life, there is hope. You are made for glory. You are being restored. You are on a glorious path to the Lord himself, and we are all in this together. So take heart, dear friends. You are tenderly and eternally loved.

Sr. Miriam James Heidland, S.O.L.T.

GOOD NEWS FOR THE AFFLICTED

*The Spirit of the Lord G*OD *is
upon me . . . He has sent me to
bring good news to the afflicted.*
—Isaiah 61:1 (NASB)

The conference room, overlooking the rolling Amish countryside in southeastern Pennsylvania, quickly filled to capacity. The nervous energy and anticipation in the room was palpable as the students settled into their seats. I felt honored to be invited to teach this course on "Sexual Healing and Redemption" for the Theology of the Body Institute and grateful to be accompanied by my good friend Fr. Mark Toups, who would serve as our chaplain for the week.

After nearly three years of preparing the material for this course, I felt a mixture of excitement and nervousness. My own feelings were compounded by the rising anxiety among the students that permeated the atmosphere of the retreat center. Most had taken other courses at the institute, but they somehow intuited that *this course* was going to involve a deeper immersion into their sexual brokenness, before experiencing the healing and redemption that the course title promised.

Sensing the nervousness among the students, Fr. Mark wisely opened with a prayer welcoming the Holy Spirit's presence. He then offered a few words of exhortation that brought immediate peace to the participants, and to me as I prepared to give an overview of the material. Here is a paraphrase of Fr. Mark's opening remarks:

> It's normal to feel anxious as we begin this course, as
> we address our sexual brokenness. We all have sexual
> wounds, and for some of us these may run very deep.
> But you don't need to muster more courage right now.
> Courage is not the opposite of fear. The opposite of
> fear is *communion*. The only answer to your fear and
> anxiety is the knowledge that Jesus is here, intimately
> present with us. He will personally walk with each of
> you through these five days.

After Fr. Mark finished his brief exhortation, he introduced me and
told the class I had been working with his seminarians for the past
several years. To encourage them, he shared about the healing and
restoration that he and his seminarians had received. As I stood and
greeted the class, I began a bit tentatively, feeling unusually nervous.
But within a few minutes, I experienced a surge of confidence, sensing
the inspiration of the Spirit as I spoke.

Piggybacking on Fr. Mark's comments, I shared that Jesus' entire
mission was one of redemption and restoration. After reciting one of
my favorite passages from scripture, from Isaiah 61, I emphasized that
Jesus proclaimed these verses as his messianic mission (in Luke 4). I
assured the class that Jesus' mission of restoration is as real today as
it was two thousand years ago.

Applying the phrases from Isaiah 61, I continued:

> If you have been sexually violated in any way, your
> trust has been betrayed and your heart has been
> wounded. Jesus desires to heal your broken heart and
> give you joy instead of mourning. If you are struggling
> with habitual sexual sins or compulsions, you are in
> captivity. He desires to bring you into his glorious
> freedom. In the place of your shame, he intends to give
> you double honor, and to offer you beauty instead of
> ashes. He desires to restore the generations of your
> family and to make you oaks of righteousness, a plant-
> ing of the Lord for his glory (see Isaiah 61:1–7).

Looking at the attentive faces around the room, I could tell these truths were deeply penetrating many of their hearts. They were also touching my own heart. I stopped briefly and allowed myself to feel the impact of these truths. In those few seconds, I reflected on what Jesus had been doing in my own life and in my family over the years, healing my broken heart, freeing me from sin, healing the generations of our family, and replacing my shame with his glory. My presence in teaching this course was evidence of all he had been doing in my life and in our family. I thought about all the ways he led me to face my sexual sins and wounds over the years and the restoration he brought about in the generations of my family. (I will share elements of this throughout the book.)

In that moment, I felt prompted to do something I had not anticipated and had never done before in public. Liberated from the shackles of shame, I began to vulnerably share with the attendees about those areas of sexual sin and wounds in my own life and in our family, and how the Lord continues to bring restoration. After my personal sharing, I emphasized again, "This is Jesus' desire for each of you. He promises to reveal his glory in the places of your shame." I continued: "That means he isn't satisfied merely eliminating your sin and healing your wounds. The area that you are most ashamed of right now is the area he most desires to reveal his glory in your life." As I spoke these words, a stillness descended upon the room. A collective sense of awe came upon all of us, as we pondered that reality. In the quietness, I encouraged everyone to reflect on the deepest area of sexual shame in their life, past or present, and to think of what it would mean not only to have that shame dispelled but also for it to become the very area of his glory shining in and through their life.

Restoring the Glory

You may be wondering why I am sharing all this with you, about an event that took place more than a decade ago. The reason is straightforward. These promises from Isaiah 61 are for *you*. The teaching from that first class at the Theology of the Body Institute is the foundation for the book you hold in your hands. Sr. Miriam, who wrote the foreword, teaches a version of this material with me at the John Paul II Healing Center. The conference is now called Restoring the Glory. (The talks and workbook are available on our website at jpiihealingcenter.org).

As Sr. Miriam can attest, every time we teach this material, we see Jesus do amazing things in the lives of the attendees. Obviously, none of us is completely restored in a week because restoration is a lifelong process. But as you will see later in the book, Jesus did visit that class at the Theology of the Body Institute (TOBI), in ways beyond anything any of us could have imagined. He continues to amaze us every time we share this teaching.

I am confident that Jesus desires to bring restoration in every area of your sexual brokenness, past or present. My continual experience as a therapist, teacher, and conference leader applying these truths assures me that he will restore you to sexual wholeness to the degree that you invest yourself in this process and actively seek his help. If you have experienced any kind of sexual brokenness in your life—and we all have—you realize that these wounds can be a source of ongoing shame and intense anguish, long after the events themselves.

Whether from broken attachments, identity distortions, sexual compulsions, sexual sins, or sexual abuse, our unhealed wounds have robbed us of the fulfillment we desire. We are left mired in shame, rather than radiating God's glory. These wounds have left each of us with a lingering belief that "something is inherently wrong with me." We may believe any of the following identity lies: "I am inadequate," "I am bad," "I am dirty," "I'm perverted," "I'm tarnished," "I'm ugly," "I'm weak," "I'm unlovable," and so forth. It is within these very areas of shame in each of our hearts that Jesus speaks his astounding words of hope and restoration: "In place of your shame I will give you double honor" (Is 61:4).

This is why Jesus came to earth: to restore the glory of our broken human nature. He is the embodiment of graciousness and truth (Jn 1:14). As Sr. Miriam is fond of saying, "Only authentic love can restore broken and distorted love." His merciful love is the antidote to our shame. But this battle between love and shame is ongoing. Christian psychiatrist Dr. Curt Thompson observes: "All that we do . . . is done in response to love and shame competing for our attention."[1]

Shame is the inner consciousness of our sin and our brokenness. Left unaddressed, it becomes a shield blocking our capacity to give and receive love. Toxic shame keeps us in hiding. It isolates us, fragments us internally, thwarts our creativity, and leaves us in constant fear of being condemned. Genuine love, on the other hand, is the only force on earth that can break through our shame and restore us to wholeness. God's love reveals the truth of our identity in a world of confusing identities. Love integrates us interiorly, while restoring our communion with God and others.[2]

After forty years of accompanying people of all backgrounds and ages on their healing journey, I am convinced that Thompson's observations are applicable to every person. We all know this fierce battle, between the competing forces of love and shame, in the depths of our being. This spiritual battle is fought most fiercely in the area of our sexuality. Have you ever wondered why sexual shame seems most powerful? Sexuality is one of God's most beautiful gifts and reveals the most intimate aspects of our person, physically, emotionally, and spiritually. When violated in any way, our sexuality becomes the target of the deepest shame.

I write in the hope that you and I will recognize the intense battle in our hearts between shame and love, especially in the area of our sexuality, and fight valiantly until we experience "the glorious freedom of the children of God" (Rom 8:21).

Overview

This book is the culmination of years of experience and study about the process of healing and restoration. In many cases, I have included stories from my own life, as well as those from family members and men and women I have accompanied in the process of restoration. To protect the privacy of individuals, I have used pseudonyms wherever necessary.

Part I begins with an exploration of the many sources of our sexual shame and brokenness and how these affect us and our relationships. The individual chapters examine areas of our sexual wounds, psycho-sexual deprivations, identity distortions, sexual compulsions, sexual sins, and sexual trauma, in light of God's design for sexual wholeness.

Part II is a guide to restoring sexual integrity. By bringing our woundedness and shame to Jesus, we discover ways to experience freedom, healing, and integration. This involves renouncing the barriers that keep us bound in shame and pain, releasing the trauma of our sexual wounds, and forgiving those who have hurt us. The appendices at the end of the book provide tried and tested prayers and activities that are essential for restoration.

My prayer is that you will find this book to be more than an insightful resource. I believe it can also lead you into life-changing encounters with the merciful love of Jesus and some of the most profound healing you have ever experienced in your life. Each chapter includes eternal wisdom from scripture and Church teaching, as well as insights from my personal and professional experience. I also draw on the knowledge and experience of those who have walked this journey personally, as well as those who have accompanied others in the restoration process. At the end of each chapter, you will find "Take a Moment" reflection questions and a "Personal Activity." I can assure you that if you will take these seriously, you will experience substantial freedom and healing.

As you work your way through this book, I encourage you to be kind and gracious to yourself and those you accompany, while remaining patient and hopeful as the process of restoration unfolds (see 1 Corinthians 13:4).

Patience and Kindness

Because this process is deeply personal and can sometimes evoke strong emotions, including stirring up shame, I offer a note of caution as you reflect and work through the activities. Be patient and kind with yourself and with the unfolding of your own story. Healing from the effects of sexual wounds and shame is not a quick fix. Rather, it is a work of deep and ongoing restoration through God's grace and mercy. Though glorious in many ways, it is not always without challenges and obstacles.

If you have been sexually wounded, are a family member or friend of someone who has been, or have participated in the sexual wounding of another, you may experience increased feelings of shame, anxiety, depression, sorrow, or anger as you read the stories of brokenness or learn about the process of healing and recovery. If this is the case, I encourage you to pause and allow some time for reflection and prayer so you can restore your peace. As Fr. Mark told the class at TOBI, *you are not alone*. Rest secure in the knowledge that Jesus is with you throughout the process. Remember his kindness and compassion revealed in Isaiah 61 and internalize these truths for yourself. Be attentive to your reactions. Notice which stories or ideas trigger these feelings and why. Also pay attention to topics you find yourself wanting to skip over or resist. These probably reveal specific areas of your shame and brokenness. The entirety of the book will help you explore where those reactions are rooted in your personal history. Appendices 1–4 will help you work through their deeper roots.

You may also benefit from one or more of the resources listed in appendix 5, including the healing conferences, books, or workbooks that are available through the John Paul II Healing Center or my *Restore the Glory* podcast with Catholic therapist Jake Khym.

As you begin, I pray you will encounter the merciful love of Jesus in every area of your sexual sins, wounds, and shame. I ask Jesus to give you an abiding confidence in his presence and in the power of the Holy Spirit to turn your mourning into joy and transform your shame into his glory. May you become his oak of righteousness, a planting of the Lord for his glory (Is 61:1–4).

PART I

REVEALING OUR SEXUAL BROKENNESS

You may have noticed the subtitle of this book emphasizing Jesus' merciful love and *our* sexual wounds. We are in this together. We all have sexual wounds. It is not hard to see that sexual brokenness is endemic to our culture and present within our Church. But if we look closely enough, we can also recognize how sexual sins and wounds have affected our families and each of us personally. I daresay that sexual wounds, and the shame they engender, have become embedded into the fabric of our souls, many of our relationships, and into our cultural norms. In this broken world, I believe we are all wounded in our sexuality in one way or another. We all need ongoing encounters with Jesus' merciful love. Part I of this book lays out the areas of our sexual woundedness.

- Chapter 1, "Shining Light in the Darkness," identifies the various ways we have been sexually wounded and how they impact us and our relationships. I share some of my personal and family experiences, as well as my awakening when I began my career as a family therapist that these realities of sexual brokenness are endemic in all families. At the end of the chapter, you will have an opportunity to identify the various sources of your sexual wounds, within two umbrella categories: sexual violations and psychosexual deprivations.

- Chapter 2, "Living the Truth in Love," focuses on our integral human development and how we can become wounded in our psychosexual identity. Many of us have hidden wounds from experiences of deprivation or distortions in love, which hinder our maturity and lead to disintegration. At the end of the chapter you will have an opportunity to understand how deprivations of love have affected your personal psychosexual development.

- Chapter 3, "Reflecting God's Image," focuses on our God-given identity as male and female and the factors that influence our acceptance or rejection of our gender. When our identity is not affirmed by our family and culture, or has been disrupted by sexual wounds, we develop distortions in our identity. Conversely, when our gender is affirmed and accepted, we become increasingly more confident in who we are. The chapter ends with reflection and application questions, allowing you to assess your own gender awareness and acceptance.

- Chapter 4, "Lured by Desires," explores how wounds in our psychosexual development and gender identity are often the driving force behind our disordered desires and sexual compulsions. Facing these underlying wounds and unmet needs enables us to experience freedom and integration in our sexual desires. You will have an opportunity at the end of the chapter to explore and reflect on how your sexual desires express unmet needs and unhealed wounds.

- Chapter 5, "Crushed by Iniquities," acknowledges the crushing reality of sexual sin and how these inevitably wound the heart of God, our own integrity, and our intimate relationships. Conversely, when we honor God's holy boundaries for sexual expression, we reverence every person as a temple of the Holy Spirit. The personal activity at the end of the chapter offers an opportunity for you to review your sexual history and receive Jesus' mercy for any areas where you have not lived according to God's design for your sexuality.

- Chapter 6, "Mourning Broken Hearts," examines the heart-shattering trauma resulting from sexual violations. In this chapter, we carefully examine the "seven deadly wounds" and corresponding "identity distortions" that remain long after the experiences of sexual violation have occurred, offering the hope of restoration when these are uncovered and the trauma is released. The activity at the end of the chapter provides an opportunity to uncover these wounds and identity lies in your own life.

Considered together, these chapters show how wounds in our psychosexual development distort our gender identity, fueling our sexual compulsions and leading to sexual sins, which inevitably cause sexual trauma. All point to our need for a Savior.

Dear Reader, I am sensitive to where you are as you begin this book. We are addressing some very tender topics related to sexuality. I have tried to balance honesty with modesty in my descriptions of sexuality, in my own story and in all the others. *The use of such stories and examples helps to illustrate the deep and lasting impact that trauma has upon the heart and life of one who suffers it. In the same moment, these stories help to make concrete what otherwise might remain only theoretical.* With that said, I realize that mentioning certain words and experiences can trigger emotional reactions. Please know that my intention is to bring you healing and not trigger you in any way. But if it does happen, feel free to pause or skip over those sections. If you are triggered in any way by the stories or descriptions in this chapter or throughout the book, you may find it helpful to go back to the appendices immediately to use the prayers and exercises there to help you return to peace.

1

SHINING LIGHT IN THE DARKNESS: IDENTIFYING OUR SEXUAL WOUNDS

Live as children of light, for light produces
every kind of goodness . . . and truth.
—Ephesians 5:8–9

When I began my career as a marriage and family therapist in the early 1980s, I had no formal training concerning how to help people heal from sexual wounds. Nor had I faced areas of my own sexual sin and wounds, or my self-righteous judgments toward family members and others in the areas of their sexual brokenness. As a result, I did not realize how much sexual shame affected nearly every person and every family, including my own. My graduate-school education focused primarily on relationship dynamics and generational patterns of family interaction. At the time, I had little understanding of how these relational dynamics and generational patterns might be intertwined with sexual wounds and shame. By the time I retired thirty-five years later, I realized that some degree of sexual wounding and shame was endemic to nearly every person and family I met with as a therapist.

My naivete from graduate school did not last long. The first three people I counseled after opening my therapy practice had experienced profound wounding from very diverse kinds of sexual violations. I soon realized that these experiences from their past were continuing to have a significant impact on their current relationships, including the way they saw themselves (identity), how they related to God (worship), and how they interacted with their loved ones (intimacy).

The first person I counseled was Susan, a female graduate student in her early twenties.[1] She told me in the initial interview that she had no religion and did not believe in God. Halfway through our first therapy session she revealed that her father had sexually molested her throughout her childhood. She added, without much emotion, that she had also been sexually involved with her three previous therapists. After that initial meeting, she never talked about these experiences again, and I was reluctant to ask. Instead, she spent session after therapy session sharing intimate details of her sexual relationship with her live-in boyfriend. Desiring to be supportive, I sat quietly and listened. But underneath my professional veneer, I felt extremely uncomfortable with the detail of her sharing. I felt bombarded by her incessant barrage of sexual words and images, but I never considered the possibility that I could redirect our conversation.

At the time, I did not realize that her sharing was stirring unresolved issues in my own sexual history. Nor did I realize until after we terminated therapy that she was unwittingly testing me to see if I would be the next therapist to sexually violate her. Thank God I was never tempted. Looking back, I am not sure I did much to help her heal during these therapy sessions, except the most important thing, which was to treat her with the dignity and respect she deserved but had failed to receive from other men.

After she graduated and moved away, Susan wrote me a letter to thank me for showing her that it was possible to have a man honor her and not use her sexually. She shared that it was a huge breakthrough for her and that, as a result, she had subsequently broken up with her boyfriend because she was feeling used in that relationship as well. She also realized in retrospect that she had been using him. It dawned on her after therapy that she had unconsciously reenacted her earlier sexual abuse with her father with her boyfriend, as well as with her three previous therapists. She expressed joy, hoping that this lifelong pattern of abuse and sexual compulsion had come to an end.

The second person I accompanied in therapy was a middle-aged man I'll call Jimmy. He came to therapy desiring to address his suicidal depression. Within a few sessions it became apparent that he carried a lot of unresolved pain and shame from his childhood. As a twelve-year-old boy he had been taunted by older boys in the locker room about his physical anatomy (while he was naked coming out of the shower). He carried the shame of that humiliating experience throughout his life, affecting not only his self-image but also his current work and family relationships. He told me he felt weak and ineffectual as a man and that his wife "wore the pants" in their family.

During one session, which will be forever etched in my memory, he painfully recounted the details of the incident when he was ridiculed by the older boys in the locker room. While describing these events to me, he suddenly stood up and pulled his pants down, as a way of reliving his traumatic experience in the locker room. To say I was shocked would be an understatement. Sitting there, I felt trapped and intensely anxious, fearfully imagining someone walking into my office to witness this scene. My fight-or-flight response immediately kicked into high gear. My first impulse was to run out into the hallway of my professional building. But then, imagining him chasing me down the hallway with his pants around his ankles and people gawking at us, I realized that was probably not a good idea. In a millisecond, I switched from flight to fight. Jumping to my feet, I sternly commanded him to put his pants back on. Though not the most compassionate response, I am thankful he did because after that I had run out of creative ideas.

Soon after he was fully clothed again, we both regained our composure (somewhat) and began to discuss the situation "therapeutically." I invited him to talk about what he was feeling and why he had acted as he did. As he spoke, my bewilderment slowly turned into compassion, realizing that my forceful reaction further traumatized him. After we both apologized, he talked through his initial motivation, which was to overcome his feelings of inadequacy and to receive affirmation for his masculinity. The more we spoke, the more he realized that his shame over his manhood went much deeper than this incident in the locker room or his physical anatomy. It originated in his father's emotional disconnection and lack of affirmation, starting in early childhood. The shower incident with the older boys only confirmed his self-doubt and his sense of impotence as a man.

The third person I met in the early months of my therapy practice was a married woman, Joyce. She came for healing from a more immediate sexual wound, one caused by her husband's infidelity. Suffering from what I now understand as betrayal trauma, she despaired over ever being able to rediscover the sacredness of their marriage or restore the broken trust with her husband. She wondered if her husband ever really meant the sacred vows he spoke to her on their wedding day. Her husband's betrayal left her feeling self-protective and insecure in her desirability. Long after the affair had ended, she struggled with her body image and felt incapable of giving herself to her husband. When they attempted to be sexually intimate, she reported feeling paralyzingly self-conscious and simultaneously disgusted with her husband.

As I listened to Joyce share her pain, I felt compassion for her. But without any training in this area, I had little to offer her regarding how she might heal from this soul-shattering betrayal wound. In the subsequent months, we made minimal progress in therapy, even after inviting her husband in for marital counseling. Several years later, I grieved hearing they had divorced. At the time I did not make the connection that this woman's situation mirrored my own family growing up. As a young teenager, I had felt helpless responding to my mom's pain following my dad's infidelity, as well as the distress in our family with their subsequent divorce.

Since that inauspicious beginning as a therapist, I have come to realize that I cannot help others heal from their sexual wounds unless I first face my own and find healing for them with God's help. I have also discovered that all of us have much more in common in our sexual brokenness than I could have imagined back then. I now see that we are all sexually wounded in one way or another. As the three stories above illustrate, these violations may occur in very different ways, and at any age or stage of our development.

Consider the different sources of sexual wounding in the three situations. The young woman, Susan, was sexually violated by her father during childhood and then rewounded in adolescence and adulthood by her previous therapists and live-in boyfriend. The middle-aged man, Jimmy, had been verbally assaulted by older boys at a crucial stage of his psychosexual development and had experienced deeper wounds in his masculine identity from his earliest years in his family. These wounds continued to impact him in adulthood and especially in his marriage. The married woman, Joyce, was wounded by her husband's adultery, shattering her trust and simultaneously desecrating their marriage. This traumatic wound tapped into areas of shame and her unaffirmed identity as a wife (and as a daughter from her earliest days with her mother and father).

I have come to believe that many of us are sexually wounded in one or more of these ways: sexual boundary violations, lack of affirmation in our gender, and/or betrayal from our loved ones. These wounds can affect us throughout the crucial years of our development and even into adulthood. Many of these wounds are caused by others. But some come through our own actions and reactions. If left untended, these sexually wounding experiences will inevitably become sources of debilitating shame and disintegration, which will bring us into a cycle of compulsive sin and effectively hinder our capacity for intimacy and authentic love.

Sexually Wounding Experiences

Our sexuality is one of the greatest gifts we have received from God. "However," as Christian therapist and author Dr. Juli Slattery observes, "we rarely see it as a gift because it has been so twisted and tainted in our personal experiences and in our culture. There is perhaps no aspect of humanity that represents more pain and shame than sexuality."[2] Slattery continues: "While some of us have not experienced anything as horrific as rape or sexual abuse, we have all been broken by the world's consistent vandalism of sexuality."[3] Catholic sex therapists Christopher and Rachel McCluskey elaborate: "We have become the proverbial frog in the pot, so used to daily portrayals of live action sexuality that we fail to appreciate how desensitized we have become."[4]

Consider all the ways our minds and hearts have been, and continue to be, sullied through sexual images. These enticing visual and verbal images bombard us from the internet, magazines, newspapers, textbooks, romance novels, music, fashions, television, movies, and our daily interactions with the people around us. Few of us escape the effects of this barrage of sexual imagery.

In addition to these pornographic images, we have been force-fed destructive sexual ideologies and agendas for decades since the so-called sexual revolution of the 1960s and beyond. These influences distort our understanding of sexuality and violate God's wholesome design for love and procreation. Immersed in this sexually obsessed culture, none of us can remain entirely untarnished. All of these sources of sexual violation, though often unconscious, leave an imprint of shame in our bodies and souls. Whatever generation we belong to, many of us have shameful images impressed in our memories. Some of us lost our sexual innocence "from the tenderest ages." And it has only gotten worse over time. "All those born in the 1970s and 1980s have grown up in a pan-sexualized and hypereroticized cultural climate. . . . Images never seen in earlier times . . . remain impressed in our memory, fantasy, and even in the subconscious of persons from the tenderest ages."[5]

Loss of Innocence

Can you recall how and when you lost your sexual innocence? Apart from original sin and generational influences, we all start off life with a measure of innocence. Personally, I do not remember any shame about sexuality until hearing obscene words in second grade from my friends at school. This was compounded by seeing images of naked women in third grade when a friend discovered *Playboy* magazines in his brother's room and secretively shared it with me. For many years, I didn't consider these experiences to be sexually wounding. No one forced me to do anything against my will. But now looking back, I see how these alluring images of naked women became implanted in my imagination and then left me feeling dirty and ashamed. I did not have words back then to describe my experience. I hid these shameful experiences from my parents and others in authority. They continued, however subtly, to color my perception of sexuality for years to come.

Can you remember how and when you were exposed to sexual experiences in ways that negatively affected your understanding of sexuality? Can you see how those incidences were sexually wounding and led you to internalize shame? In addition to images and words, many of us have been touched or touched others in ways that violated appropriate sexual boundaries and awakened sexual desire before its proper time and place.

I vividly remember my initial awkwardness and then the exciting sexual touches in eighth and ninth grade with my first two girlfriends. These experiences awakened my sexual desires as well as those of my girlfriends. Though I justified my actions as "normal for my age," I knew even then they were not in accord with God's protective boundaries for sexual expression. I now believe these experiences were "violations" of my sexuality as well as that of my girlfriends, even though we were mutually consenting.

These kinds of experiences usually aren't considered to be sexually wounding by many in our society. Many consider them normal developmental experiences. Since no one forced anyone to do something against their will, we naively think there are no lasting effects. But after some healthy soul searching, under the guidance of the Holy Spirit, I have come to believe differently. Any time we violate God's intention for sexuality, we harm ourselves and others in the process. Any sexual act outside of God's will constitutes a desecration of our body as a temple of the Holy Spirit (see 1 Corinthians 6:19). Whether we are consciously aware of it or not, shame and disintegration inevitably accompany these violations against purity.

During my early teen years, I had other experiences of sexual violation that could more classically be defined as sexual abuse. The first occurred when a teacher and coach from grade school tried to molest me on a camping trip while I was sleeping. Though I woke up and got away, I was troubled by the experience. The fact that I did not tell anyone about it is a clear indication I felt overwhelmed and ashamed. For a long time, I didn't perceive that I was wounded by his attempt to violate me, because I got away after he touched me the first time. But years later, when I heard he was in jail for molesting other students, I realized I too had been groomed to be one of his victims. I began to blame myself for being so naïve and not telling someone. I never thought that my telling could protect others.

Around this same time, I had other indirect sexual experiences that I now realize further stole my innocence and distorted my view of sexuality. After being invited into a neighbor's tent, I watched a male neighbor, who was my brother's age, perform oral sex on my brother. I was sworn to secrecy. I felt both curious and repulsed by what I saw but remained silent and told no one.

Similarly, I remember being at a bowling alley a few miles from home when a middle-aged man came up and offered me money in exchange for oral sex. I felt repulsed by his request and left immediately. I now realize this too was a form of sexual abuse, even though I told myself at the time that it didn't bother me. In reality, I felt violated by his proposition, even if nothing further came of it. Collectively these violations of my sexual boundaries affected me even if I didn't realize it at the time. The fact that I kept them hidden shows that they left an ongoing impression of shame. They also exacerbated the hidden shame and pain resulting from my psychosexual wounds.

Psychosexual Wounds

Most of the above incidents were onetime events and impacted me less than the subtler psychological wounding of my sexuality that was part of living within my family during school-age and teenage years. At the time, I never thought of these as being sexually damaging interactions, but now I see them in a different light—that is, God's light that "produces every kind of goodness . . . and truth" (Eph 5:9).

In the darkness of the night, when I slept at my grandparents' house, I would be startled awake by my grandfather raging at my grandmother for refusing him sexual intercourse. My young mind and heart raced with anxiety overhearing his tirades. Though an otherwise good man in many respects, these outbursts affected my view of my grandfather and contaminated my perception of masculinity and sexual intimacy. I vowed I would not be a sexually aggressive man as he was. As often happens with such vows, this led me to repress my sexuality in subtle ways that were not healthy.

Another deeply damaging situation was my father's adultery. His unfaithfulness to my mom and violation of their marital covenant devastated our entire family and many in our social network. It shattered my trust in my father and the positive view I held regarding the sacredness of marriage. Moreover, it ruptured our intact family when I was a young teenager. As a result, I lost respect for my father who had been my primary role model and protector. I loved my dad and always wanted to be like him, but when I found out about his adultery, I feared I would become sexually out of control, as he was. To protect myself, I resolved that I would never be like him. In overreaction, I suppressed my sexual desires and felt shame about them when they came to the surface. In many ways this hampered my normal psychosexual development as a teenager, almost as much as not having my father around to guide and protect me and lead me in virtue.

When my parents divorced, we were all deeply hurting. I felt responsible to tend to my mother's emotional needs, taking on a role that was inappropriate for my stage of development. This too, I have come to discover, was a type of psychosexual wounding, often referred to in the literature as *emotional incest*.[6] According to Dr. Dan Allender, it involves "using a child as a spouse surrogate (confidant, intimate companion, protector or counselor)."[7] Feeling responsible to meet my mom's needs was not healthy for me or for her. This violation of emotional boundaries has impacted me more than I imagined. This wound, hidden in my consciousness for so long, has been difficult to acknowledge and therefore to overcome. It has led to me feeling overresponsible for others who are in emotional pain.

I am sharing all this to help you identify your own sexual wounding experiences and to let you know it is good and freeing to bring it all into God's redeeming light. Are you aware of any similar circumstances in your life that you did not consider sexually wounding at the time the incident occurred but now realize tainted your innocence, violated your sexual boundaries, left you feeling ashamed, or hampered your psychosexual development in some way?

Do you have clear or even vague memories of other kinds of sexual violations (whether verbally, visually, or physically)? I encourage you to explore these areas, with the guidance of the Holy Spirit and trusted people in your life, and then ask yourself some honest questions. Contrary to how you may feel, you are not dishonoring your family members, coaches, teachers, or clergy by speaking the truth about what happened. Being honest is honorable and is a necessary step in eradicating shame.[8]

Seeing the truth of our sexuality with greater clarity, we can realize that anything that desecrates God's intention for our sexuality is a violation of our dignity as a person. Any sexual interaction, whether physical, mental, or spiritual, that does not respect our body and soul as the temple of the Holy Spirit is a source of sexual wounding.

Types of Sexual Wounding

As you can see from the preceding examples, sexual wounds are caused in a variety of ways and can occur during any stage of life. For our purposes of understanding, these wounds can be classified into two general categories: sexual violations and psychosexual deprivations.

Sexual violations are direct experiences of sexual wounding. They may include any of the following:

- *Forceful sexual abuse.* The breaching of sexual boundaries when one or more person(s) overpowers the will of another (e.g., rape, sex trafficking, ritual abuse, sexual harassment, unwanted fondling, violations of consent).

- *Seductive sexual abuse.* The violation of sexual boundaries through molestation, seduction, or unhealthy attachments (e.g., incest, pedophilia, emotional incest, suggestive sexual overtures).

- *Sexual sin.* Any transgression of God's protective boundaries for sexual intimacy with conscious intent (e.g., lustful looks, voyeurism, exhibitionism, adultery, fornication, prostitution, pornography, masturbation, homosexual activity, bestiality, orgies).

- *Sexual play.* Any transgression of God's protective boundaries for sexual intimacy, entered into without full awareness of it being wrong (e.g., playing doctor, exploring pleasure, early childhood sexual interactions).

Psychosexual deprivations are indirect sources of sexual wounding. These may also affect our psychological development and cause distortions in our gender identity, while being a source of sexual shame and compulsion. They may include any of the following:

- *Attachment wounds.* A lack of healthy attachment to mother or father or both.

- *Gender confusion.* A lack of affirmation and confidence in one's gender identity.

- *Poor modeling.* A lack of identification with same-sex parent.

- *Isolation.* A lack of belonging and affirmation by siblings and peers.

- *Peer rejection.* A lack of acceptance by members of the same or opposite sex.

- *Self-rejection.* A rejection of our body, gender, or sexual identity.

- *Suppression of desires.* A suppression of our sexual desires or attractions.

- *Disordered desires.* Any sexual desire that is not in accord with God's design.

Each of the above listed sexual wounds is a source of pervasive shame in our life until it is brought into the light and eventually healed. Throughout the rest of part I we will look at God's design for our sexual wholeness and how these various sources of sexual wounding impact our psychosexual development, gender identity, sexual desires, and sexual behavior. In part II we will explore how these wounds can be healed, allowing Jesus' love and truth to dispel our shame and restore our sexual integrity.

Before turning to the next chapter, where we will explore psychosexual development, I encourage you to first spend some concentrated time reflecting on the content of this chapter. Ask God to shine his light in the darkened recesses of your mind and heart as you identify the different manifestations of sexual wounding and shame. As you go through this activity you may experience intense memories or feel completely numb. Either way, be patient with yourself. Accept yourself. Trust that as we work through the rest of the book, the healing process will unfold. For now, honor the pace of your heart and don't try to rush the process.

I pray the following Take a Moment reflection, personal activity, and prayer will help you bring whatever you are experiencing into the light. Rest in the heart of the Father's mercy, knowing he loves and accepts you in this moment, and at every moment of your life.

Take a Moment

1. Which of the stories in this chapter did you relate to most? Why?

2. What is your opinion of this statement? "We have all been sexually wounded."

3. How do sexual images and cultural distortions about sexuality affect us?

4. What did you read about in this chapter that stirred feelings of anxiety or shame?

Personal Activity

1. Ask the Holy Spirit to guide you in this activity of identifying your sexual experiences.

2. Review the various kinds of sexual wounding at the end of the chapter (sexual violations and psychosexual deprivations) to see which of them you have experienced.

3. Name the various wounding experiences and write them down.

4. Describe the shame you experienced and what you believed about yourself.

5. Are you aware of any sexual compulsions or sexual sins you struggle with related to these wounds?

6. Write down how you are feeling after completing this exercise.

7. As you finish the activity, pray the following prayer (or write one yourself and pray through it):

> Father, I bring you my entire history of sexual experiences, all that I have identified and anything else that remains hidden in the darkness. I ask you to shine the light of your truth into this darkness. Please reveal your merciful love and compassion in these areas of my woundedness and shame. Help me to remember that Jesus does not condemn me and that he has never abandoned me. Though I may not fully understand now, I pray that I will come to know his love and presence in time, especially in these areas of my sexual wounding and shame. I also ask that you heal and forgive any person who has been a part of my sexual history. I ask all this, in the name of the Father, Son, and Holy Spirit. Amen.

2

LIVING THE TRUTH IN LOVE: UNDERSTANDING OUR PSYCHOSEXUAL DEVELOPMENT

Living the truth in love, we should grow in
every way into him who is the head, Christ.
—Ephesians 4:15

Even if your family growing up seemed healthy to you, no one (aside from Jesus) had a perfectly loving family. None of us received the abundance of love and nurturance we needed to develop to our full capacity. This is the reality we all live in due to original sin (*CCC*, 402). None of us are perfectly integrated in our sexuality. We all have psychosexual wounds. For some of us, these wounds, caused by a deprivation of love, are more debilitating than we realize. They can be easily overlooked because our childhood experiences seemed normal to us.

Some of us are aware of these wounds but hesitate to face them because they feel too painful or threatening. That's why we need the assistance of supportive people to help us acknowledge and work through these areas of deprivations in our development. We also need to understand what healthy development looks like, so we can become aware of what we are lacking and where our development has been hindered in any way.

Christian psychologist Jim Wilder and his associates proposed the "Life Model" to help us understand our developmental love needs and the traumas we experience when these needs are not adequately met.[1] After laying out the process of healthy development, they identify two main categories of trauma, which they refer to as "Type A" and "Type B" traumas.[2] We are mostly aware of Type B traumas since these are the noticeably *bad events* that disrupt our development and sometimes rock our world. But few of us give adequate attention to what they refer to as Type A traumas. The *A* refers to the *absence* of the good things we needed for our healthy maturation.

Type A traumas may include things like a chronic lack of affection, unmet needs for affirmation, poor role modeling, or a lack of parental guidance and discipline. These deprivations from one or both parents result in psychosexual wounds. Deprivation wounds can also come from a paucity of nurture from other significant people in our life. These traumas can begin in the earliest days of childhood, even in the womb, and their effects can be passed down from one generation to the next. You may be surprised to discover that some of your deepest and most pervasive sources of shame and woundedness have their origin in these Type A traumas.

Impact of Type A Traumas

In the stories from the beginning of last chapter, notice that all three people had some significant Type B traumas. These *bad* traumatic events—sexual abuse, public humiliation, and spousal betrayal—rocked their world, leaving them with intense pain, shame, and confusion. But in addition to these soul-shattering traumas, all three experienced Type A traumas as well. Though they seemed less impactful, they may have caused even greater damage in their overall emotional well-being and relational capacities.

With Susan, the young graduate student, the obvious trauma in her life was her father's sexual abuse. But her relationship with her mother also played a significant role in her life. I now wonder whether she experienced a lack of bonding with her mother (a Type A trauma) that left her more susceptible to being sexually abused by her father and unable to tell her mother. Did she feel protected by her mother? Did she feel emotionally secure with her? Or did she feel abandoned and unprotected by her? Did she pull away from her mother due to shame, guilt, or fear of her mother finding out? Those are questions I didn't ask at the time. But later in my career, as I worked with people who had been sexually abused, I realized that uncovering these earlier developmental deprivations was essential for healing the wounds of sexual abuse and restoring the survivor's capacity to trust again.

Jimmy, who was humiliated by older boys in the locker room, also experienced Type A traumas in his earlier development years. Perceiving himself as a weak and ineffectual man, it is clear that he was deeply wounded in his masculine identity from the earliest ages. The event in the locker room as a young teenager was an obvious source of intense shame for him. Less obvious but even more insidiously shameful was his lack of bonding and affirmation from his father (a Type A trauma). Because he did not form a strong attachment with his father or receive the necessary affirmation from him, Jimmy lacked confidence in his masculine identity. As an adult this lack of self-confidence manifested in his marriage and work career. The healing of his marriage and the ridicule from older boys could not be adequately resolved until these deeper issues of shame from the Type A traumas were also brought into the light.

Joyce, who was betrayed by her husband, also had underlying psychosexual wounds. Her relationship with her parents, as well as her early dating relationships, contributed to her rejection wounds. These underlying wounds needed to be healed before she could heal her relationship with her husband. At that time, I did not have the experience or the awareness to explore these earlier wounds, or to bring them to Jesus for healing.

What I have learned over the years has helped me to understand that sexual wounds are part of a more comprehensive understanding of the human person. God's intention from the beginning of creation and for all generations has been for us to grow as whole persons, integrated in body and soul. It is not enough to address the traumatic wounds. We must also find ways to restore each person's sexual integrity.

Sexual Integrity

Sexual integrity involves "living the truth in love" (Eph 4:15). When we are wounded by the ravages of sin and trauma in our psychosexual development, we experience a loss of integration. This in turn causes us to hide in shame. Shame is the awareness that we are not what we are meant to be. Healthy shame is based in truth. When we honestly acknowledge our sexual shame, in light of God's truth, we grow in integrity. Unhealthy shame, on the other hand, is based in identity lies that distort the truth of who we are. These identity lies block our capacity to give and receive love, which inevitably leads to further disintegration.

Only in the light of Christ's mercy and truth can we be fully restored in our sexual integrity—to what God intended for us in creation. St. John Paul II was fond of quoting the Second Vatican Council in this regard: "Christ . . . fully reveals man to man himself and makes his supreme calling clear."[3] Just as Jesus was fully integrated in his sexuality, we are all called to *live the truth in love.* In Christ, we discover our true identity and become sexually integrated. Jesus is our prototype for integral development. Growing up, he experienced fully what St. John Paul II referred to as the "fairest Love," the love that God intended for every human being from the beginning.[4] His human nature was formed through the pure and faithful love of the Holy Family. Their "fairest love" is the model for all families. Like us, he was conceived in the womb of his mother and went through a lifetime of maturation from infancy to adulthood. But unlike us, his mother's immaculate womb and heart nourished and protected him without deprivation. His father Joseph loved him purely and faithfully.

Living the truth in love throughout every stage of his development, Jesus' sexual integrity (i.e., his ability to love purely) remained unblemished. He was without sin. He was also free from its debilitating effects. His innocent soul did not become fragmented by

disordered desires. Unlike the rest of us, he did n
and ominous shadow of shame. He had no hint of c
hood in his nature. He desired love and intimacy, but
his desires to become hijacked by unruly compulsio
remained "full of grace and truth" throughout his develo ̣ years
(Jn 1:14). He "grew and became strong, filled with wisdom; and the
favor of God was upon him" (Lk 2:40). Securely loved, he matured
gracefully and manifested the greatest possible purity.[5]

Though Jesus is our model for sexual integrity, none of us were
perfectly loved and nurtured in our families the way Jesus was in
his family. Nor have any of us developed with complete integrity
the way Jesus did. Unlike him we are infected by sin's debilitating
effects within ourselves and in the generations of our family. That is
why I can confidently assert that you and I both lack complete sexual
integrity. We have each experienced at least some deprivations or
distortions of love at different points in our development.

The cumulative effects of Type A and Type B traumas in our
development, coupled with our immature responses to them (including our sins), leave us with divided hearts and darkened minds (see
Ephesians 4:18–19). As a result, each of us has experienced a certain
amount of *disintegration* in our souls. We each exhibit some degree
of insecurity, immaturity, and impurity in our overall development.
This deficit of "living the truth in love" has profoundly affected our
sexual integration. As a result many of us walk around with hardened
hearts, immature attitudes, disordered desires, and areas where we
lack freedom and purity in our sexuality. But we are not mere victims
of our fallen natures and developmental deficits. *We always have a
choice.* We can keep these areas of our life hidden in darkness and
shame, or we can courageously bring them to Jesus to receive his
healing love and truth.

To fully live the truth in love, we need to first understand and then
restore each of the stages of our psychosexual development.

Stages of Psychosexual Development

Jesus grew and developed from conception to mature adulthood through the same stages of human development that we undergo. During this process of maturation we learn to trust and imitate (attachment), discover who we are (identity), and learn how to love and be loved with increasing purity (integrity). We grow from totally dependent infants into capable adults who are called to care for the needs of others while maintaining the ability to care for ourselves and receive love from others.

The table below highlights the stages of psychosexual development that naturally unfold in an environment of self-giving love.[6] Notice that each stage is accompanied by a corresponding developmental task appropriate for that age range. As you read through the table, think about how Jesus, in his humanity, matured through each of the stages in fullness and how each of us proceeds through those stages with some measure of both fulfillment and deprivation. In order to be sexually integrated, each of us needs to develop secure attachments with our parents, be blessed and affirmed in our gender identity, experience acceptance and belonging with our siblings and peers, develop self-mastery, and grow in our capacity for committed self-giving love and generativity.

Table 2.1. Stages of psychosexual development

STAGES OF PSYCHOSEXUAL DEVELOPMENT	AGES	PRIMARY DEVELOPMENTAL TASKS
ATTACHMENT	0–2	Developing secure love bonds with parents
GENDER IDENTIFICATION	3–5	Development and blessing of gender identity

STAGES OF PSYCHOSEXUAL DEVELOPMENT	AGES	PRIMARY DEVELOPMENTAL TASKS
PEER GROUP BELONGING	6–12	Acceptance and belonging with peer group
SEXUAL EXPLORATION	13–22	Self-mastery and integration of sexual desires
SELF-GIVING LOVE	Adult	Sexual fidelity, intimacy, and generativity

Attachment

From the time we are conceived in our mother's womb and throughout the first years of our life, our most important need is to form a secure attachment with our parents, first with our mother and then later with our father. Healthy attachment enables us to feel wanted and to receive the nurturance that is vital to our sense of security. We all need to know from the earliest ages that we are a treasured gift and a source of delight to our mother and father. According to the authors of *The Life Model*, "In the child's first two years, *the desire to experience joy in loving relationships is the most powerful force in life*" (italics added).[7]

During the first two years of life, we all have a basic need to develop a secure love bond, first and foremost with *our mother*. The mother bond is crucial for cultivating a sense of being in children, as they learn to trust in their mother's tender love and nurturance. This develops through a mother's consistent and caring responses, warm affectionate touches, a soothing tone of voice, and attentive gazing that she communicates to her young child on a daily basis. It is through these activities and many more that a secure mother-child love bond is formed. When these interactions are consistent over time, children experience themselves as beloved daughters or sons.

These expressions of tenderness and nurture are also vitally important in the father-child relationship, though Dad is typically a secondary influence during the earliest months of his child's life. His role becomes more prominent in the subsequent stages of development. As the child grows, the father-bond becomes increasingly more important for providing a sense of identity, safety, and security. Good fathering helps the child separate from his mother and attach to their father. This develops naturally when the father affirms the child's goodness and gender and enters into the child's world of wonder and play, setting healthy boundaries of self-expression, while providing opportunities to expand the child's world of adventure. All these are essential for children's healthy psychosexual development which will remain with them throughout life.

Biologically the father determines the child's gender through x/y chromosomes; psychologically he also plays an important role, along with the mother and extended family, in the child's developing gender identity. When we are affirmed first as persons and then in our gender, we come to experience a basic sense of our own goodness. When affirmation is lacking, we internalize a sense of shame as a person and in our sexuality. Dennis Linn et al. observe: "Affirmation is not something we do, but something we are. . . . We cannot become our true selves until another person affirms us. . . . We become our true selves when we see our goodness reflected back to us in the eyes of another person who loves us."[8]

To the degree to which nurturing love and affirmation are missing from either parent, our attachments become insecure. Because most of us lack cognitive memory from this early stage of development, the effects are often felt and experienced later in life. Researchers have found that attachment difficulties persist (until they are healed) throughout our life, affecting all of our intimate relationships.[9] When our love needs are grossly unmet during this stage, children become vulnerable to disordered desires and sexual compulsions of various kinds, which can manifest many years later.[10]

Attachment and affirmation tremendously influence the next stage of development: gender identification.

Gender Identification

During this second stage of development, children learn about masculinity and femininity from their parents, siblings, and other role models. This is facilitated when children separate their identity from their mother and attach to their father. They will soon learn to model after their same-sex parent. Masculine and feminine identity is more caught then taught. With a secure attachment, a boy will intuitively model masculinity after his father (or father figure) and the girl, femininity after her mother (or mother figure). They will then have this affirmed and nurtured by their opposite-sex parent. When this growth proceeds in a healthy manner, the child instinctively accepts his or her sexuality and gender identity. When that attachment is lacking, children will have difficulty identifying with their same-sex parent and, in more severe situations, reject the influence of their same-sex parent. As a result they may develop confusion in their gender identity.

This process of identification, along with the blessing of one's gender, is essential for integrated development. It influences our ability to accept our own gender and feel confident in it. Over the years, serving as a therapist, I saw these patterns of poor attachment and disrupted identification play out over and over again, resulting in lack of confidence, identity confusion, gender dysphoria, sexual compulsions, sexual dysfunctions, and same-sex attractions. I also came to understand it is during these first two stages of development that sexual shame is most deeply rooted.

Andrew Comiskey, who has spent his entire career assisting people in their pursuit of sexual wholeness, underscores the importance of these early years in psychosexual development. "Breaches in relationship with the same-sex parent . . . can block a lifeline of intimacy and identification which in turn obstructs a child's secure gender development."[11]

Leanne Payne likewise spent her career helping people heal from gender distortions. In her book *The Broken Image*, she describes a variety of situations where healthy identification is often disrupted for boys and girls. "A mother, overly protective and peculiarly or injuriously intimate with a son—unless a strong and affirming father figure is close at hand—can render a son unable to separate his sexual identity from hers."[12] She goes on to note that a harsh or unavailable father cannot bless his son's emerging identity as a boy. These wounds of shame and inadequacy, if left untended, are brought into the next stage of development and influence children's sense of belonging with their peers. Conversely, according to Comiskey, "An affirming relationship with the same-sex parent proves affirming to one's gender."[13] An affirmed child is able to proceed confidently into the next stage of development: peer group belonging.

Peer Group Belonging

Children who have secure attachments and identification through the first two stages find it easier to develop a sense of acceptance and belonging with their siblings and peers in this third developmental stage. During these preschool and school-age years, a healthy sense of belonging allows a boy or girl to receive affirmation by their peers, not only as a person, but also in their gender identity. A boy will feel he belongs as a boy among boys. And a school-age girl will see herself fitting in and included as one of the girls. Conversely, boys and girls who feel inadequate are often rejected, ostracized, or labeled during this stage. This wounding can deeply affect their sexuality and gender identification for years to come.[14]

In the situation with Jimmy, who was ostracized and ridiculed by his peers for his lack of masculine development, we see how this pattern plays out. He had no brothers and felt alienated from his father. His delayed physical growth, along with his immature emotional development and lack of athletic ability, left him feeling deeply insecure around other boys. Their ridicule only served to reinforce his lack of confidence and shame. Similarly, Susan, with her lack of bonding with her mom and the incestuous relationship with her father, would naturally carry a sense of pervasive shame about her sexuality. It is not hard to see how both might withdraw their hearts from intimate relationships with the boys and girls at school and in the neighborhood during this stage of development, all the while feeling like an outsider with their peers.

For both Jimmy and Susan, psychosexual injuries during this third stage merely built on their wounds from earlier stages and set them up for even more humiliation and sexual vulnerability during the next phase of development, where they would become more acutely aware of their deficiencies in the world of adolescent sexuality.

Sexual Exploration

In normal psychosexual development, we mature physically, emotionally, and spiritually throughout our teenage years. We also develop an integrated social and sexual identity. In this normative pattern, we expand our social circle from the largely same-sex peer group of pre-adolescence to include more intense attractions with the opposite sex. When development matures in a healthy way, we naturally gravitate to opposite-sex attractions during these teenage years. Comiskey notes, "The capacity to maturely relate heterosexually isn't something we possess at birth. . . . We thus develop into our intended heterosexual identities . . . one stage at a time."[15]

With the onset of puberty and the upsurge in hormones resulting in significant changes in physical anatomy, many developing adolescents can be overwhelmed by intense feelings of sexual attraction and desire. With puberty comes the need for growing self-awareness in order to develop a balanced self-mastery. This is especially necessary in times of heightened arousal and attraction. It is during this stage that self-mastery is most severely tested and yet also most important. Without the healthy development of chaste love during this stage, disordered sexual desires may give way to isolation, fantasy, masturbation, pornography, same-sex attraction, sexual compulsions, promiscuity, unplanned pregnancy, contraception use, and abortions.

Though this stage of sexuality is largely peer centered in focus, family relationships continue to play a crucial role in the emerging adolescent's sexual development and identity. Fathers especially play an essential role in guiding and protecting their children and helping them grow in their identity and self-mastery during this stage. Payne observes:

> The loss of an affirming father is a terrible one at any point in the growing years . . . [but] the loss is especially crucial for both boys and girls during and after puberty. As the mother's warm presence and love is so crucial during the first weeks and months of life, so is the father's during adolescence. The finest and most capable mother, try as she may, cannot repair the gap an absent or emotionally remote father leaves on the young teenager. She simply cannot affirm a son or daughter in the way a *whole* father can. This is one of the awful tragedies of divorce and broken homes. There is seldom a father substitute who is both capable and willing to affirm the struggling adolescent boy or girl.[16]

When I first read Payne's words, they struck a chord in me, as it was during this stage of early adolescence that I lost contact with my father for several years. Though I felt confident in my masculine identity during the earlier stages of development, my dad's absence left me without guidance and protection during this crucial stage of my psychosexual development. After my sexual boundary crossings and subsequent betrayals by girlfriends in early adolescence (which I mentioned in the previous chapter), I responded by suppressing my sexual desires and withdrawing from intimate relationships with girls my age for the next few years. This delayed my psychosexual growth. I know I am not alone in this. Many teenagers lack the support and psychosexual integration to move confidently into the next stage of development, where we are challenged to mature in our capacity for self-giving love.

Self-Giving Love

When all goes according to God's design in our development, we continually mature in our capacity to *live the truth in love*, throughout adolescence and into adulthood. We become ever more capable of giving and receiving God's self-donating and generative love for the good of others and for our own joy and well-being. The secure and mature person, enjoying the wholeness of their sexual identity according to God's design, is able to grow in purity in whichever state or vocation of life to which they are called.

God's intention from the beginning of creation and for all generations has been for us to grow as whole persons, integrated in body and soul. He created us, male and female, to express ourselves authentically in love. This integral vision of our humanity and sexuality is what St. John Paul II referred to as the "Theology of the Body." "Purity," he says, "is the glory of the human body before God. It is the glory of God in the human body, through which masculinity and femininity are manifested."[17]

For many people purity (i.e., chastity) is perceived as a restriction of sexual desire. But from God's perspective it is just the opposite: the freedom to live sexually fulfilling lives. Chastity is the antithesis of all that contributes to our sense of shame and lack of integrity. It is the fulfillment of our integral development revealed in mature, self-giving love.

A mature person learns how to offer their love as a gift to bless others. When we express the fullness of our nature as men and women, we become capable of authentic intimacy and generativity, glorifying God with our bodies (1 Cor 6:20). Our bodies are designed to communicate love and generate new life. Whether we are married or celibate, each of us is called to love chastely in this way.

Chaste Marital Love

Chastity, by definition, involves freedom from adultery and what Pope St. John Paul II referred to as "adultery of the heart," which he says is

a disordered way of looking at others as an object for sexual gratification. This can even include looking at one's spouse in that way.[18] For
the married person, chastity involves an emotionally and spiritually
intimate love that is expressed physically in the marital embrace and
in every other aspect of marriage. Chaste love is free, full, faithful,
and fruitful.[19] The chaste couple remains open to generating new life
and committed to nurturing and educating children until they reach
their full development.

Catholic sex therapists Christopher and Rachel McCluskey
contrast the difference between a marriage that is based in integral
self-giving love and one that has not yet matured in this stage of
development:

> We have already noted that lovemaking as God
> designed it is rooted in a *healthy covenantal mar-*
> *riage*. This does not mean a perfect marriage, but one
> in which both partners *are completely committed to*
> *each other for life and to being known, which means*
> *being real, transparent and intimate with each other.*
> *Their relationship is built on trust*, requiring absolute
> honesty. . . . A marriage cannot facilitate lovemaking
> if it is marred by uncertain commitment, lack of trans-
> parency, a controlling spirit or dishonesty (all which
> breed fear). *This couple may have sex but will not be*
> *able to make love, because the spirit is wrong.* There
> is no fear in love (1 Jn 4:18).[20]

As you read these insights from the McCluskeys, think of the relationships of Susan (who was living with her boyfriend) and Joyce
(whose husband betrayed her in adultery). Both struggled in their
sexual intimacy because, in both cases, an authentic commitment and
transparent honesty were lacking. As a result they both felt used and
insecure, rather than securely loved. As a marital therapist, I observed
this pattern over and over again in the sexual relationships of the
couples I served. When intimacy and transparency were missing, one
or both spouses would end up feeling like an object for the other's

consumption. They would eventually become disinterested in sexual intimacy with their spouse. Sexual intimacy can only flourish in a covenantal marriage, where there is honest and vulnerable sharing of time, affection, thoughts, feelings, desires, and experiences. Only then can sexual intimacy be called lovemaking. Everything else, no matter how gratifying for a season, is a counterfeit and will eventually lead to emptiness and disinterest in sexual intimacy.[21]

For those who are single, consecrated, divorced, or widowed, chastity is expressed in wholesome celibacy, marked by emotional and spiritual intimacy and spiritual generativity.

Chaste Celibate Love

For the single or celibate person, sexual integrity means respecting one's state in life and the meaning of their consecrated sexuality. Daniel Keating, a consecrated man, observes:

> Unlike erotic love, which is rightfully exclusive between spouses, friendships in community ought to be warm and affectionate but genuinely open to others. . . . If a consecrated man has not set his heart on purity, then there is little hope that he will remain faithful to his commitments. If he harbors secret desires at odds with the life he has chosen to live, deep conflicts will emerge. An essential condition, then, for a consecrated man to live a life of sexual integrity is a commitment to seek purity of heart and body on the one hand and on the other a commitment to specific practices that help him live purely.[22]

Susan Muto, a single woman, elaborates: "It is important for singles to show how and why sexual expression means much more than merely 'having sex.' It is to reveal in decisions and deeds how to be a masculine and feminine person radiant with self-respect and respect for others."[23] And Dominican sister Sara Fairbanks adds, "As a celibate lover, I need to share intimacy in self-giving ways as much as a married person does."[24] When celibate love is self-giving, it is also spiritually generative.

Generativity

Mature self-giving love is always generative. This is as true in marriage as in celibacy. Mother Adela Galindo, foundress of the Servants of the Pierced Hearts of Jesus and Mary, explains: "The freedom which the vow of chastity offers, is that of a heart, which is free of self-love, exclusive or conditional, that can love with universality, giving itself to others, according to God's love, from God's love and with God's love."[25] This is the way that Jesus, Mary, and Joseph loved each other in the Holy Family two thousand years ago and continue to love each one of us now.

Every mature person, whether single, celibate, married, widowed, or divorced, is called to a similar generous self-giving love in all of their relationships. In spiritual generativity, we look to pass on to the next generations all that we have received. We help those dependent on us to grow in sexual integrity. In doing so, we live the truth in love and become representatives of God's creative and nurturing charity inside and outside our families, in our local communities and beyond.

As we continue into the next chapter, we will build on these understandings of our psychosexual development with a specific focus on gender identity. Before proceeding to the next chapter, however, I encourage you to take a moment to reflect on our psychosexual development and how trauma affects it. Then in the personal activity, reflect more deeply on the graces and disruptions in your own psychosexual development.

Take a Moment

1. How have sin, shame, and trauma interfered with your sexual integration and development?

2. Can you identity a specific Type A and Type B trauma that you or members of your family experienced?

3. Which married couple and celibate person in your life have exhibited mature chaste love? How do their examples inspire you?

Personal Activity

Reflecting on the stages of psychosexual development, examine your own growth and integral development over the years.

STAGES OF PSYCHOSEXUAL DEVELOPMENT	AGES	PRIMARY DEVELOPMENTAL TASKS
ATTACHMENT	0–2	Developing secure love bonds with parents
GENDER IDENTIFICATION	3–5	Development and blessing of gender identity
PEER GROUP BELONGING	6–12	Acceptance and belonging with peer group
SEXUAL EXPLORATION	13–22	Self-mastery and integration of sexual desires
SELF-GIVING LOVE	Adult	Sexual fidelity, intimacy, and generativity

1. Attachment/modeling: What was your relationship like with your parents? Were they emotionally attuned to you? Growing up, did you feel securely loved and delighted in by each of them?

2. Gender identification: How did your parents affirm or not affirm gender identity? Did you see your same-sex parent as someone you admired and wanted to be like?

3. Peer Group Belonging: Describe your relationships with siblings and same-sex peers. What experiences of rejection/alienation or shame do you remember during your elementary-school years? Who welcomed and accepted you during those years?

4. Sexual exploration: Whom were you attracted to during your teen years? How did you experience acceptance or rejection (or both) by those you desired to have relationship with? How did your parents assist you (or fail to) in guiding you and setting healthy sexual boundaries during those years?

5. Self-giving love: How do you experience relational intimacy in your life in the present? In what ways is your love generative? In what ways do you lack chaste love and generativity?

6. Prayer: Offer any specific areas of shame and brokenness to Jesus, asking him to restore you. Thank him for your parents and other role models and for the ways your development has been blessed by their love. Forgive them for ways they have not loved you well (see appendix 2).

3

REFLECTING GOD'S IMAGE: AFFIRMING OUR GENDER IDENTITY

*God created mankind in his image . . . male
and female he created them.*
—Genesis 1:27

In the opening chapter of Genesis, the inspired author makes it clear that God created us as one of two genders: male and female (Gn 1:27). In the very next verse he affirms the purpose of *gender*, which is for *generativity*: "Be fertile and multiply" (Gn 1:28). Our sexuality does not make sense when divorced from these realities. But, for various reasons, not everyone in our world accepts this understanding of gender and generativity. Moreover, many do not feel at home with their God-given gender.

Over the years I have known and counseled many who were either not affirmed in their gender or felt confused about the nature of their gender identity. As we noted in the last chapter, our self-understanding (i.e., identity) unfolds throughout our psychosexual development. Our varied experiences throughout life—both good and bad, loving and harmful—can tremendously influence the way we view our gender. For example, if we have been sexually abused or rejected by parents or peers, this can and often does significantly impair the way we experience our masculine or feminine identity. That is why we each need to receive gender affirmation.

Gender Affirmation

As a grandfather of eight, I love observing how each of my grandchildren develops in their unique personality. Since I am not directly responsible for their care and discipline, I am freer to delight in them at each stage of their development. Recently, we celebrated the nineteenth birthday of my oldest granddaughter, Anna. She is now in college and living out her femininity in a beautiful way, exploring a whole new world of relationships with other young men and women.

The week before her birthday, we celebrated the fourth birthday of my youngest grandson, Will. He is unabashedly all boy. Just the other day he was wrestling with his older brothers and father on my living-room floor after Mass during our weekly family brunch. Though it made his mom and sisters a bit nervous to see them roughhousing, the males in the room enjoyed watching them wrestle.[1] Will thrives on rough-and-tumble play, especially with his dad and older brothers, much more than his three sisters did at the same age (or at any time in their development). He loves swords and dinosaurs, toy trucks, rock climbing, and every kind of sport, including anything that involves action and movement. But as active and aggressive as he is each day, he also loves to read and snuggle with his mom and dad and with his older siblings throughout the day. Every morning when he wakes up, he makes a beeline for his parents' bed. At night he has a routine of reading and snuggling with his mom or dad before falling asleep. His life is fairly simple, and mostly joy filled, though not without many physical (and sometimes emotional) bumps and bruises each day.

As the youngest sibling, Will has grown up observing the many unique ways that boys and girls express themselves without preconceived judgments or prejudices about gender or sexuality. At this stage of his development, he is simply satisfied being a little boy and knowing he is loved and free to express himself. Occasionally he reminds himself and everyone at the dinner table that he is a *boy*, like his dad and brothers, and *not a girl*, like his mother and sisters. In doing so, he is affirming not only his own gender but also that of everyone in his family. It is a matter of fact for him, just like learning about colors, numbers, and the alphabet.

After naming the gender of everyone at the table, Will seems satisfied to have gotten a perfect grade on his self-initiated test. Even without fully realizing it, he is fulfilling some of the most important challenges of this critical stage of development for a four-year-old: affirming and being affirmed in his gender, identifying with other males, and relating to both sexes as a way of living out his masculine identity. As we will see, this process of gender identification does not always go smoothly for children in this stage.

Gender Identity Formation

Will's gender identity formation started before he was born, as it does for each one of us. Gender affirmation begins with the generations of our family, with the way our parents, grandparents, and siblings relate to their own gender as well as to the opposite gender. This accumulated family culture is transmitted to each child through all the ways these relatives live out their own sexual nature and then either affirm or disaffirm each child's gender development.

Reflect for a moment on how this took place in your family. As far as you know, did your relatives accept and seem comfortable in their God-given gender? Were they able to model for you a healthy and holy image of masculinity or femininity? When you were born, did they celebrate your gender, or did they have some ambivalence or outright rejection of you because they wanted you to be the opposite sex? I know a woman who never knew her father because he left the family when he found out she was a girl and not a boy. These early influences can profoundly affect the way we accept or reject our own gender identity.[2]

As Will's birth was approaching four years ago, his parents (my daughter Carrie and son-in-law Duane) decided to wait to find out his sex until after he was born. We all waited with anticipation and wonder. His sisters, Lily and Elle, *really* wanted a younger sister. Their four older brothers and oldest sister were accepting either way. After hearing they had a baby brother, the boys and Anna cheered, but the younger girls spontaneously burst into tears. Lily, who was five at the time, became uncharacteristically angry. She felt deeply disappointed because she had asked God to give her another sister.

This could have been a real crisis later in Will's life had his sisters rejected their baby brother or treated him like a girl because they wanted a sister. There is no telling how that might have affected him. This kind of thing happens in families much more often than you might imagine and can leave a lasting impact. But thankfully their "aunt Kissy" (my daughter Kristen) had spent the night with them and was there to intervene when they became upset. Before responding, she asked the Holy Spirit to give her wisdom, and then she explained to the girls (with their older siblings listening), "I know you are disappointed because you wanted a sister, and it is OK to be sad and angry. But we do not get to choose whether a baby is a boy or a girl. That is God's decision." Upon hearing Kristen's explanation, the girls calmed down almost immediately. Feeling affirmed that it was OK to be disappointed, they accepted their beloved aunt's explanation and the truth behind it.

Later at the hospital, each of the older children took turns holding their new baby brother—all with looks of awe on their faces. Having heard the story from earlier that morning, I was intently watching to see how Lily and Elle would react. When it came their time to hold him, I saw no trace of disappointment on their faces or in their body language; instead, they each beamed with delight.

While at the hospital we found out that his parents had chosen the name "William Joseph" and that he would be called "Will." On the way home from the hospital, ten-year-old Jack, who was present during the girls' morning tirade and heard Kristen's explanation, remarked to his younger sisters, "Do you get it? His name is 'Will.' He is a boy because it is God's *will*." From that day forward no one in the family has expressed any ambivalence regarding Will's gender. But what if they had? What would be the impact of them rejecting his fundamental identity as a boy? I have counseled several people who were not accepted by a parent or another relative in their gender. The impact has been wide ranging but often significant.

Obviously, there is much more to gender identification than simply being born a boy and receiving a boy's name. Affirmation of gender identity is a lifelong process. All of Will's interactions with his mom, dad, siblings, grandparents, aunts, uncles, teachers, and friends contribute to the formation of his gender identity, and it will continue to unfold and solidify as he interacts with God in prayer and with other people throughout his life. This is the way it is for all of us when things proceed naturally, according to God's design. But it does not always go this smoothly for children deprived of affirmation and adequate love. As we all know, gender identity can be a source of great angst and shame, especially in our culture that is fraught with so much confusion about sexuality and gender.

Gender Confusion

Having accompanied a number of people over the years who have struggled in accepting their God-given gender, I have grown in understanding and compassion for the confusion and suffering that entails. They and their families have experienced the agonizing pain and alienation that inevitably comes with gender confusion. When our gender identity is not affirmed, the experience of shame can be a controlling factor throughout life, affecting all our relationships.

Most of us have experienced some amount of affirmation in our gender, allowing us to function somewhat normally in our day-to-day life. But living in our culture today, with the breakdown of families and widespread confusion about gender,[3] many of us have some degree of uncertainty about how to live fully in our masculine or feminine identity. This can be disquieting and bring a degree of shame in the areas where we believe we are not measuring up as boy or girl, man or woman.

Donna, who has a strong faith in Jesus' merciful love and has gone through a lot of healing related to her gender identity, wrote me this note after reviewing this chapter. I think it is worth sharing (with her permission) because it is deeply insightful about the experience of many:

> So often times people will say, "I always felt this way." . . . That is true for me. I felt like a little boy by the time I was five. I was always a tomboy. I think it is important to clarify that for many our sexual formation and understanding is already present before our cognition is fully functioning. Children absorb their environment, both conscious and subconscious messages about their family, parents, and the world at large from early stages of brain development. The parent may not objectively state an opinion about gender. For example, because of my mother's depression and emotional instability, I remember a specific moment I detached and rejected my mom because she was unsafe to attach to. I was only four to six, but I did reject her. I remember always wanting to be a boy. Subconsciously, I thought my mom wasn't as strong. I never would have said that. I don't even think that was spoken; it was just my experience from living at home. In addition, my brothers, who were ten to fifteen years older, often disrespected my mom. They wrestled with me and gave me attention. I just somehow absorbed these messages without anyone telling me. By the age of five, I wanted to be a boy and wear boy's underwear. . . . So this process is multifaceted. These dynamics are often not overt.

Donna now embraces being a woman. She is dating a man and has solid confidence in her feminine identity. If she had submitted to today's cultural distortions, who knows how much more confusion she might have experienced and where she might be in her gender affirmation process? Life can become a living hell for those who have become deeply confused or outright rejecting of their gender. Gender distortions can affect one's capacity for relationships and in severe situations can literally destroy a person's life. Depression, anxiety, alienation, and shame are common side effects in these situations. And the suicide rate is higher for those with same-sex attraction and gender dysphoria than for the rest of the population.[4] If this is your personal struggle, my heart goes out to you. But know that hope and healing are real possibilities.

I have been touched lately hearing the sobering stories of those who have lived through this hellish conflict but have finally found peace in their God-given identity. An example is the story of Walt Heyer, who grew up in the 1950s tormented by tremendous inner conflicts and confusion about his masculine identity. When he was four (the same age as my grandson Will and the critical stage for gender identification), his grandmother used to dress him in purple dresses. She "affirmed" him in being "her little girl." Later, at the age of ten, when his uncle found out about this, he taunted and sexually abused Walt, which only "reaffirmed" in his mind that he was not a real boy.

Later in life, Walt would be diagnosed with "gender dysphoria," which according to the American Psychiatric Association "involves a conflict between a person's physical or assigned gender and the gender with which he/she/they identify."[5] Like many with gender dysphoria, Walt believed he was a woman trapped in a male body. Yet despite his inner turmoil, he grew up, got married, had children, and was highly successful in his career. Through those forty years, he remained inwardly troubled and felt he was living a lie.

Around this time, with the shift in society regarding transgenderism and the cultural encouragement to "come out" and receive transgender hormone treatments and surgeries, Walt felt a glimmer of hope that his inner and outer worlds could be congruent. This misguided "affirmation" from society was all the encouragement he needed to receive the treatments and transition into becoming a transgendered woman. Walt was so desperate that he gave up everything to find relief from his inner torment. He forfeited his marriage, his relationship with his children, his career, and all of his friends. Eventually he became homeless.

After receiving more than a hundred surgeries, including being castrated, Walt lived for the next eight years as a transgendered woman. After an initial euphoria, he began to realize that he had made a grave mistake. He had sacrificed everything, without finding any peace of mind or soul. His inner conflicts were not resolved by the numerous surgeries, hormone therapies, the name change, or wearing dresses as he always dreamed he could. In his words, "I lived as 'Laura' for eight years, but, as I now know, transition doesn't fix the underlying ailments. After de-transitioning, I know the truth: Hormones and surgery may alter appearances, but nothing changes the immutable fact of your sex." Walt now concludes, "*There is absolutely nothing good with affirming someone in a cross-gender identity, because it will destroy their life*" (italics added).[6]

Walt's experience is both tragic and illuminating. The tragedy is multifold: he endured gender abuse by his grandmother and verbal and sexual abuse by his uncle, and then, in seeking help, he was further "abused" physically, emotionally, and spiritually by our culture and the medical community. In the name of medical care, they "disaffirmed" his true identity while "affirming" his identity *distortions*. Then with his consent, they mutilated his body and encouraged him to deny his immutable God-given identity. In addition to the devastating impact these abuses had on his body and soul, they also had a shattering impact on his wife, family, career, and livelihood. Having counseled spouses, parents, and children of people who suffer from gender confusion, I have seen the layers of damage firsthand when gender is not affirmed.

The Vital Role of Affirmation

Walt's experiences and testimony illustrate the powerful influence of affirmation—for good or for evil—in each of our lives. When we are not affirmed in our true identity as boys and girls by our authority figures and our peers, we can develop any number of distortions in our awareness of our sexuality. Walt's example is an extreme one. But in this broken and confused world, we can all suffer with some degree of confusion regarding how to live fully and authentically in our gender. The effects may range from low confidence, shame, striving for approval, or social awkwardness to promiscuity, same-sex attraction, gender dysphoria, suicide, and violence. All of these effects and more can be severely damaging to individuals, families, and our society as a whole.

Conversely, when children are deeply and consistently affirmed in their personhood and gender, they are more likely to be accepted by peers and confident in their identity. They have a greater capacity to relate well to family members and friends and are more capable of chaste love as they grow and develop. Gender-affirmed children and adults grow into generative men and women serving their families, church, and society.

This understanding of the essential role of affirmation is what prompted Fr. Dan Kogut, a priest in the Diocese of Lansing, Michigan, to write a pastoral letter to the parents in his parish and school. I received his permission to share it with you.

> Healthy affirmation is an important aspect of your role as a parent. The way in which a girl is delighted in as a daughter helps to establish her identity as such. The way in which a young man is affirmed as a son helps to establish him as such. This affirmation of the sexual identity of your child is a blessing to them. This blessing is very important for them to receive both from their same-sex parent and their opposite-sex parent. The affirmation of a child in their sexual identity helps them to establish a secure identity as a young man or a young woman, and it allows them to experience the joy of being delighted in as they were created. . . . This need not lead us to shallow stereotypes unless we desire to impose them ourselves. In fact, over-restrictive stereotypes can undermine affirmation and cause confusion. When we offer healthy affirmation to children and young people, it is an affirmation of what God has done."[7]

I celebrate Fr. Kogut's wisdom and courage addressing these issues with his parishioners. After thirty-five years as a therapist, I can testify to the realities he highlights in this pastoral letter. Each of us needs to know we are personally loved and affirmed in our gender. If we do not receive this affirmation, we will continually strive for approval and will seek affirmation in a myriad of unhealthy ways, including sexually disordered relationships.

An unaffirmed boy who is insecure in his masculinity may grow into a teenager or young man who is self-centered and constantly searching for approval.[8] He may seek to receive his affirmation through an exaggerated emphasis on his talents and accomplishments. He may embrace false stereotypes of masculinity by trying to prove his masculine identity through gangs or in sexually disordered relationships with women. Sexual fantasy, promiscuity, and sexual compulsion are some of the bad fruits of an unaffirmed gender identity. When the damage to masculine identity runs deep, the boy moving into the teenage years may envy other boys' masculinity and eroticize his attraction in same-sex fantasy or homosexual behavior. Furthermore, he may become a "macho male," domineering and demeaning in his relationship with women, or present a weak and passive persona, allowing himself to be controlled by them.[9]

Likewise an unaffirmed girl will be more prone to seek her affirmation through boyfriends, or in promiscuous relationships with men. When gender confusion results from poor attachment or identification with her mother or from traumatic relationships with men, the teenage girl may identify more with men, or turn instead to other women and eroticize her longing for affirmation and comfort in a lesbian relationship. Or she may suppress these sexual desires, turning her energies into striving to receive affirmation through her achievements or people pleasing. Without confidence in her sexual identity, she may eventually allow herself to be used and dominated by men, or in the opposite direction contemptuously control and manipulate her sexual partners (male or female) to get the nurturance and acceptance she desperately needs.[10]

In the most severe situations, like that of Walt Heyer, the deeply confused boy or girl may reject their gender altogether and believe they are a female trapped in a male body, or a male trapped in a female body. (Even writing this feels confusing.) There are many men and women in our modern era who are struggling because of a lack of affirmation of their gender. This lack of affirmation in their psychosexual development is reinforced by the cultural confusion about gender that we see in our world today.

Cultural Distortions about Gender

Many in our culture today have rejected the traditional Judeo-Christian view of gender and sexuality that understands gender as God given, binary, and fixed to biology.[11] The "new gender theory" proposes that gender is determined by the subjective disposition and choice of the individual. This change in the definition of gender is novel in the history of the world. But it has been evolving rapidly over the past fifty years. Fr. Walter Schu identifies a key moment in the cultural shift around the turn of the millennium: when Bella Abzug gave a passionate speech at the United Nations conference in Beijing, China. Stating her opinion as though it were a universally accepted fact, she said, "The meaning of the word gender has evolved and differentiated from the word sex to express the reality that men and women's roles and status are socially constructed and subject to change." Commenting on this, Fr. Walter Schu remarks: "Incredible as it may seem, the claim is made that there are not merely two genders but five . . . male, female, homosexual, lesbian, and bisexual or transsexual."[12]

But even now, this "new" definition of gender has become obsolete. Many have come to realize that labels describing non-normative sexual orientation (i.e., gay, lesbian, bisexual, transgender, and queer) are not fixed identities but instead changeable conditions over time.[13]

Accounting for this reality, the new cultural norm is *gender fluidity*, "the ability to freely and knowingly become one, or many of limitless number of genders, for any length of time, at any rate of change. Gender fluidity recognizes no borders or rules of gender."[14]

Walt Heyer would be an example of someone who changed his gender identity multiple times. His witness, among a host of others, demonstrates that our culture's affirmation of *gender distortions* is not genuine affirmation. While the new gender theory may be well intended by many proponents, as a compassionate attempt to alleviate shame and confusion for those suffering from gender identity confusion, it actually does more harm than good. Findings from a comprehensive review of research on sexual orientation demonstrate that these redefinitions of gender can be extremely hazardous to one's health and emotional well-being.[15]

Research is beginning to show that hormone treatments and transgender surgeries are not only destructive but also shortsighted. In his thought-provoking book *When Harry Became Sally*, Ryan Anderson summarizes available research:

> Parents are told that puberty blockers and cross-sex hormones may be the only way to prevent their children from committing suicide. Never mind that the best studies of gender dysphoria (studies that even transgender activists cite) show that *between 80 and 95 percent* of children who express a discordant gender identity will come to identify with their bodily sex if natural development is allowed to proceed. And never mind that "transitioning" treatment has not been shown to reduce the extraordinarily high rate of suicide attempts among people who identify as transgender (41 percent, compared with 4.6 percent of the general population). In fact, people who have had transition surgery *are nineteen times more likely* than average to die by suicide. These statistics should be enough to halt the headlong rush into "transitioning" and prompt us to find more effective ways to prevent these tragic outcomes.[16]

Far from being the liberating freedom it is purported to be, gender obfuscation compounds rather than alleviates the imprisonment for the person who is suffering. Rather than accept their true identity from the Father, the person suffering in this way ends up suppressing the truth of their nature (see Romans 1:18). To rediscover the truth about gender we only need to turn to the source of that truth: God himself.

Reflecting God's Image

We began this chapter with these foundational truths from the book of Genesis: "God created mankind in his image . . . male and female he created him" (Gn 1:27). Despite the world's confusion over gender, the Bible and natural law are very clear in revealing the reality that there are only two genders: male and female. Even when medical interventions or fallen humanity distort gender identity, as in Walt Heyer's case, science affirms what the Bible reveals. No matter how we feel subjectively, we remain objectively our God-given gender throughout our lives. Every child who has not been deeply wounded in their gender identification knows this to be true, as my grandson Will demonstrated.

Arguably, no one has spoken more articulately about sexuality than St. John Paul II. His profound insights on this passage in Genesis shines through in all his writings, especially in his epic work popularly known as the "Theology of the Body."[17] John Paul II begins the Theology of the Body by laying out a portrait of our human nature before sin disordered it. He observes that in our state of original innocence man and woman realized they shared a common human nature, but with *sexual distinctives*.

The original Hebrew words for male and female, in the Genesis passage, shed considerable light on God's design and intention for sexuality. These words speak of not only the different physical natures of men and women but also something of the essence of each one's soul and calling to reveal God's love. We will explore first the biblical meaning of masculinity (*zakar*) and then the nature of feminine receptivity (*neqebah*).

Zakar

The Hebrew word for male used in the book of Genesis is *zakar*. It literally means "to remember." As strange as it may sound at first, the word actually has a rich meaning. *Zakar* provides great insight into how authentic masculinity reflects God's faithful covenant love, as our eternal Bridegroom and Father. According to Dr. Larry Crabb, a Christian psychologist who has studied the meaning of these Hebrew words for gender, *zakar* means "one who remembers and moves in to bless."[18]

God created man to remember his covenant and to bless those in his care. Think of Abraham, being blessed by God and then blessing those around him, as well as the generations to follow him. Each male in the Old Covenant was called to do the same. But each of them failed to be faithful to God's covenant at some point, starting with Adam and including Abraham, Moses, and David, reaching a climax of distortion in the evil King Ahab, a descendant of David. The unfaithful actions of each of these men betrayed their identity as representatives of God's faithful covenant love. Their actions hurt those they were called to serve and bless. Undeterred, God re-established his plan of faithful love in the New Covenant. It began with St. Joseph, a shining example of a man who lived the reality of God's tender compassion and fidelity throughout his life. Remembering the Father's love, he continually moved in to bless Mary and Jesus, and all he encountered. He modeled the Father's love for Jesus with humility, love, and faithfulness.[19]

Jesus, the New Adam, is the ultimate example of redeemed masculinity. As the fulfillment of God's promise to Abraham, Jesus was blessed by his Father in order to bless the whole world. He fully expresses the image of God—a man who sacrificially offers himself in self-giving and generative love, faithfully remembering God's covenant and living constantly from his true identity to bless those he serves.[20]

Following the example of St. Joseph and Jesus, every man is called to live out his essential masculine nature, as *zakar*. This is the true meaning of spiritual headship about which St. Paul speaks so eloquently (Ephesians 5:23). It is a call to serve and bless as Jesus serves and blesses. Our authentic masculinity develops from the earliest days of life, as a boy is blessed and affirmed in his identity by his father and other male figures.[21]

As the young man grows in security, maturity, and purity, he can then offer himself in pure and faithful love to those entrusted to his care (see Ephesians 5:25–28). Authentic masculinity faithfully provides, protects, nurtures, and blesses. Whenever males remember God's covenant and move into bless those around them, they embody authentic masculine strength. Everything else is a counterfeit.[22]

Counterfeits of authentic masculinity are evidence that a man has not been truly affirmed in his masculine identity. It can be manifested in a tendency to exhibit one of two extremes: *hyper-* or *hypo*masculinity. King Ahab exemplified both, as he worshipped the gods of sex and power and yet remained passive in the face of his overpowering wife, Jezebel. Some men become intoxicated by sex, power, and prestige (hypermasculinity), while others retreat timidly out of fear and weakness (hypomasculinity). In both distortions the man becomes disconnected from God and from his true self. As a result, he loses his spiritual strength and God-given authority. Forgetting the Father's love and blessing, he becomes incapacitated to bless those around him and uses or neglects them instead. He may become passive and ineffectual or dominating and exploiting (which are compensations for inadequacy).[23]

Noting this disordered tendency of males to become intoxicated by power, John Paul II observes, "Male domination is a consequence of original sin. Both men and women are diminished . . . in their *own* personal dignity [by this misuse of power]."[24] In Mulieris Dignitatem (*On the Dignity and Vocation of Women*), St. John Paul II warns against women reacting to male domination by trying to control the men who have hurt them. "Even when women rightly oppose domination 'in the name of liberation,' women must not appropriate to themselves male characteristics contrary to what is uniquely feminine, lest they 'deform' and lose what constitutes their essential richness."[25]

That essential richness of femininity is expressed in the Hebrew for female: *neqebah*.

Neqebah

According to Dr. Larry Crabb *neqebah* (or *n'kebah*) means "one who is open to receive and nurture."[26] This is every woman's core nature: to be *receptive* in body and soul, capable of giving and receiving nurture. In her receptivity, woman reveals the beauty and mystery of God.[27] She is called by God to incarnate his tenderness and to be the initiator of communion, complementing the masculine gift in upholding the covenant. St. John Paul II observes, "On the human level, can there be any other *'communion'* comparable to that *between a mother and a child* whom she has carried in her womb and then brought to birth?"[28]

Eve was called the mother of the living. However, when she broke communion with God, she closed her heart, setting up a chain reaction in the female race throughout much of the Old Testament. The evil Queen Jezebel (Ahab's wife and partner in idolatry) is the archetype of a hardened and controlling woman (see 1 Kings 21). She deformed her feminine nature by taking on male characteristics contrary to what constituted her essential nature. Instead of imaging God, she imitated the "goddesses" she worshipped. These included Ashtoreth, the fertility goddess known for temple prostitution, and Lilith, the goddess of death and destruction.[29]

Our current culture worships these "goddesses" through the sexual revolution (Ashtoreth) and abortion (Lilith). These "goddesses" have been aptly described by Dr. Carrie Gress as the anti-Mary spirit. They represent distortions of femininity, where marriage and motherhood are demeaned and so-called sexual liberation actually leads to sexual enslavement. The anti-Mary spirit pridefully flaunts femininity and uses it to seduce and control rather than to reflect the beauty of God. Contraception and abortion are the antithesis of receptivity.[30]

A woman who blocks her receptivity in these ways (seduction, control, and contraception) cuts herself off from genuine love and her capacity to nourish and be nourished. In doing so, she loses touch with her essential feminine nature and denigrates her inward beauty. In desolation and loneliness, she may look to men rather than God for fulfillment. Grasping for validation and love, she leaves herself vulnerable to being used and discarded. Or she may have contempt for men and become hardened, seeking instead to seduce and control, or disdain men altogether.[31]

By contrast, femininity as God intended it in creation is fully redeemed and shines forth in the person of the Blessed Virgin Mary. She who is "full of grace" reveals the perfection of the feminine genius.[32] Her fiat, "May it be done according to your word," is the essence of feminine receptivity and beauty (i.e., *neqebah*). Her receptivity to the Holy Spirit at the annunciation was not just a momentary response but a reflection of her entire way of life.

Mary is the redeemed mother of all the living and the archetype of the Bride. She is often described by those who encounter her in apparitions as the most beautiful woman who ever lived. Yet her beauty is pure gift, reflecting the essence of God and inviting all into her immaculate heart. Unlike Eve, Mary remained in communion with God throughout her life. She reveals herself in history as the daughter of the Father, the mother of the Son, and the spouse of the Holy Spirit. Fully submitted to the Trinity in every respect, she maintained communion with her chaste husband, St. Joseph, while being humbly submitted to his spiritual headship (see Matthew 2:13–18).

Every woman is called, through the power of God's grace, to follow the example of Mary. In humble receptivity and enjoying intimate communion with the Trinity, she communicates her feminine receptivity and nurturance within her family and community. Her true nature is revealed in "the hidden character of the heart . . . which is precious in the sight of God (1 Pt 3:4). Far from being a doormat, a restored woman "is clothed with strength and dignity. . . . She opens her mouth in wisdom; kindly instruction is on her tongue" (Prv 31:25–26).

We can only recover the essential richness of our gender by affirming and practicing what God intended from the beginning. For the woman, the opposite of closing is to remain open and receptive. An open heart is a tender heart that remains in humble submission to

Christ and in communion with loved ones (see Ephesians 5:22–24 and 1 Peter 3:3–6). For the male, the opposite of dominating and passivity is faithful, self-giving love (see Ephesians 5:25–27). Acknowledging our weaknesses, we can draw on the power of God's grace to strengthen us, so that we in turn can bless those in our care (see 2 Corinthians 12:9).

There is a lot here for us to reflect on and apply. Take a moment to ponder God's design for masculinity and femininity and the confusion inherent in our culture; then go deeper in your reflection in the personal activity, examining the ways you have been affirmed or unaffirmed in your gender identity and how you are currently living out your authentic identity as God intended.

Take a Moment

1   What was your reaction after reading the story of Walt Heyer?

2. Do you feel gender affirmation is essential to psychological health? Why or why not? What happens when it is lacking?

3. In what ways do you relate to Joseph and Mary's revelation of authentic masculinity and femininity? How do Ahab and Jezebel demonstrate the antithesis of authentic masculinity and femininity?

Personal Activity

This activity is to help you examine how and when you experienced affirmation or dis-affirmation in your gender identity. It is an opportunity for you to look back over your life and examine the varying influences that have shaped your gender identity.

1. When you were born, did your parents celebrate your gender?

2. In what ways did your parents model authentic masculinity and femininity?

3. When you were four, were you happy to be the gender God gave you? Was there any internal conflict you were aware of at that age or any time since then?

4. As you grew up, did you feel as if you fit in with your peers and siblings? How did they affirm or disaffirm you in your gender?

5. When you were a teenager, how well did you relate to those of the opposite sex? Your same-sex peers? Did you feel affirmed in your gender by other teenagers of both genders?

6. As an adult, how do the people around you affirm or disaffirm you in your gender identity?

7. Do you accept and celebrate your gender today? When do you recognize the counterfeits of masculinity or femininity in yourself?

8. What attributes of Jesus, Mary, and Joseph do you admire and desire for yourself?

4

LURED BY DESIRES: EXPLORING OUR SEXUAL COMPULSIONS

Each person is tempted when he is
lured and enticed by his own desire.
Then desire . . . brings forth sin.

—James 1:14–15

Over the years, I have accompanied numerous men and women seeking freedom from their unruly desires and sexual compulsions. These men and women have typically experienced wounds in their psychosexual development and distortions in their gender identity, though they are often unaware of how much these wounds and distortions are driving their compulsions. They typically feel out of control and enslaved by these compelling desires. The nature of their sexual compulsions may vary considerably. Some may involve an exaggerated attraction to certain people or to sexual images. Others have a compulsive aversion to sex altogether. These compulsions may involve persons of the opposite sex or those of the same sex, people of different ages or certain body types, or even animals or fetish objects of some kind.

Doug Weiss, a leading expert in treating sexual compulsions, tells the story of a young boy who masturbated outside his house, looking down at his galoshes. After repeated acts, he became habituated to feeling aroused every time he saw his galoshes. This is an example of how people develop sexual fetishes, which are simply compulsions connected to objects. Fetishes are an example of classical conditioning. Even though the person feels intense shame about these fetishes, once the conditioned response is brought to light, the shame can be lessened significantly and the fetish loses its power. A similar kind of conditioning and habituation to images takes place in any kind of sexual compulsion.

In all these situations, the person coming for help desires freedom from their particular compulsion but feels powerless despite many attempts to overcome this struggle in their own strength.

The natural tendency when someone experiences unwanted sexual compulsions is to painstakingly suppress and control these disordered desires and fantasies, all the while keeping them hidden behind a wall of shame and isolation. But this strategy rarely works for long, if at all. Suppression actually increases the force of compulsions. It is akin to holding a ping-pong ball under water, only to have it explode to the surface once you lose your grip. The force of compulsion is a lot like that ping-pong ball, pushing against all attempts to suppress those highly charged sexual desires, as well as the underlying pain and distortions that are driving the compulsion.

Among those who work in the field of sexual addiction, it is well known that shame and isolation are the driving forces behind sexual compulsions. Christian sex therapist and researcher Jay Stringer explains, "The type of sexual behavior we pursue is a direct reflection of how highly or poorly we think of ourselves. When abandoned we are convinced that we were left because of the deep flaws that exist within us. This shame-based identity is then woven into all our choices and eventually becomes the lens through which we see our lives."[1] Stringer wisely advises that we need to see beyond our shame to the legitimate desires underlying our lust: "Lust exposes your demand to be filled. But if you listen to your lust, it will reveal a holy desire for belonging."[2]

Recognizing these factors at play in sexual compulsions, we often start our Holy Desire conferences at the John Paul II Healing Center with these words: *"Behind every disordered desire is a holy desire, an unmet need, an unhealed wound, and a hidden pattern of sin."* This approach to exploring sexual compulsions breaks through the veil of shame while serving as a road map to healing. We can more readily explore the underlying roots of our sexual compulsions, by honestly and humbly exploring the origins of these disordered desires and the holy desires that underlie them.

Origins of Disordered Desires

Reflecting on the meaning and purpose of sexuality, St. John Paul II observes that our bodies and souls are designed to participate in intimate communion. That means our desires for love and communion are holy. However, when Adam and Eve broke God's covenant and lost communion with him and each other, shame, pride, and loneliness became a part of our universal heritage. Since then, all of us have divided hearts due to what St. John Paul II refers to as the triple concupiscence: "the lust of the flesh, the lust of the eyes, and the pride of life" (1 Jn 2:16 NIV). On this side of Eden, we all struggle with lust and pride in one way or another.[3]

Lust distorts what God intends for our sexuality. It perverts our God-given desires for communion, fragments our bodies and souls, and separates sexual arousal from its ordered fulfillment in personal love and procreation. Lust is based on a consumer attitude of using the other, while seeing them as an object for our pleasure. It seeks the sensation of sexuality apart from genuine communion and covenant with another person.[4]

Pride is often a close companion of lust. Believing we are the masters of our own destiny, we seek fulfillment apart from God. We arrogantly act as though our bodies belong to us and that we can use them any way we want. We delude ourselves into believing we can fulfill our own needs and satisfy our own longings. In pride, we deny the consequences of our misguided sexual expression and justify our disordered thoughts and behaviors. When our pride and lust remain unchecked, our desires sooner or later become compulsive. All too easily we can find ourselves bound by these compulsive desires.

Don't we all know this struggle with conflicting desires? St. Paul speaks eloquently of our internal battle: "For the flesh has desires against the Spirit, and the Spirit against the flesh" (Gal 5:17). Due to concupiscence our hearts have become a battlefield of desires struggling between the opposing forces of lust and love. Concupiscence by itself is not sin, but these disordered desires can lure us into sin if we are not aware of their strong pull. After repeated indulgence of the "lust of the eyes" and "lust of the flesh," our pride can leave us in denial that we have become sexually addicted.

Sexual Addiction

Sexual addiction is an enslaving of our minds, emotions, and spiritual affections to sexual desires and pleasure.[5] Mentally, our thoughts become obsessively fixated on sexual imagery as our brains habituate to seeking greater and greater variation and novelty.[6] Emotionally, we become attached to the euphoric feelings of satiation as we continue to seek pleasure for its own sake, all the while becoming less able to enter into intimate relationships with real people. Withdrawing from intimacy, we become isolated. Spiritually, our hearts become hardened, we turn our affections away from God, and we lose interest in things pertaining to God.

Before long, we find ourselves caught in an addictive cycle. Self-indulgence leads to shame, which gives way to isolation, which seeks relief in self-indulgence, which only causes more shame and even more isolation. Deeply ashamed, we hide our disordered desires behind a mask of pride, causing us to further isolate, while being cut off from the nurturing human relationships we so desperately need. Pride and self-deception prevent us from humbly asking God and others for help.

Russell Willingham, who has spent his career helping people find freedom from sexual addiction, warns of the dangers of keeping our struggles hidden while denying our brokenness. Willingham observes:

> If you deny your brokenness,
>
> - You will lie constantly for fear that someone will see how messed up you are.
> - You will lead a double life—one that is Christian and one that is hidden. . . .
> - You will feel constant guilt [and shame] about your sexuality. . . .
> - Sometimes you will hate yourself and believe that God hates you.
>
> If, however, you humble yourself and face your brokenness, you will begin a road to true freedom:
>
> - You will not need to hide. . . .
> - You will seek out other honest people whom you can trust with your brokenness. . . .
> - You will know that your sexuality is broken and it will take time to heal. . . .
> - You will be gracious toward others instead of being critical and self-righteous. . . .
> - You will know that maturity and wholeness are a process and not an event.

Breaking out of isolation, turning to God, and trusting others is the way we gain freedom from sexual compulsions and addictions. God's merciful love is the only remedy that can penetrate the dark shadows of our shame, break through the walls of our isolation, and fill our inner emptiness. As we share our struggles in a safe environment, we enter into a process of listening attentively to the deeper heart motives underlying our sexual compulsions. When we do this, we discover the futility of our self-reliant attempts to meet our deepest needs apart from God and other people. These universal and often unmet needs for love and belonging are expressed uniquely in each of our stories.

Though often hidden from our awareness, our unmet needs make perfect sense once we come to understand them without self-condemnation. Sexual compulsions almost always expose hidden areas of our woundedness and shame. They also frequently reveal unhealed traumas in our psychosexual development. Additionally, they highlight areas where we have not been adequately affirmed in our gender identity. Finally, sexual compulsions often expose habitual patterns of sin and may reveal essential details of past sexual abuse experiences.[7] Steve's story illustrates how these intertwined dynamics often become the raw material for our sexual compulsions.

Steve's Story

Steve was a young man who had a life-changing encounter with Jesus in high school and felt a call to spend his life serving him in ministry.[8] When I met Steve, he was already in seminary and doing well in every area of his formation, with one major exception: he had been battling a raging sexual addiction since puberty. Though he had made progress, he was not free from its grips. Because of this area of enslavement, he despaired over ever being able to be ordained when it was time for him to do so.

Steve's lust-driven sexual experiences began at the age of twelve, after finding his father's pornographic magazines in his parents' bedroom. Though shocked, he was also mesmerized by the compelling images of naked women. Curiosity and sexual arousal overpowered his better judgment. Rationalizing that it must be okay because his father kept these magazines in the house, he began sneaking into his parents' room on a regular basis to look at the pictures in the magazine. Over time, his arousal escalated into masturbation and sexual fantasies. In his fantasies, Steve imagined himself desired and pursued by these seductive women (unlike his real-life experience of feeling inadequate and remaining isolated from girls his age). He also imagined himself having a strong masculine physique in his fantasies (like some of the more athletic boys at school, who ridiculed him for being "a puny weakling"). By the time Steve entered high school, he had access to other forms of pornography, including videos of sexual acts. With increased exposure, his shame increased proportionately, thus fortifying his sexual compulsions. Before long, watching strong men participate in various sexual acts with beautiful, inviting women became Steve's daily routine after school. As his sexual addiction escalated, he found himself drawn to watching muscular men engaging in sexual acts with smaller, younger men and boys.

As Steve's compulsions became increasingly enslaving, his fantasy life centered more and more on imagining himself as both the initiator and recipient of every imaginable sexual activity between the men on the screen, including acts of sodomy and violence. At times he would see himself as a powerful man, overpowering younger boys. At other times he saw himself as a smaller and weaker boy, dominated by bigger and stronger boys and men. Shortly after indulging these fantasies and reaching climax in masturbation, Steve felt an extreme emptiness. He saw himself as dirty and perverted. He hated himself and began to wonder if these fantasies meant he was "homosexual," or perhaps "bisexual." He knew he was attracted to women, but he felt inadequate and ashamed to ask a woman out on a date.

Throughout these middle-school and early high-school years, Steve remained deeply divided within his mind and heart. While he continued to portray a respectable image in public, he inwardly despised himself for his sexual desires and compulsions. He was horrified by the thought of anyone knowing about his secret fantasies, or what these might possibly indicate about him. Even after his profound spiritual conversion, and a subsequent Confession where he acknowledged these sins in a general way, he could not imagine revealing the details of his fantasy or compulsions to anyone.

Although his compulsions continued (to a lesser degree) throughout college and seminary, Steve was finally able to open up about his struggles with a trusted spiritual director. His spiritual director recommended he go to therapy, which is where Steve began to explore some of the details of his fantasies, seeing how these imaginary scenarios were related to his childhood traumas and self-rejection. He discovered that these wounds, incurred at different stages of his psychosexual development, were the driving force behind his compulsions.

Wounds in Psychosexual Development

As Steve explored his attachment and identification with his parents, he discovered several important factors underlying his sexual compulsions and identity confusion. Steve felt a loyalty to both of his parents, but his emotional connection with his mom was much stronger than his bond with his dad. He realized that his mom had idolized him, by looking to Steve rather than her husband to meet her emotional needs. Steve and his mom developed an unhealthy attachment, sharing negative judgments about his father, while looking to one another for comfort and protection.

Steve felt deprived of the affirmation he needed from his father. His dad's anger, criticism, and emotional distance left Steve feeling afraid and alone. To protect himself from the pain of abandonment and rejection, Steve emotionally detached from his dad. He erected walls around his heart to guard against further hurt. In therapy, Steve began to see how these self-protective reactions had cut him off from a vital relationship with his dad, the one person who should have been the source of his masculine identification and affirmation.

Steve's experience is not uncommon among those who struggle with sexual compulsions and corresponding confusion about their sexual identity. Andrew Comiskey, the founder of Desert Streams Ministry,[9] has walked this journey himself and now helps many men and women find freedom from sexual compulsions and distortions in gender identity.

In his workbook *Pursuing Sexual Wholeness*, Comiskey identifies the key components of "defensive detachment" (i.e., emotional disconnection):

> - Breaches in relationship with the same-sex parent . . . can block the lifeline of intimacy and

identification, which in turn obstructs a child's secure gender development.

- When a child responds defensively to this breach by detaching him/herself, the legitimate need for same-sex love is repressed. This leaves the child with a tremendous need for that love. Yet the child distrusts this love due in part to deficient or hurtful relationship with their same-sex parent.

- The child's interpretation and response play a big role. What is interpreted by the child may or may not be based in the reality of the parent's treatment of the child.

- This defensive detachment may obstruct the child's capacity to take on characteristics of the same-sex parent, which generalizes onto other members of the same sex.

- Inner vows, such as "I will not be like him/her/them," may strengthen to the point that the child develops an aversion to identifying with their own sex. . . .

- The child's repressed need for same-sex love and unresolved gender identity issues express themselves erotically later in adolescence in the form of sexual compulsions.[10]

I have found Comiskey's observations to be particularly true in situations where people struggle with sexual compulsions and with confusion about their sexual orientation and gender identity. Each one of these factors Comiskey identifies was influential in Steve's sexual compulsion and identity confusion. Steve's sexual fantasies involving men were partially expressions of his longing for the connection with masculine love, a love he never adequately received from his father. His use of pornography and fantasies also revealed his self-rejection over his body image and the powerlessness he felt as a child as the recipient of his father's mistreatment and emotional distance. Steve's perceptions and responses to feeling hurt by his father contributed significantly to his emotional detachment, his self-rejection, and his longing for masculine love. But Steve's broken relationship with his father was only part of his wounding. His relationship with his mother and peers also played an important role. Being overly enmeshed with his mother emotionally, Steve was not able to fully go through the normal separation that would allow his masculine identity to mature. This became evident in the critical developmental stages of identification and peer group belonging.

Identification and Peer Group Influences

In the normal course of psychosexual maturation, children naturally desire to imitate their same-sex parent. When this identification is unhindered, it gives children confidence relating with their peers. For girls, this is often expressed in feeling accepted in relational activities and having a sense of belonging with other girls. For boys, some of this confidence is expressed in competitive games, including sports and other active behaviors where they feel included with other boys. Because Steve's dad was distant emotionally and did not play with him, Steve did not develop the necessary coordination or confidence to enter into active or aggressive peer activities with other boys his age.

Without being fully conscious of it at the time, Steve internalized a feeling of shame and inferiority as a young child and carried this identity into his relationship with his peers throughout grade school. When he got to middle school, he found relating to both male and female peers too threatening. He isolated himself, believing he didn't fully belong in the masculine world, one in which the other boys seemed much more comfortable and capable. When these same boys called him names and questioned his masculinity, it only exacerbated Steve's sense of shame and feelings of inadequacy.

Though he may not have been able to verbalize it at the time, he internalized these beliefs into his identity: "I am not as good (strong, capable, and athletic) as the other boys. I'm too small, weak, and uncoordinated. I'm not like the other boys. I don't fit in. I must be gay." As a result of these beliefs and his feelings of inadequacy, Steve found himself pulling back from engaging in activities with the other boys at school or in the neighborhood. He chose instead to hide behind the security of his mom and sister and spent the majority of his time with them or by himself. Once he began to look at pornography, he isolated even more out of shame. He found that these fantasy relationships were much safer.

Through these sexual fantasies, Steve could envision himself as the man he always wanted to be, without risking rejection. But in reality, these fantasies, coupled with masturbation, only furthered his shame and sense of inadequacy. They also stunted his psychosexual development, as C. S. Lewis explains:

> For me the real evil of masturbation [and sexual fantasy] would be that it takes an appetite which, in lawful use, leads an individual out of himself to complete and (correct) his own personality in that of another (and finally in children and even grandchildren) and turns it back; sends the man back into the prison of himself, there to keep a harem of imaginary brides. And this harem, once admitted, works against ever getting out and really uniting with a real woman. For the harem is always accessible, always subservient, calls for no sacrifices. . . . Among these shadowy brides, he is always adored, always the perfect lover, no demand is made on his selfishness, no mortification ever imposed on his vanity. In the end they become the medium through which he increasingly adores himself.[11]

Steve's sexual fantasies with women certainly fit this profile described by Lewis. Through his fantasy, he was temporarily able to escape the shameful feelings of inadequacy around girls his age. His healthy desires to be confident in his masculinity and to feel desired by women could never be fulfilled in fantasy. Instead, these fantasies only reinforced his lack of confidence, which in turn fueled his same-sex compulsions.

Same-Sex Compulsions

Steve's compulsions, driven by his accumulated wounds, shame, and fantasies, were directed to members of both sexes. But his fantasies with men created the most shame for Steve. His desires for masculine affection and love were good and holy. He needed to be accepted by males in order to feel confident and affirmed in his masculine identity. But when these needs remained unmet, they became eroticized through pornography and fantasy. Wounds of peer rejection, ridicule, and self-hatred are common for those who struggle with same-sex fantasies and compulsions.[12] In his book *Growth into Manhood*, Alan Medinger explains how a lack of confidence can lead to same-sex compulsions: "A man who feels he lacks complete manhood satisfies his need for it through his homosexual behavior [or fantasy] hoping to acquire some of the other's manhood. The key point however is that this craving for another's manhood is only present in a man who lacks his own manhood."[13]

David Foster, like Medinger, struggled with same-sex compulsions through his early adult years. He offers further insight into the psychosexual development of those with same-sex compulsions:

> The typical scenario for the development of homosexual inclination is one where the child has a distant and cold parent of the same sex, and no other significant same-sex figure to take the place of the parent in the emotional bonding process that must take place in the life of every child, somewhere between the ages of two and ten. The child fails to receive the emotional (not sexual) bonding—the emotional assurance that he or she is a full and acceptable member of his or her own gender. A concomitant result is that they miss the modeling of same-sex behavior that accompanies such a bonding process.[14]

These descriptions from Foster and Medinger fit not only Steve's experience but also the experience of many who become enslaved by same-sex compulsions. The more severe the wounding, the more intense the compulsion. What is sought initially to satiate needs and medicate wounds ends up in a sexual addiction. While Steve did not act out his fantasies and compulsions with others directly, many do act out these compulsions through homosexual acts and pedophilia. Others with opposite-sex compulsions may live out their sexual fantasies through fornication, adultery, incest, rape, and prostitution. Many suffer silently in isolation and self-loathing, suppressing their sexual desires.

Though sexual compulsion has traditionally been considered more of a male struggle, many women also struggle with disordered sexual desires. Sexual compulsion among women is becoming increasingly more visible in our culture today.

Sexual Compulsion among Women

Historically, women's lust has been expressed more relationally than visually, more romantically than physically, and more subtly than overtly.[15] The traditional forms of pornography for women—romance novels, soap operas, and romantic movies, spiced with seduction and racy sex scenes—are often subtler and more socially acceptable, in contrast to the hard-core porn that has been the usual purview of men.

Karin Cooke, the author of *Dangerous Honesty*, explains: "The female mind does not typically descend swiftly down the funnel of arousal with a total focus on body parts and the physical act of sex. She descends more slowly, taking into account a wide variety of sensorial factors. Her focus is on the whole of the relationship."[16] These preferences of women naturally draw them to the soft-core porn that has been easily accessible for decades. But now that internet pornography has moved beyond the images of naked bodies (such as in magazines) to include live-action sex scenes and sexually charged chat rooms, there is a great increase in women's engagement in hard-core pornography, including sexual violence and the degradation of women. Cooke continues: "The popularity of *Fifty Shades of Grey* suggests that, even when a storyline is riddled with violence, humiliation, coercion, and manipulation (images women do not 'typically enjoy'), the existence of a narrative is, in itself, reason for women to read it and enjoy it."[17]

In my years as a marriage and family therapist, I was often troubled and bewildered when particular women shared that they were compulsively drawn to sexually demeaning kinds of activities and fantasies like sadomasochism, or to books and movies like *Fifty Shades of Grey*. When I explored with these women their desires and unmet needs behind these compulsions, it finally made sense. Some told me these activities expressed their unconscious desires to be pursued or forced into submission, as opposed to being in control. Others recognized their disordered desires for sexual degradation as an unconscious reenactment of past physical or sexual abuse experiences.

Christian therapist and sex researcher Jay Stringer verified these responses: "Whereas men tend to pursue pornography to find *power over* their shame and harm, women tend to pursue violent pornography to repeat their shame and harm."[18] I have observed this pattern of reenactment quite often for women (and men) who have been sexually abused, most of the time with little or no awareness of the connection between their current sexual compulsion and the earlier abuse. Like Susan, the graduate student I mentioned in chapter 1, most women (and men) who have been sexually violated develop sexual compulsions and are more susceptible to further abuse later in life. These sexual compulsions may be expressed in any number of ways: fantasy, masturbation, pornography, promiscuity, prostitution, acting in pornographic films, rape, lesbianism, or even in the participation in BDSM (bondage and submission; sadism and masochism).

I have also noticed that some of the women (and men) who have been sexually abused become enslaved by an opposite kind of compulsion: an aversion to sex. This is more common among Christian women who are afraid of acting out their sexual desires in any kind of sinful activity. In my marital therapy, this form of sexual compulsion came to the surface often when the wife had not yet found healing from her sexual abuse trauma or other damaging sexual experiences. Feeling contemptuous toward her own body and her sexual desires, she would compulsively and unconsciously shut down her erotic impulses, while remaining disinterested in intimacy with her husband. I have discovered similar dynamics among single and consecrated women, who have compulsively resorted to masturbation as an outlet.

In all these situations, fear and shame are often the driving force behind a compulsive aversion to sex. Observing this pattern, Comiskey adds this insight: "For young girls and women, the abusive sexual advances of men can easily create in her a fear, hostility and aversion to men."[19] Matt Fradd interviewed a teenage stripper who speaks of her aversion to men, while stripping in a night club: "It makes me feel sick. I always have thoughts like, 'I hate you so much. Please die. I want to castrate you. Stop looking at me.' While I'm in front of them, smiling and staring into their eyes, I feel nothing but loathing."[20]

Lesbian relationships are another way that women who have been sexually violated or deprived respond to their aversion to sex with men. Many of those who self-identify as lesbians prefer sexual intimacy with women as an escape from their anxiety and hostility toward men. It is not only a compulsion to avoid harm but also a desire for what they hope will be a more nurturing sexual intimacy with women (though this is not always realized, since many lesbian relationships eventually become violent and abusive).[21]

Not all same-sex compulsions among women are driven by their hatred or fear of men. Payne notes that some women are compulsively attracted to women as a result of unmet needs from an earlier developmental breach in relationship with their mothers. They long for maternal tenderness and approval, to feel safe, cherished, nurtured, and known.[22] These are holy desires and legitimate needs that can become disordered only when God's protective boundaries for sexuality are violated, whether in fantasy or in practice.

It must be emphasized that none of these responses to sexual wounding that we have been discussing throughout this chapter are inevitable. No matter how compromised we are by past wounds and disordered sexual desires, we always have free will. "No one experiencing temptation should say, 'I am being tempted by God'; for God is not subject to temptation to evil, and he himself tempts no one.

Rather, each person is tempted when he is lured and enticed by his own desire. Then desire conceives and brings forth sin, and when sin reaches maturity it gives birth to death" (Jas 1:13–15). In summary, sexual compulsions are *deadly* serious and must not be ignored.

We will address this topic of sexual sins and their deadly consequences in the next chapter. Before turning there, however, I encourage you to take a moment to reflect more deeply on the origins and consequences of our sexual compulsions. I also strongly encourage you to reflect on your personal history by further applying Steve's story in the personal activity.

Take a Moment

1. In your experience, how can you tell the difference between a holy sexual desire and a disordered sexual desire?

2. What stood out to you regarding the differences in sexual compulsions for men and women?

3. Do you believe same-sex compulsions (including same-sex attraction) are "inborn" or are the result of psychosexual wounds and cultural influences? Explain.

4. How do you understand this statement that is often used at John Paul II Healing Center conferences? "Behind every disordered desire is a holy desire, an unmet need, an unhealed wound, and a hidden pattern of sin." Can you see all these elements in Steve's story? See the personal activity for more on this.

Personal Activity

Honesty met with mercy is the antidote to our shame. We need to humbly explore our personal history in light of Christ's merciful love. In this activity, you will have an opportunity to explore Steve's story and apply it to your own experience with sexual desires and compulsions. Ask the Holy Spirit to guide you as you work your way through this activity.

Steve's Story

1. Describe the details of Steve's *sexual compulsions*.

2. What *disordered desires* were involved in those compulsions?

3. What were Steve's *holy desires* underlying his sexual fantasies and compulsions?

4. What were the *unmet needs* Steve was trying to meet through pornography and fantasy?

5. What were Steve's *unhealed wounds* and *identity lies* that were driving his sexual compulsion?

6. What were the *hidden patterns of sin* behinds Steve's sexual compulsion?

Your Story

Identify any area in your history where you have or had a disordered sexual desire or sexual compulsion of any kind. Then walk through the same questions for yourself.

1. Describe the details of your *sexual compulsions or fantasies* (even if minor).

2. If you have viewed *pornography*, when did it start? Are you currently involved?

3. What *images*, interactions, and fantasies were/are you drawn to? Be specific.

4. Have you ever *masturbated*? If so, at what age did you start? Is it still ongoing?

5. Describe your *sexual attractions*. What are the characteristics of people you are attracted to? Is there any compulsive aspect associated with these attractions?

6. Have you ever had a *sexual fantasy* involving someone who is not your spouse? Explain.

7. Have you ever had sexual fantasy toward someone of the *same sex*? What were you desiring?

8. What were/are the *disordered desires* involved in your fantasies and attractions?

9. What *holy desires* were/are underlying your sexual fantasies or compulsions?

10. What *unmet needs* were/are you trying to meet through pornography and fantasy?

11. What *unhealed wounds* were/are driving these sexual compulsions or fantasies?

12. What *hidden patterns of sin* were/are behind these sexual compulsions and fantasies?

13. *Invite Jesus* into any area of your sexual compulsions or disordered desire (past or present). How does he look at you? What does he say to you? What does he desire for you? Write this down.

5

CRUSHED BY INIQUITIES: ACKNOWLEDGING OUR SEXUAL SINS

He was pierced for our transgressions, he
was crushed for our iniquities
—Isaiah 53:5

A wide chasm exists between the world's perspective and God's perspective regarding sexuality. Before addressing God's perspective, we need to acknowledge how much the world's perspective has influenced our own attitudes. The world's viewpoint, ruled by the "father of lies" (Jn 8:44), mocks God's intention for sexuality, while denying the deadly consequences when we violate his design.

Jesus made it clear that from the beginning God intends sexual intercourse to be the sign of the sacred covenant between a man and a woman (see Matthew 19). He desires for this bond to last a lifetime so that both children and spouses may experience God's love and protection. His protective boundary for sexual intercourse (i.e., covenant marriage) is intended for the good of both spouses (communion and fidelity), the good of children (procreation, protection, provision, and nurturance), and the good of all people (social welfare). Any violation of these boundaries inside or outside of marriage constitutes sexual sin and has destructive consequences.

The influence of the world's culture is one of the main hindrances to acknowledging the reality and scope of sexual sin. If the world accepts a particular sexual practice, we can more easily rationalize it as normal and acceptable. Like Adam and Eve, we want to be our own gods and decide what is good and evil, apart from God. Since studies show that the majority of people in the world engage in sexual practices outside of marriage, it can be easy to believe that God's word in the Bible and the two-thousand-year teaching of the Church are outdated.

When we are operating from the world's perspective, we refuse to acknowledge that God is the Lord of everything, including our sexuality. We arrogantly claim a false freedom to do whatever we please with our minds and bodies. We try to overcome our shame by rationalizing our actions and denying they have any consequences for ourselves or others. We freely engage in shameless sexual behavior. We justify ourselves, while condemning others. We resent people who remind us of God's truth and resist any exposure of our shame.

For this reason Dr. Sam Fraser, a Christian family therapist, identifies four specific "denials" that must be overcome in the process of acknowledging our sexual sins and wounds. He says,

1. We must overcome the *denial of facts* by acknowledging the reality of our sexual sins.

2. We must overcome our *denial of culpability* by acknowledging our personal responsibility for our sexual sins and the wounds they have caused.

3. We must overcome our *denial of the consequences* by acknowledging the way our sexual sins have hurt God, ourselves, and others.

4. We must overcome our *denial of hope* by acknowledging that nothing is impossible with God.[1]

All of this begins as we accept what God considers sexual sins.

Sexual Sins

Sexual sins are offenses against God's holy justice and violations of the personal dignity of each person affected. These transgressions against the natural and moral law violate our integrity, while desecrating the gift of sexuality itself (*CCC*, 2337). Each of these specific sexual sins listed below are violations of chastity and are (direct or indirect) transgressions against the sixth and ninth commandments, which God gave to Moses. They have been consistently acknowledged for thousands of years in Judeo-Christian teaching (*CCC*, 2351–59, 2380, 2388, 2399–2400) and have been the basis for most laws in Western civilization for centuries.

You may notice that some of the sexual practices mentioned are now acceptable in our culture, while others are not. But a hundred years ago, the laws of our land would have upheld that each of these sexual practices is an offense against justice and a violation of our human dignity. (Note: Lust is nearly impossible to legislate, but lewd and lascivious behavior in public is still against the law.) I encourage you to go through the following list a couple of times. First go through and pay attention to your reaction to the list. What troubles you or causes a reaction? Then go through a second time and ask the Holy Spirit to gently show you when and how you have participated in any of these sexual activities, past or present. And then a third time, acknowledge which of these sexual sins have been committed against you, or by members of your family, that have had an effect on your psychosexual development.

As you go through this examination of sexual sins, keep in mind God's merciful love and compassion. Recall Jesus' interactions with the woman caught in adultery (Jn 8). Jesus did not condemn her, and he does not condemn you or your family members. So do not condemn yourself or members of your family, or others who have hurt you by their sexual sins. The list is taken from scripture and the *Catechism of the Catholic Church*, so if you desire to gain a greater understanding, you can review those sections under Life in Christ.[2] These are specific sexual sins:

Lust (including sexual fantasy, impure looks and thoughts, and using others sexually)

Masturbation (sexual stimulation of self or others outside marriage)

Fornication (sexual intercourse among unmarried people, including cohabitation)

Adultery (sex with someone not your spouse, including unlawful remarriage)

Pornography (immoral images received visually, verbally, or in written form)

Prostitution (paying for sex; desecrating another as an object of sexual gratification)

Rape (sexual assault; forcing another into any kind of sexual act, including date rape)

Homosexual activity (erotic sexual interactions with someone of the same gender)

Incest (sexually stimulating interactions with a family member other than spouse)

Pedophilia (sexual violation of a minor, through seduction or force)

Satanic ritual abuse (severe forms of abuse incorporating all forms of sin and idolatry)

Bestiality (sexual contact with an animal)

Polygamy (having multiple spouses, either at one time or consecutively)

Contraception and sterilization (intentional blocking of conception)

In vitro fertilization (artificial insemination outside of the sexual act)

Once you have acknowledged the fact that these are sins, the next step is to humbly accept personal responsibility for them. As a practical way of doing this, I encourage you to prepare for a *whole-life confession* (see appendix 1). Do not blame anyone else for your personal sins. Likewise, do not take responsibility for another's sexual sins, unless you were a willing participant. It took me many years to finally acknowledge some of these sexual sins in my life and within my family, and to examine their consequences for all of us. When I finally did acknowledge my personal responsibility for my sins, confessing them to God and then to a priest in the sacrament of Reconciliation, I experienced freedom from guilt and shame and gained a greater appreciation for God's mercy.

I now find joy helping others face their sexual sins, shame, and guilt, in order to experience the mercy flowing from God's wounded heart.

God's Wounded and Merciful Heart

Devotion to the Sacred Heart of Jesus is popular in the Catholic Church. It depicts God's compassionate love and mercy toward each one of us. No matter how grave our sins, his mercy is even greater (see Psalm 136 and James 2:13). And yet his tender heart also reveals the real consequences of our sins. Have you ever reflected on how your sexual sins pierce Jesus' tender heart? Take a moment now to contemplate this reality. If you look closely enough at the image of the Sacred Heart, you will notice the crown of thorns around Jesus' heart. He suffers with and for us. Because his heart is tender, our sins wound him more than we can possibly comprehend.

With your inspired imagination, I invite you to envision him bloodied and broken on the Cross. Can you see and feel the unfathomable physical, emotional, and spiritual suffering he is experiencing? "He was *pierced for our sins, crushed for our iniquity*" (Is 53:5; italics added). Let that reality sink in as much as you can. He absorbs our sins into his body, soul, and spirit. They cause the pain of a whip tearing his flesh. They have the force of a spear, piercing his heart.

They have the weight of nails puncturing his hands and piercing his feet. These sins crush his spirit.

Perceiving even the slightest glimpse of this reality can be overwhelming. How can we be so nonchalant about our sexual sins? God is certainly not indifferent to them. Even before Jesus came to earth to fully reveal and heal the horrific effects of our sins, the *prophets stood in the place of God. They intimately knew God's heart and felt the pain of our sin.* Hosea was called to marry a prostitute to experience God's broken heart in relation to our unfaithfulness (Hos 1:2). Jeremiah felt the intensity of the Lord's anguish over our sexual immorality (Jer 2:19–20). The prophet Nathan had to overcome his fear of death to confront King David about his adultery with Bathsheba.

When David realized he was offending God personally, he was humbled and acknowledged his offense: "Against you [God], you alone have I sinned; I have done what is evil in your eyes" (Ps 51:6). Like David, we too have offended God's goodness and pierced his tender heart. Our sexual sins wound others and ourselves, and desecrate God's name in the eyes of an onlooking world. Think about how people now view the entire Church, in light of the sexual abuse scandal involving a minority of priests. It causes many people to doubt the goodness of God and the trustworthiness of his Church.

Also consider those who are the victims of any form of sexual abuse. For each sufferer, there is a perceived abandonment or betrayal by God. Susan, from chapter 1, didn't believe in God, largely because of the sexual abuse she experienced from her father. She couldn't believe in a God who either wouldn't or couldn't protect her (we will address this more in the next chapter).

Most of us are willing to acknowledge that these grave sins of sexual abuse, pedophilia, and adultery blaspheme God's name and desecrate his intention for sexual love. But isn't this also true about *every sexual sin*? Can we also humbly acknowledge that our perverse sexual practices transgress God's will, wound his heart, and bring scandal to his name? By its very nature, sexual sin bears false witness to God, who is self-giving love, and hinders our capacity for authentic love. With each sexual sin, we are diminished in our personhood, experiencing some measure of disgrace and disintegration.

Disgrace and Disintegration

Disgrace and disintegration are inevitable consequences of our sexual sin. All of us experience a measure of unworthiness when we violate God's design for sexuality—*whether we acknowledge this reality or not.* Each time we engage in unholy sexual practices (in thought, word, or deed), we become increasingly more *disintegrated.* We lose intimacy with God and lessen our own internal integrity. We deprive ourselves of God's indwelling grace. Our awareness of shame (i.e., disgrace) is actually a gift from God—working through our consciences, letting us know that our relationship with God has been weakened. Some (venial) sins weaken grace in our souls, while other (mortal) sins completely cut us off from a vital relationship with the Holy Spirit, depriving us of integrity, charity, and grace (see *CCC*, 1849–63).

With a divided heart and darkened mind we lose some capacity to love chastely. This inevitably opens us to more sinful inclinations and sexual compulsions, driving us deeper into desolation. C. S. Lewis explains:

> Every time you make a choice you are turning the central part of you, the part of you that chooses, into something a little different from what it was before. And taking your life as a whole, with all your innumerable choices, all your life long you are slowly turning this central thing [your heart and soul] either into a heavenly creature or into a hellish creature: either into a creature that is in harmony with God, and with other creatures, and with itself, or else into one that is in a state of war and hatred with God, and with its fellow creatures, and with itself. To be the one kind of creature is heaven: that is, it is joy and peace and knowledge and power. To be the other means madness,

horror, idiocy, rage, impotence, and eternal loneliness.
Each of us at this moment is progressing to the one
state or the other.[3]

Lewis's words are extremely sobering, aren't they? Every sexual
choice really does matter. Our choices have both temporal and eternal
consequences. If we are honest with ourselves, we can see how our
sexual sins, and the effects of others' sins upon us, have exposed us
to hellish influences. Our misguided choices not only weaken God's
grace in us but also become the doorway for demonic spirits. These
demons darken our minds and divide our hearts. This is not medie-
val superstition. Demons are real, and they are invited into our souls
whenever we give into temptation and participate in any form of sin
(see Ephesians 4:27). God's words to Cain testify to this reality: "Sin
lies in wait at the door: its urge is for you, yet you can rule over it"
(Gn 4:7).

This notion of spiritual entryways may seem foreign to many of
us in our "enlightened" world, but it is really very simple. Our free
will is the gateway to good and evil. When we open a door to evil by
engaging in sexual sin, we inevitably lose some measure of our interior freedom. Jesus expresses this rather succinctly: "Everyone who
commits sin is a slave of sin" (Jn 8:34). Our sexual sins eventually
enslave us in sexual compulsion. For most of us, this experience of
losing control may occur without our full awareness.

Andy Reese, who has accompanied many in the process of restoration, understands well the dynamics leading to our enslavement:

Loss of control normally starts small and grows over
time in visible control. A lie is planted and believed. A
temptation is acted out. A wound is incurred and left
to fester. We seem to be living a lifestyle dictated by
this area of our lives. It is willful sin; then we derive
some perverse pleasure from it even if it is bringing
havoc in other parts of our life. The draw to God and
the things of God is being deadened.[4]

This process of giving into temptation and losing control is illustrated in Steve's experience (described in the previous chapter). His sexual compulsion started with one moment of temptation when he found his father's pornographic magazines. There was a natural curiosity, but he also had a choice. The voice of the Holy Spirit in his conscience whispered to him that it was wrong, but he ignored it. He immediately rationalized his actions. With that choice, he opened the doorway of his soul to demons of lust. As he continued feeding his lust, he further opened to spirits of bondage and perversion, bringing him into a lifestyle bound by this sin. His sexual integrity was compromised, as his sexual desires became increasingly more compulsive.

Though he derived a perverse pleasure from his sexual fantasies and masturbation, he was also tortured with shame and desolation from that point on. The pleasure was fleeting, but his feelings of shame persisted and increased. As Steve continued to ignore the voice of the Holy Spirit in his conscience, his mind became increasingly darkened and his heart hardened through the "deceit of sin" (Heb 3:13). Each time he returned to his compulsion, the draw to God and the things of God became deadened. We would be naïve to assume this all happened in a moment.

Steve's loss of control actually began many years earlier, with his response to the wounds he experienced from his father and peers. Remember that behind every disordered desire there are unhealed wounds and a hidden pattern of sin. Steve incurred wounds early in his life. These were untended and left to fester. His unresolved hurt and anger toward his father and peers turned into bitterness. His envy for other boys turned into hating his own body and lusting after theirs. His self-reliance became a source of pride, creating isolation. His lack of initiative to remedy those situations was fueled by the sin of sloth. The father of lies was at work in Steve's heart well before the moment he found his father's pornography.

It's sobering to think about what might have happened in Steve's life if God had not intervened in a powerful way to bring him back into relationship. Steve received the grace of the Holy Spirit in Baptism and had enough faith formation to remain open to God until the grace was restored in the sacrament of Reconciliation. This allowed him to still seek God, until he could eventually find freedom from his compulsions.

There are some, however, who become so hardened by repetitive sins that they completely deny and reject God and his moral law. Others feel so unworthy of God's love that they believe it is impossible for them to be set free. Yet even in these situations God is always desiring to draw us back to him (*CCC*, 1). No one is without hope, or beyond redemption, except those who persist until death in their hardness of heart (see Matthew 12:31).

In my previously published book about the healing power of the sacraments, *Be Transformed*, I recount the miraculous healing and restoration of a man named Hank (and his family) who had grievously sinned by sexually molesting his four daughters throughout their childhood.[5] I have witnessed similar kinds of transformation in many other seemingly hopeless situations. There is always hope when we are willing to acknowledge our sins and face how they pierce the tender heart of God. When we do this, we become capable of acknowledging the crushing consequences of our sexual sins.

Consequences of Sexual Sins

Sexual sins always have consequences; in many cases these consequences can be deadly. Overcoming Fraser's third denial (identified on page 76) requires that we take an account of the many consequences of our sexual sins. We have already seen how they offend God, cause a false witness, and cause disintegration within us. Now we will look at some of the other major consequences. Sexual sins offend the human dignity of all involved, inflict trauma that can last a lifetime (if not healed), and impact generations of family and society.

Violation of Human Dignity

As we will see in the next chapter, even a single incident of sexual violation can leave a profound and lasting impact on the dignity of each person involved (until healing occurs). The far-reaching damage touches the victims, perpetrators, family members, friends, community members, and society as a whole. We see this most clearly in the sexual abuse scandal that has rocked the Church in recent years. In this case, the reverberations are global.

As a family therapist, I worked for many years with sexual abuse survivors. I saw firsthand how profoundly it affected their personal lives and their relationships for years to come. Without exception, each survivor had to overcome layers of trauma, judgments, and identity distortions before they could trust again (we will further address this in chapter 6). I also discovered how deeply it affected the "non-participating" family members. I was surprised to discover that many parents and siblings of victims had been sexually abused during their childhood or had experienced other serious traumas or compulsions that remain unhealed and had compromised their sense of security and dignity.

But as severely wounded as the survivors and family members were, I found that the most damaged by sexual abuse were the perpetrators themselves. Many were nearly entirely crippled by shame, though they often remained in denial because it was overwhelming for them to acknowledge. My experiences are confirmed by others who have ministered to perpetrators of sexual abuse. David Foster, in his book *Sexual Healing*, notes that perpetrators of sexual abuse are "riddled with judgments, vows, bitterness, guilt, depression, fatalistic mentality, and unforgiveness. Many are victims of physical or sexual abuse, suffered from alienation, self-hatred, and deep powerlessness, needing to control others to 'prove their self-worth' and get gratification."[6]

Hank, mentioned above, fit this profile identified by Foster. For many years, he denied his sexual sins and their crushing consequences. When his wife found out and confronted him, he literally wanted to die rather than face his intense self-hatred. His wife may have wished he were already dead rather than face their family nightmare. But when she began her own healing process and invited her husband and children to participate, this gave Hank and their daughters a glimmer of hope. After working through his intense self-hatred, Hank entered into the hard work of facing his judgments, bitterness, and need for control, as well as his loss of dignity. Only after addressing his own wounds could he listen with an open heart to the unspeakable damage he had caused his wife and children.

Seeing the damage caused by his sexual sins nearly crushed Hank. But he courageously acknowledged his actions and how they affected his loved ones. He allowed each family member to express their anguish and share how his sins had robbed them of the dignity that a daughter should receive from her father, and a wife receive from her husband. After several years of addressing these heart-crushing realities, one by one the family members began to experience renewed joy and trust in their relationships (I will share more about this healing in chapter 8). But before their joy and trust could be restored, they all needed to face the deeply painful betrayal trauma they each experienced.

Betrayal Trauma

By breaking the foundations of trust, sexual violations often result in severe traumatization and betrayal. Sexual abuse and incest are far from the only sources of this trauma, however. I have discovered that there is some degree of betrayal trauma in nearly every form of sexual sin. For example, betrayal is endemic in situations of adultery. Joyce, from chapter 1, was crushed after finding out about her husband's unfaithfulness. The fact that he lied about it made it worse. Her husband and his illicit lover were also deeply impacted. In addition their children were deeply hurt by the betrayal from their father, the bitter tirades from their mother toward their father, and the subsequent divorce that shattered their trust. Moreover, those in the couple's extended family and social network were also harmed, either directly or indirectly.

Pornography has many of the same effects as adultery, though often to a lesser degree. The betrayed spouse, children, and relatives are often deeply impacted and are left to deal with the trauma for many years to come. Additionally, pornography does "grave injury to the dignity of its participants" (*CCC*, 2354). It damages the actors and producers of the pornography, as well as the consumer. Each one participates in the sin of prostitution. As we saw in the last chapter, those who are the actors and producers of pornography are also likely to have a history of sexual abuse and compulsion. And they become increasingly hardened by their participation in this form of sexual sin.

Perhaps less obvious in its impact, but still extremely damaging, are the effects of nonmarital sexual relationships, whether homosexual or heterosexual in nature. All forms of fornication (sex outside the bounds of marriage) have much more serious consequences than anyone realizes. It *always* causes harm to the intimacy and trust in the relationship. Even for those who delude themselves into believing there are no effects, there is always an impairment in the capacity of both participants to give themselves freely, fully, faithfully, and fruitfully to each other in covenant love.

Furthermore, premarital sex is *a betrayal of one's future spouse.* The breaking of intimate bonds after breakup decreases each person's capacity to give and receive love, and progressively deadens each one's heart, thus hindering further relationships. Fr. Raniero Cantalamessa observes, "Anyone who has been betrayed or hurt once is afraid to love again and be loved, because he knows how much pain another betrayal would mean. And so the numbers of those unable to believe in God's love, or any love, go on increasing."[7]

I have counseled many couples in premarital and marital counseling who have come to realize these damaging effects in their capacity to love because of previous broken sexual relationships. They feel betrayed by their spouse's (or future spouse's) past relationships. Many have become paralyzed with anxiety at the prospect of trusting again in subsequent relationships. They intuitively fear that their trust will be broken and their heart crushed again, as they try to open themselves another person who may betray them.

Once married they may also fear their own or their spouse's infidelity, since they have experienced a history of unfaithfulness in previous years. If once married they are betrayed again by unfaithfulness, their worst fears have been realized. The heart of the betrayed spouse is crushed and then hardens in response, due to the overwhelming pain of rejection. The unfaithful spouse meanwhile deadens their own heart as they deny their conscience and close themselves off from the light of God's truth and mercy.

For each of these sexual sins and more, the effects on unmarried lovers, spouses, and children can last for generations, and the cumulative effects can eventually destroy society as a whole. Does this sound overblown? Many families, including my own growing up, have been devastated by generational patterns of sexual sin. And many cultures, including our own, have been destroyed through sexual sins as well.

Generational and Cultural Impacts

King David's family offers a snapshot of both the generational and societal effects of sexual sin. His sin with Bathsheba, and his multiple marriages and concubines, had profound consequences for his family as well as for the nation of Israel (see 2 Samuel 11). First and foremost, David's sexual sins damaged his own integrity and hindered his relationship with God. His multiple lovers were also diminished by being treated as objects for his sexual satisfaction. This undoubtedly affected the children born to these women as well. As we will see in the next chapter, with his son Amnon and daughter Tamar, sexual sin spread like a deadly cancer to the next generation of David's family.

Though David's sin was forgiven, the effects were not acknowledged and healed. As a result the generational impacts increased over time. The sexual perversion, division, and rivalries in David's family line continued down through the generations, resulting eventually in the disintegration and fall of the entire nation of Israel.

This biblical example with David and his family is repeated in many families. I have experienced it personally. After my father's adultery, sexual sin permeated our family for several years. The amount of wounding through my dad's sexual sins and then each of ours is staggering. Until this pattern is stopped and brought to the Cross, sin will continue to have an increasing impact down through the generations.

In King David's family, we see generation after generation of disintegration and disgrace as a result of their sexual sins and idolatry. David's heir Solomon, who at one time was considered the wisest man who ever lived, became a fool as a result of his sexual sins. Through his many concubines and foreign wives, he invited false worship and sexual perversion into the nation of Israel. Generation after generation of kings and queens in Israel then followed suit, with few exceptions. The ultimate example of perversion is evident in the lives of the evil King Ahab and his treacherous wife, Queen Jezebel. They are among those who allowed idolatrous worship to nearly obliterate the worship of God in the nation of Israel.

Christopher and Rachel McCluskey chronicle the idolatrous worship under the leadership of Ahab and Jezebel's reign:

> Altars and idols were erected, even in God's holy temple, to Baal and the vile gods Molech, Ashtoreth, and Chemosh. (It appears that sacred stones symbolized the male testicles or possibly the entire genitalia, and an Asherah pole may have been a phallic symbol, a wooden penis used in worship. A gigantic one had apparently been placed in the Holy of Holies, and there were living quarters for male shrine prostitutes within the temple!)[8]

These idolatrous practices are an outrage against God. They are a direct offense against his goodness, kindness, and purity. But these vile practices are not past tense. They did not end with the Old Covenant. From the beginning to end of the Bible, God warns against sexual immorality because our human nature is prone to this weakness, due to concupiscence. That's why St. Paul exhorts us, "Avoid immorality. Every other sin a person commits is outside the body, but the immoral person sins against his own body. Do you not know that your body is a temple of the holy Spirit within you, whom you have from God, and that you are not your own? For you have been purchased at a price. Therefore glorify God in your body" (1 Cor 6:18–20).

Worshipping with Our Body

Worshipping God is rendering to God his due. Worship is also for our own good and for the good of our family and society. As the *Catechism* explains, it is only in adoration of God that we can become integrated (i.e., whole) people. "Human life finds its unity in the adoration of the one God. The commandment to worship the Lord alone *integrates man and saves him from an endless disintegration. . . .* An idolater is someone who 'transfers his indestructible notion of God to anything other than God'" (*CCC*, 2114; italics added).

We worship God when we *live the truth in love* by obeying his design for our sexuality, offering our whole being—body, soul, and spirit (Rom 12:1). Conversely, when we engage in sexual sin, we participate in idolatrous worship. We vainly worship ourselves rather than God. In the process we idolize human bodies, sensual pleasures, and intense orgiastic experiences (i.e., the idolatry of the body). Whether we intend to or not, we end up worshipping Satan rather than God. The McCluskeys expound, "When sexual union expresses love within covenant Christian marriage, God is glorified. When it expresses lust, selfishness, disobedience or lies, Satan is glorified. Remember we worship with our bodies (Ro. 12:1). The question we must always ask is who is being worshipped in spirit by this physical act."[9]

Few set out to worship Satan directly, though I have counseled some who have been brought up to engage in Satanic worship with all of its sexual perversion. The great majority of us participate in worshipping Satan in less obvious ways. We are deceived by the world we live in and accept what the world teaches rather than what God says will bring us fulfillment. We unwittingly worship at the altar of Baal and Ashtoreth (in sexual immorality) or offer sacrifice to Molech and Lilith (with contraception and abortion).

Acknowledging these realities in a world filled with deceptions can be quite sobering. Our culture and the generations of our families are more similar to the Israelites under King Ahab and Queen Jezebel than we would like to acknowledge. We, like the Israelites of old, engage in something akin to temple prostitution. We have erected vile images in God's holy temple. Many of us have allowed phallic images in our holy temple (our body and mind) through pornography or fantasy. We have also engaged in ritual prostitution (pornography is a form of prostitution because the actors are paid for having sex). These sexual sins and many others are evidence of our idolatry. When we engage in them, we are worshipping and glorifying Satan with our bodies, while being unfaithful to our baptismal covenant with Jesus.

All of the sexual sins we have addressed in this chapter are forms of idolatry. Each of these physical acts violates God's design for our sexuality in one way or another. They are ways of worshipping demonic "gods" and "goddesses." They dis-invite the Holy Spirit and invite demonic powers into our bodies, minds, and spirits. They desecrate Christ's body in the very act. They also create *unholy soul bonds* with the person(s) with whom we were sexually involved. (See appendix 3 for renouncing unholy soul bonds). These realities should bring us to our knees before our crucified Lord and motivate us to acknowledge our sexual sins and their deadly consequences. As we do we can also help others see clearly.

For the past fifteen years, I have been teaching these truths to seminarians. They are zealous for God's ways, but many of them, like the seminarian Steve, are still recovering from a lifetime of living in our sexually polluted culture and are in fierce battle to overcome sexual compulsions that began in puberty or earlier. When I speak about the passage in Corinthians referring to our bodies as temples of the Holy Spirit, I can see there is a disconnect between their spiritual life and their understanding of their own body, resulting from their shame over past and current sexual sins.

Looking for a way to speak to their hearts, I offer this analogy: "Suppose someone walked into the chapel while we were worshipping God and took Jesus' sacred Body (the Blessed Sacrament) from the tabernacle. Then you watched them desecrate his body by spitting on it, putting dirt on it, and screaming obscenities." I then ask them, "What would you do?" Seeing the anger and horror in their eyes, I know what they would do. They love Jesus and believe he is bodily present in the Eucharist. They would do everything in their power to stop the one desecrating Christ's body. Then I say to them, "You are Christ's body. What are you going to do to protect against anyone or anything defiling and desecrating your body? How are you going to fight for each other, so that none of you are allowing Christ's body to be desecrated?" I can tell it registers for many of them.

I bring that same question to you. Do you see your own body as a sacred temple housing the presence of God's Holy Spirit? Do you see the bodies and souls of your brothers and sisters in Christ in this same way? Or have you been so deceived by living in our world that you believe your body is your own and you can do whatever you please with it? Do you also believe other people can do whatever they want with their bodies, without any consequences?

I doubt many of us are consciously aware that we are desecrating God's holy temple when we engage in sexual sin. I do not believe most of us have the intention of worshipping Satan or desecrating Jesus' body. Like Adam and Eve we have been deceived. But we all have a choice. At any moment we can turn our hearts back toward God and worship him.

After acknowledging and confessing my sexual sins, I saw a chain reaction of God's grace released into my family. I began to pray for the generations of our family and asked for God's mercy (see Daniel 9:8–10). I believe what happened was more than psychological, as demonic strongholds over our family were broken. God released an outpouring of grace. Over the next several years, each of my brothers and sisters, and then my parents, also acknowledged their sexual sins and began to make changes in their lives and lifestyles. One by one they came into a renewed relationship with Jesus and the Church. This in turn brought incredible healing within our family.

I offer my experience as a word of encouragement for you, as you take a moment to reflect on this chapter and to engage in the personal activity. Every step you take in this process is going to bear great fruit in your life, and the effects will be multiplied in your family and in our world. You are the light of the world (Mt 5:14).

Take a Moment

1. Why do you think it is important to acknowledge our sexual sins? What happens when we remain in denial?

2. Do you perceive God's commandments regarding sexuality as restrictive or protective? Are there any sexual practices on the list you think should not be considered sins?

3. How have your sexual sins impacted your relationship with God, yourself, and your family?

4. What do you see as the similarities and differences between ancient Israel and our modern culture with regard to sexual sin and idolatry?

Personal Activity

1. Ask the Holy Spirit to guide you as you reflect on your personal history of sexual sin.

2. Begin by reflecting on Jesus' death on the Cross as the atonement for your sins. Take in the depth of his love as he is willing to be pierced and crushed for your sins to free you from them. Spend time actively thanking Jesus for his mercy toward you and for taking on your sin.

3. Reflect on the story of the woman caught in adultery in John 8. Imagine yourself as the woman and walk through the entire story, identifying who is accusing you and who is throwing stones, and see how Jesus responds.

4. With the help of the Holy Spirit, review your life and identify specific areas of sexual sin.

5. Inspired by the Holy Spirit, identify who was harmed by these sexual sins and how it affected them.

6. Write these reflections in a journal or on a piece of paper (you can burn it later if you want).

7. Plan to make a general life confession to a priest (if you are Catholic) or to a therapist, a trusted friend, a spiritual director, a twelve-step sponsor, or a mentor. Tell them what you are wanting to do so you can both set aside sufficient time and prepare your hearts. (See appendix 1 for a more detailed explanation.)

8. When you make your confession, acknowledge your sexual sins (of thought, word, and deed, and what you have failed to do) and the consequences of those sins. Humbly accept Jesus' forgiveness with gratitude. Then forgive yourself, and where it is beneficial ask for forgiveness from those you hurt.

9. Firmly resolve to "sin no more" and ask for God's help to overcome habitual patterns of sexual sin. If you have a sexual compulsion, commit to work through it, with the help of a support community, counselor, and the sacraments. (See appendix 5.)

10. Pray for your family, friends, and society that all of us may truly worship God with our bodies.

6

MOURNING BROKEN HEARTS: RELEASING OUR SEXUAL TRAUMA

The LORD is close to the brokenhearted,
saves those whose spirit is crushed.
—Psalm 34:19

Shame attempts to cover up our sexual wounds and bury the trauma associated with them. But the Bible never shies away from uncovering these painful realities. In fact, there are numerous accounts of sexual violations revealed throughout scripture, including descriptions of incest, rape, adultery, prostitution, homosexuality, ritual abuse, and much more. It is clear from both the Old and the New Covenant that God strongly condemns these acts of sexual sin and abuse (see Deuteronomy 27 and 1 Corinthians 5:1–5). His fatherly heart yearns to protect us from harm and comfort us when we have been violated (see Isaiah 4:11; 2 Corinthians 1:3).

Biblical accounts of sexual violation can be quite shocking at times. The story of Amnon and Tamar is a vivid example. We are introduced to them immediately following the narrative detailing David's sin with Bathsheba. It is as if the author wants us to see how the effects of sexual sins cause devastation down through the generations of a family. The story of Tamar and Amnon begins with these words: "David's son Absalom had a beautiful sister named Tamar, and David's son Amnon loved her" (2 Sm 13:1).

Sounds innocent enough, but we soon discover this was not a healthy brother-sister love. Rather, Amnon is obsessed with lust for his beautiful half sister. With the help of a friend, he schemes to lure her to his bedroom so he can rape her. King David, who is seemingly out of touch with these family dynamics, tells Tamar to go into her brother's room to care for him. When she arrives outside his room, Amnon orders all the servants out and pleads with her to come in. Within minutes Tamar's innocence is stolen and her heart is shattered. Allow yourself to empathize with her anguish:

> He seized her and said to her, "Come! Lie with me, my sister!" But she answered him, "No my brother! Do not shame me! That is an intolerable crime in Israel. Do not commit this insensate deed. Where would I take my shame? And you would be a discredited man in Israel." . . . Not heeding her plea, he overpowered her; he shamed her and had relationship with her. Then Amnon conceived an intense hatred for her which far surpassed the love he had for her. "Get up and leave," he said to her. She replied, "No brother, because to drive me out would be far worse than the first injury you have done to me." He would not listen to her. . . . Tamar put ashes on her head and tore the long tunic in which she was clothed. Then, putting her hands to her head, she went away crying loudly. (2 Sm 13:11–19, NAB)

This heart-wrenching description of incest and rape brings us right into the depths of the intense anguish inherent in many forms of sexual violation. Tamar's heart is pierced by Amnon's sin. She is traumatized by the experience and absorbs the identity lies resulting from all seven of the deadly wounds.

Seven Deadly Wounds

In *Be Healed*, I introduced the "seven deadly wounds" (powerlessness, shame, rejection, abandonment, confusion, fear and mistrust, and hopelessness)[1] as a way of describing what happens within our souls when we experience the impact of sin and trauma.[2] In *Be Transformed*, I elaborate that these wounds are universal and originate in the fall of mankind due to original sin.[3] And yet these wounds are uniquely experienced in each of our lives in response to specific traumatic events, as well as the long-standing patterns of our relationships within our families and culture. These wounds are deadly because they rob us of the joy of life and cut us off from freely giving and receiving love. They are the source of much of our human suffering. I believe all seven deadly wounds are present in nearly every incidence of sexual violation, most clearly within the victim and probably also in the perpetrator and the family members who are impacted, directly or indirectly.

In the sexual victimization of Tamar, each of the seven deadly wounds is present, though some are more obvious than others. Two of these devastating wounds—shame and powerlessness—are mentioned explicitly in the passage, whereas the others are implicit in the story. In drawing them out, my desire is to uncover the pervasive wounds inherent in nearly every act of traumatic sexual violation. If you have been sexually wounded in any way, my desire is to help you put into words what you have experienced in order to facilitate your healing process. If you are a support person or family member of someone who has been sexually wounded, my intention is to assist you in understanding the hidden effects of trauma so you can understand what your loved one has experienced and provide the compassion and empathy they need.

Since it is obvious in the story of Tamar and Amnon, we will begin by uncovering the deadly wound of powerlessness.

Powerlessness

By definition, sexual violation leaves victims feeling powerless. That is the nature of victimization.

> *Sexual abuse is any activity—verbal, visual, or physical—engaged in without consent, which may be emotionally or physically harmful and which exploits a person in order to meet another person's sexual or emotional needs. . . .* Consent is the key issue in this definition of sexual abuse. A person does not consent if he or she does not have the ability either to choose or to refuse the sexual activity. Age, circumstances, level of understanding, dependency, and relationship to the offender are all factors that limit a person's ability to choose.[4]

Sexual violation compromises our free will, whether through force or seduction. This can happen in any relationship. Date rape, sexual coercion within or outside of marriage, incest, pedophilia, and sex trafficking are all examples of sexual violations where free will is violated. In each case, the victimized person experiences the painful effects of powerlessness. In this situation with Amnon and Tamar, both seduction and force are in play. Tamar is seduced to come to Amnon's room. She is then physically overpowered when he doesn't heed her plea. Note the descriptions in the narrative: "He overpowered her. . . . He would not listen to her."

Tamar's words speak for every man or woman who feels powerless to stop someone from violating them. Sexual violations may or may not involve force. A long pattern of seduction, what is often called grooming, is also a way of being coerced without consent. The unsuspecting victim is seduced, and before they know it, they find themselves involved in something they would not freely choose on their own accord. There comes a point when they are convinced to do things they do not want to do. They may have been told by their abuser that because they went along with it and felt pleasure, they really desired it. *This is not consent.* Often the perpetrator makes them feel responsible and gives them a false sense of control by making choices that are not made in freedom. They feel trapped. If they try to speak up, they are silenced or shamed. If they try to resist, they are overpowered or told they want it. If they are tempted to tell someone they are threatened with harm, they are convinced it would not be a good outcome.

The wound of powerlessness is one of the greatest traumas that victims of sexual abuse experience. The following are some of the thoughts and expressions of someone struggling with this wound of powerlessness:

- I feel (felt) trapped.
- I feel helpless.
- Everything feels chaotic and out of control.
- I can't stop this.
- I am too weak or small to resist.
- They are too strong.
- There is no one to help me.

These experiences of powerlessness can become long-standing beliefs (i.e., *identity lies*) if they are not immediately worked through (see appendices 3 and 4). These beliefs are often accompanied by other wounds and identity lies, including shame. I believe shame is inherent in every act of sexual violation; it is certainly evident in Tamar's experience.

Shame

Notice the emphasis on shame in Tamar's speech. Once she realizes Amnon's intentions she begins to internalize his disgraceful behavior as her shame. "Do not *shame* me." "Where would I take *my shame*." "Not heeding her plea he overpowered her and *shamed* her." Tamar's shame is displayed powerfully in the imagery of her tearing her tunic and putting ashes on her head. Her shame is now public. She feels permanently tainted and robbed of her dignity and virginity.

Tamar intuitively knows that her encounter with Amnon will leave her feeling tarnished long after the event has passed. Every victim of sexual violation recognizes that they have been stripped of their dignity and desecrated in ways they can't describe. Depending on the age and type of violation, this deadly wound of shame can be internalized in many different forms. For some, shame can act like a shroud that keeps their pain buried. For others, shame is expressed in the belief that they are somehow responsible for the abuse. For still others, shame is an intuitive awareness that they are irrevocably damaged, desecrated, and tarnished. The following phrases are often felt and uttered by those who have been sexually violated, once they can verbalize their experience:

- I am damaged and tainted; I will never be normal again.
- I hate my body (my gender, my sexuality) because of what happened to me.
- I felt pleasure so I must have wanted it (ambivalence over pleasure/pain).
- I am bad, dirty, worthless, unlovable, ruined, and so forth.
- It's my fault because I was naïve, didn't stop it, and didn't tell anyone.
- I'm perverted, my desires are twisted, my body betrayed me, and so forth.

These expressions of shame by the victims of sexual abuse are often ways of avoiding the experience of powerlessness and mitigating the pain. They are also ways of internalizing the perpetrator's shame. Notice in the story with Tamar that she recognizes the shame Amnon will bring to himself, their family, and to the nation. "That is an intolerable crime in Israel. . . . You would be a discredited man in Israel." Every perpetrator (who is not completely disconnected from their heart) experiences intense shame at some unconscious level, whether they acknowledge it or not. And yet, like most perpetrators of abuse, Amnon refuses to acknowledge his own shame. Instead, he projects it onto Tamar by disgracing her in the act, and then projects his shame as contempt for her.

Dr. Dan Allender speaks of the dark cruelty inherent in contempt: "Contempt is condemnation, an attack against the perceived cause of shame. The attack is laced with hatred, venom, and icy cruelty."[5] Contempt can be turned inward against oneself, in the form of self-hatred. Or it can be projected outward against the one who reminds the person of their shame. Contempt is often present in both the perpetrator and the victim of sexual abuse. Both hold contempt for themselves and also toward the other. This is evident in Amnon's chilling contempt for Tamar, which left her feeling even more rejected.

Shame and contempt are closely related with the wound of rejection. I have met many men and women who have experienced intense rejection from their abuser following the act of sexual violation. Many are also mired in self-contempt. This is a form of self-rejection.

Rejection

Everyone wants to be loved. And no one desires to be rejected. Yet in many cases of sexual abuse, a strange mixture of being chosen and rejected is present at the same time. Amnon desired Tamar because he found her attractive. Yet he treated her like an object for his own satisfaction—thus degrading her. Then, after violating her, he completely rejected her. "Then Amnon conceived an intense hatred for her which far surpassed the love he had for her. 'Get up and leave,' he said to her. She replied, 'No brother, because to drive me out would be *far worse* than the first injury you have done to me.' He would not listen to her."

It is hard to imagine how anything could be more degrading than being raped and humiliated, but Tamar feels the second rejection "would be far worse." I am not sure that is true in every situation of sexual violation, but I have heard similar comments from victims of incest to realize it is a common experience. We can all relate to this if we have ever experienced being used and then discarded. Being used and treated like an object is already an experience of rejection. This experience of rejection increases when we are despised and then discarded after being used. Lust always uses and then discards. In sexual abuse, the stakes are higher. The venomous contempt of the abuser following the abuse drives the rejection deep into the victim's heart. These thoughts and phrases give voice to the experience of rejection:

- I'm not loved.

- I'm not desired.

- I'm not wanted.

- I'm not good enough (good-looking enough, smart enough, etc.).

- I'm not valued.

The wound of rejection can extend beyond the experience of sexual violation. Abuse victims (and their perpetrators) can also be severely wounded by the rejecting responses of family members and community. As I write this I am thinking of many men and women I know who were abused and then felt the rejection from their family members or faith community. When they finally mustered the courage to speak about the abuse, they were not believed, or they were blamed or told to shut up. These reactions from those from whom we desire comfort and understanding perpetuate the wound of rejection and add another deadly wound—abandonment.

Abandonment

In addition to the searing pain of rejection, sexual abuse victims (and perpetrators) often experience the anguish of feeling abandoned before, during, and after the abuse experience. They may experience abandonment by their family, their friends, and their community. The greatest damage comes when they feel abandoned by God.[6] This is the deepest and most difficult pain that abuse victims (and perpetrators) face in their healing process. It is often experienced as rage (we will discuss this more in chapter 9).

Many times, these deeper abandonment wounds precede sexual violation and make the person more susceptible to being seduced. Allender asserts, "The typical home where abuse occurs is relationally distant and empty. The variations of the pattern are many, but the fact remains that legitimate, healthy intimacy is rare or non-existent in abusive homes. The environment is a breeding ground for deep soul hunger."[7]

Adding to this ongoing sense of abandonment, survivors (and perpetrators) often feel isolated in the aftermath of sexual violation. If the abuse is shrouded in secrecy, the child or adult may feel they are living a double life, hiding their painful inward reality while putting on a mask to avoid being seen and known by the world around them. This isolation and hiding creates a deep loneliness and a feeling of not being understood in the deepest recesses of one's soul. Many survivors have told no one about their abuse or how they feel. Others have tried to tell someone in their family or community and have been ignored, called a liar, or ostracized. If we read further about the story of Tamar, we discover that her father, David, and her mother, Maccah, did nothing to comfort or protect her after they were told what happened. Instead, they protected Amnon and their family image.

The response by King David and Tamar's mother is far too common in situations of sexual abuse, whether in families or in the Church or society. Therefore, it is not unusual for the person abused to feel unprotected by a parent, church authorities, the law, or even by God. The lament of Jesus from the Cross can be echoed by all those who have been abused and feel abandoned: "My God, my God, why have you abandoned me?" (Ps 22:2). In other words, why didn't you—God or your representatives (mom, dad, pastor, bishop, etc.)—protect me from this abuse, or at least comfort me when I told you? This has been the experience of many in the Church and within families.[8]

Abandonment is reflected in the following thoughts and words of those who have been sexually violated (as well as the perpetrator):

- I am all alone.
- No one cares about me.

- No one understands me.

- There is no one to help me (or comfort me).

- God has abandoned me.

- No one protected me.

- I feel lost and disconnected (dissociation).

These last two statements (feeling lost and disconnected) are often an indication that the pain of abandonment is deeply embedded and the victim has dissociated from their pain. In his insightful book *The Body Keeps the Score*, Dr. Bessel van der Kolk explains that *dissociation* is normal with severe trauma, especially for young children. It is the self-protective mechanism of our brains and bodies to handle an overwhelming situation. It contributes to "feeling lost, overwhelmed, abandoned, and disconnected from the world and in seeing oneself as unloved, empty, helpless, trapped and weighed down."[9] Dissociation is usually associated with early childhood trauma and is more likely in families where the child has not been seen, known, and adequately attached and attuned to by his parents, especially by their mothers.[10]

Dissociation protects the victim at the time of abuse from feeling powerless and terrified, but over time it reinforces the victim's sense of abandonment. In a certain sense, it becomes the way the abused person *abandons themselves*, by disconnecting from their pain. It also cuts the person off from an awareness of God's presence in the area of wounding, thus contributing to the experience of feeling abandoned by God.

In addition, dissociation is often marked by a sense of bewilderment that adds to the inevitable confusion experienced in the aftermath of sexual trauma.

Confusion

It is not at all uncommon for confusion to cloud one's ability to process what is happening in the midst of an unwanted sexual experience and then to remain as an ongoing condition until healing occurs. Particularly for a young child it is very difficult to understand what they are experiencing with all the conflicting feelings and relational distortions.

Confusion is present in nearly every form of sexual violation, not just with young children. Here are the thoughts and phrases that indicate that the wound of confusion is operative:

- I don't understand what is happening.

- This doesn't make sense.

- I don't know what to do.

- I can't figure this out; I can't put the pieces together.

- I can't concentrate; it's hard to focus.

- Everything seems disjointed and chaotic.

- My thoughts are racing, and I can't think straight.

Sexual violation is often a very confusing experience, especially when the abuser manipulates the mind of his or her victim as a means of controlling them. The victim internalizes this confusion with contradictory thoughts and feelings that may not even be articulated: Am I wanted or rejected? Is this pleasurable or painful? Is this love or betrayal? Am I good or bad? Did I ask for this, or was I deceived and forced? Am I chosen or discarded? Long after the event has passed, this kind of confusion can remain in the heart of a survivor for years to come (until they receive healing). The confused survivor may try to regain control of the situation by trying harder to figure out what is happening, but this rarely works. It only adds confusion.

Van der Kolk explains the neurological impact of trauma by describing how our brains become incapacitated in the midst it. "The overwhelming experience is split off and fragmented so that the emotions, sounds, images, thoughts and physical sensations related to the trauma take on a life of their own."[11]

This fragmentation from trauma and the resulting confusion adds to the overall sense of mistrust and a pervasive fear of trusting others in relationship, as well as the fear of trusting one's own perceptions and experiences.

Fear and Mistrust

Fear and mistrust go hand in hand with violation and betrayal, and these are central features of sexual violation. This is especially true when the relationship is with someone previously trusted. Allender observes:

> All abuse is a violation of the sanctity and whole-ness of the human soul, but when sexual abuse is perpetrated by a member of one's own family, or by someone who has gained one's trust, the loss is even more severe. Sexual abuse is always a violation of relationship. The violation always damages the soul, irrespective of the severity, nature of the relationship with the perpetrator, use or non-use of violence, or duration of the abuse.[12]

After an experience of betrayal in relationship, the problem becomes, *How do I trust again? How do I open myself to love if I am in danger of being violated again? How do I trust my own perceptions and experiences?* These are common struggles with all trauma, but especially when sexual abuse is involved. Can you imagine the fear and mistrust Tamar must have felt? Could you see her dating or marrying someone after this happened? Can you imagine her fear of being alone in the presence of any man? The anxiety would be overwhelming; she might spend hours obsessing over what might happen to her in these relationships if she were to let her guard down.

Learning to trust again is more than a matter of the will. It requires deep healing of the underlying trauma. After years of research, van der Kolk concludes:

> Trauma by definition is unbearable and intolerable. Most rape victims . . . and children who have been molested become so upset when they think about what they experienced that they try to push it out of their minds. . . . It takes tremendous energy to keep

> functioning while carrying the memory of terror, and
> the shame of weakness and vulnerability. . . . While we
> all want to move beyond trauma, the part of our brain
> that is devoted to ensuring survival . . . is not very
> good at denial. . . . Feeling out of control, survivors
> of trauma often begin to fear that they are damaged to
> the core and beyond redemption.[13]

Notice the feeling words that van der Kolk describes: *unbearable, intolerable, terror, vulnerability, out of control,* and *fear.* These are all symptoms related to the deadly wounds of powerlessness and fear. When betrayed and violated, it becomes difficult to be vulnerable again. Panic arises whenever the victim feels out of control. This is true in the face of ongoing and repetitive violations, as well as for years after the abuse has stopped. Flashbacks of the abuse can be a source of terror that leads the survivor to narrow their life experience.

Anyone who has experienced severe trauma can relate to this experience to some degree. When we feel out of control, our instinctual response is to grasp for control in order to feel safe and secure. The problem is that this self-perpetuated security becomes a prison. We form fortresses of self-protection and barricade our hearts against the possibility of being deceived or violated again. These are some of the ingrained thoughts and beliefs that help fortify this stronghold of fear and mistrust:

- I feel anxious, terrified, and out of control.
- If I trust again, I will be hurt (devastated or die).
- I need to protect myself.
- I will never trust [a man, a woman, a priest, a teacher, God, etc.].
- If I open myself, I will be betrayed again.
- Something bad is going to happen (pervasive sense of dread).
- I'm afraid I'm going to die.

For anyone who has been deeply wounded through sexual abuse, having to trust again is their worst nightmare. Will they be deceived and betrayed a second time? But the alternative is even worse. Closing one's heart in fear and mistrust results in greater isolation and shame, and eventually gives way to the wound of hopelessness.

Hopelessness

"Tamar put ashes on her head and tore the long tunic in which she was clothed. Then, putting her hands to her head, she went away crying loudly." What a graphic and heart-breaking description, revealing how the wound of hopelessness has already taken root in Tamar's heart. She is mourning her broken heart and her loss of innocence. Tearing her tunic symbolizes her shattered heart. Putting ashes on her head is a symbol of death and despair. Wailing in this situation is an expression of intense loss, but even more the deep-seated belief that what is lost cannot be restored.

Hopelessness is an experience of death, as part of the survivor's soul has already tasted death. Hopelessness is frequently manifested in a desire to die.[14] At this point in the story, Tamar has experienced the death of her dignity, her dreams, and her desires. Her reaction gives voice to the hopelessness that resides in the heart of many survivors of sexual abuse (and their perpetrators). The descriptions are varied, but they all reveal a deep sense of despair and never-ending pain:

- My life is ruined.
- I can never recover from this.
- No matter what I do, this will never get better.
- I can't stop the pain; things will never change.
- I have nothing to look forward to.
- I feel dead inside; nothing brings me joy.
- There is nothing to live for anymore; I just want to die.

For many victims of sexual abuse, suicidal thoughts are expressions of this deadly wound of hopelessness. Other signs are depression, withdrawal from family and friends, self-harm (like cutting), addiction, eating disorders, promiscuous sex, and apathy—a loss of drive or purpose. Hopelessness is driven by the belief that nothing matters and there is no hope in sight for anything to change. While these beliefs are not ultimately true, they feel very real in the aftermath of sexual violation and for many years to come until healing can occur.

Even once the healing process has begun, this wound of hopelessness can effectively block treatment or lead the survivor to give up easily if they do not see progress quickly enough. The wound of hopelessness often emerges each time a new area of pain or shame is uncovered. (This wound of hopelessness is often even greater for the perpetrator of abuse when they finally seek help.[15])

Hopelessness is a signal that a person has shut down due to all the pain and shame. This was the condition of Rita's heart, a woman I met several years ago who was sexually abused twice—once as a child by her brother and the second time as an adult by a priest who offered to help her overcome her childhood abuse. When you hear her story you will understand why she spent many of her days contemplating suicide. Several times she came close to dying. But thank God, due to his continual pursuit of her heart and the grace of perseverance, she is alive and beginning to thrive again.

Rita's Story

Sweet and innocent, Rita was four years old when her older brother began to sexually violate her. Dan was thirteen. Their parents both worked during the day, so Dan watched his younger sister after school. She was not allowed to go out and play. She figured it didn't matter much because there were no children her age in the neighborhood. Instead, she loved to play with dolls in her room by herself. This made her happy and kept her from facing her underlying loneliness.

Dan resented his younger sister for having to "babysit" her, since it prevented him from hanging out with his friends after school. When their parents came home from work each evening, they were tired and would retreat to the bedroom or the living room to watch television.

Although their parents met the children's basic needs, neither Rita nor Dan received the attention and love they needed from their parents. This lack of affection and attention left them feeling both alone and unloved. Rita internalized her hurt, while Dan acted his out, manifesting in angry outbursts and rebellion, often taking out his rage on his younger sister.

In the afternoons, after school, Dan would come into Rita's room unannounced. At first, she liked the attention but soon became confused when he would entice her to take off her clothes. She became further confused when he began to stimulate her physically. She liked the attention and found the physical touching comforting and pleasurable but felt embarrassed about it at the same time. She knew she needed to hide these secrets from her parents. Dan reinforced her resolve by telling her that something terrible would happen if she told them.

As time went on, Dan's actions became more violent and agonizing to Rita. She no longer liked the attention. In fact she dreaded it; the moments of pleasure were few and far between. But she felt powerless to stop her brother and feared for her life. Dan would insert painful objects into her body and laugh sadistically when she cried out in pain. He threatened that if she ever told anybody, he would do much worse. I was horrified when I heard the details decades later. In describing what happened she writes, "This included all forms of sexual activity and what my longtime therapist called 'sexual torture.'"

The abuse went on for several years and became increasingly more violent until Dan left home at the age of eighteen. Rita told no one about their secret. She was convinced there was no way she could share it with her parents or anyone else. But later as an adult, she found a compassionate priest in her parish. Feeling safe, she began to open up for the first time. She had never had anyone care for her emotionally as he did. But even as she began to share about the abuse in general, she found it extremely difficult to talk about the specific events. She felt embarrassed and confused, as well as terrified by the pain she would inevitably feel. She also feared he might think less of her. But he encouraged her to seek therapy, and this enabled her to begin a process of healing.

During this time, Rita mustered up her courage to tell her parents what her brother had done to her as a child. Instead of supporting her, her parents stayed neutral, which felt like an even greater rejection and abandonment. She went into deep depression and attempted suicide and ended up in the hospital. Years later she attempted therapy several times, but whenever the memories became overwhelming, she would quit.

Many years later, while living in different city, she met another priest who offered to help her work through her abuse memories. Fr. Tony earned her trust by his patience and understanding. She found herself sharing details she never imagined she would tell anyone. Fr. Tony offered to help her heal, and after hearing the details of her story, he began praying for her in spiritual direction. This soon became confusing when he talked about "laying hands" on those parts of her body that had been severely abused. When she consented, this led to what he called "therapeutic touch" to help her overcome her shame and fear of sexual pleasure. Before long, he began to gently stimulate Rita to the point of orgasm and encouraged her to do the same with him. This soon led to sexual intercourse—all in the pretext of healing Rita's childhood wounds.

Because of Fr. Tony's compassion and gentleness, Rita believed at first that this was God's way of healing her, so she continued to trust him despite her feelings of shame, confusion, and fear that felt eerily similar to her early childhood experiences with her brother. When she brought these feelings to Fr. Tony, he reassured her that they were just her feelings from childhood coming to the surface, and it was all part of her healing process. Because Rita had long ago lost trust in her own intuition, she dismissed her feelings of discomfort and continued the relationship. It was both exhilarating and confusing, comforting and agonizing.

Finally in prayer one day during adoration, she realized she was afraid to face Jesus because of her shame. That is when she finally realized that Fr. Tony had been sexually violating her. She hated herself for trusting him and allowing herself to be deceived. This spiritual-father-turned-lover had exploited her vulnerability, betrayed her trust, and violated the nature of their spiritual-direction relationship. In many ways this experience with Fr. Tony was more damaging than the first abuse with her brother, making it extremely difficult for Rita to trust any other priests or therapists, or God for that matter. For several years afterward, she returned to the world of isolation and shame that had been her refuge and prison as a child. She soothed herself in compulsive masturbation and vowed she would never share her pain with another human being. (As we will see in chapter 9, she eventually experienced deep healing, but not without a raging battle with God over feeling betrayed and abandoned by him.)

Layers of Suffering

Let's reflect on Rita's experience, in light of everything we have been discussing in this chapter. Notice the context of her family environment before and during the abuse experiences. She was lonely and had a lot of unmet emotional needs in relationship with her parents. She did not feel safe or secure enough to go to them for protection. These abandonment and rejection wounds (Type A traumas) left her feeling unprotected and alone in her life, even prior to being sexually abused by her brother. Because of these factors, she had nowhere to go to share what was happening to her once her brother began to abuse her.

Rita also felt powerless in all the situations of her abuse and in her family. Her brother used seduction at first and then overt power and domination. Her parents and Fr. Tony exerted their authority, and she felt she had no voice. Fr. Tony seduced her into sexual acts in the name of healing her. These all contributed to her wound of powerlessness. Also notice the multiple betrayal traumas (wound of fear/mistrust) she experienced. First she felt betrayed by her brother, Dan; then with her parents, who refused to believe her; and finally with Fr. Tony, who seduced her into trusting him with her sexual wounds and betrayed his priestly relationship with her.

In a sense, the betrayals by her parents and Fr. Tony were even more damaging than her brother's betrayal because they also affected her spiritually. A priest, like parents, is called to be an icon of Christ and an image of the faithful and protective Father. Fr. Tony appeared to be the emotionally engaged father she never had growing up but always desired with her dad. She trusted Fr. Tony and cared for him more than any other person in her life. She vulnerably revealed her heretofore undisclosed secrets to him. She shared her shame, her fears, and her deepest pain, and she trusted his words that he was there to help her. These factors made his betrayal much more damaging.

The incidences with Fr. Tony affected her ability to trust her own discernment and thus made it extremely difficult to trust in any other relationship. They also shattered her trust with the Church and with God. This may have been the deepest impact of her sexual abuse experience. Worst of all, she felt abandoned by God. Every child and adult who is sexually violated has legitimate questions about how God, who is ultimate Father and protector, could "stand by and allow this to happen." (God is not guilty of this, of course; however, it is a very legitimate question in the heart of every abused person that needs to be addressed.) This pain of perceived abandonment from God is perhaps the deepest pain in sexual abuse. Abandonment from God can also be experienced by the perpetrator and by family members when they find out about the abuse.

As we will see in part II, all the wounds and identity lies need to be fully addressed and resolved for healing to reach the deepest recesses of each person's heart. Before proceeding to part II, I encourage you to take a moment to reflect on the impact of sexual violations and then apply this knowledge personally in your life in the personal activity.

Take a Moment

1. Describe how Tamar and Rita experienced each one of the seven deadly wounds.

2. Which of those wounds do you think their abusers and family members experienced?

3. How have you experienced shame, contempt, and rejection in your life? What identity lies perpetuate these wounds?

4. What has been your experience (if any) of dissociation? What were some of its benefits and handicaps?

Personal Activity

1. Did you identity with anything in the story of Tamar or Rita? Explain.

2. Describe when and where you experienced any of these deadly wounds in your life.

   Powerlessness: The experience of feeling trapped, helpless, overwhelmed, and weak.

   Shame: The experience of feeling deficient, dirty, tainted, and disgraced.

   Rejection: The experience of feeling unwanted, devalued, discarded, and unloved.

   Abandonment: The experience of feeling alone, uncared for, unseen, and misunderstood.

   Confusion: The experience of feeling lost, bewildered, chaotic, and fragmented

   Fear and mistrust: The experience of feeling threatened, insecure, unprotected, and unable to trust.

   Hopelessness: The experience of feeling dead, disappointed, distraught, and despairing.

3. How are these wounds and identity lies affecting your relationships in the present?

4. Are you aware of how dissociation has been evident in your life? How has it affected you?

5. What are you feeling after reading through this chapter? I encourage you to express it by writing it out as a prayer to Jesus or to God the Father.

PART II

RESTORING SEXUAL WHOLENESS

As you prepare to read about and engage the process of restoration in part II, I encourage you to reflect on part I as a whole. So far we have been addressing sexual traumas, sins, compulsions, and identity distortions as separate areas of sexual brokenness, but in reality they are interrelated and must be addressed as a whole. The following diagram is a summary of the layers of sexual brokenness identified in part I and how they are interrelated in our lives.

Layers in the Process of Sexual Restoration

Notice how these areas of sexual brokenness are arranged hierarchically. *Sexual sins* are on the top of the pyramid because they are often the most visible manifestation of our sexual brokenness—the fruit on our tree. Underlying these sins are *sexual compulsions*, which fuel and propel sexual sins. Directly below these are *gender identity distortions*, which are often the driving forces behind our disordered desires and sexual compulsions. Below identity distortions are *sexual abuse and betrayal traumas* (Type B traumas) and *psychosexual wounds* (Type A traumas). They are at the bottom of the diagram because these are the deepest area of our sexual brokenness. They are often the most hidden and challenging wounds to face and resolve.

Your personal healing journey may start at any of these levels and move up or down in progression as the Holy Spirit leads you, but all five areas of brokenness must be addressed for sexual integration to be complete. Restoration is rarely a linear process. Rather, it is a uniquely personal and ongoing encounter with Jesus in the areas of our particular brokenness.

Having identified and discussed the various sources of our sexual wounding in part I, we turn our attention now toward Jesus, our Divine Physician and Good Shepherd, who heals our deepest wounds and guides us on the path to wholeness.

- Chapter 7, "Anointed by the Spirit," delineates Jesus' personal mission of restoration (Isaiah 61) and how it applies to each one of us. In this chapter you will learn about the necessity of our spiritual poverty and how his power is made perfect in our weakness.

- Chapter 8, "Beauty Instead of Ashes," focuses on the process of gaining freedom from our sexual sins and compulsions. Surrendering our sexual brokenness to Jesus, he progressively sets us free from our enslavement to sexual compulsions, sins, wounds, identity lies, and the many barriers to healing.

- Chapter 9, "Joy Instead of Mourning," details the often-intensive process of healing our sexual trauma. Jesus, who is intimately close to the brokenhearted, comforts us in our deepest pain. His love and truth heal our wounds and identity lies.

- Chapter 10, "Oaks of Righteousness," provides a vision for restoring sexual integrity. United with Jesus, we find our security in the Father's love, maturity as we grow in Christlike virtue, and purity as we learn to live in union with the Holy Spirit.

- Appendices 1–4 provide specific prayer activities and spiritual tools to assist you in the process of restoration. These include (1) a guide to a "Whole-Life Confession," (2) a process for "Giving and Receiving Forgiveness," (3) prayers for "Renouncing Barriers to Healing," and (4) a prayer process for "Healing Identity Wounds." These are valuable tools to be used immediately and throughout your life as you continue to grow in sexual wholeness. Appendix

5 is a compendium of "Additional Resources" for continuing the journey of restoration.

As we begin this process of restoration, I encourage you to begin in prayer:

> Heavenly Father, as we examine our sexual broken-ness in the light of Christ, help us to understand that our identity lies keep us confused about who we are and bound by our sins and compulsions.
>
> Give us the fortitude to resist temptation and to break free from unholy physical and/or emotional attachments to people that keep us separated from you.
>
> Assist us in forgiving others, so we may be receptive to your mercy.
>
> Help us see ourselves as you see us.
>
> Provide us the courage to break down the walls we have built around our hearts that have protected us so well for so many years, and give us the confidence to put our faith in you, knowing that you will now be our protection and will guide us safely to true freedom, peace, and happiness.
>
> We ask this in Jesus' name. Amen.[1]

7

ANOINTED BY THE SPIRIT: ENCOUNTERING JESUS' MISSION OF RESTORATION

*The Spirit of the Lord is upon me, because he
has anointed me.*

—Luke 4:18

Each of us naturally longs to be delivered from the ongoing suffering caused by our sexual sins, wounds, identity distortions, and compulsions. But as we eventually discover, we cannot free or heal ourselves. We need a savior. Like Adam and Eve, we remain trapped by fear and shame and cut off from God—the source of our love and freedom.

When our first parents broke covenant with God, he didn't reject them. Rather, he pursued them in order to restore them. But they were not willing. Adam's words have echoed down through all of human history: "I was afraid, because I was naked, so I hid" (Gn 3:10). Since the onset of original sin, this is our common plight as fallen human beings. We feel exposed in our sin and wounds, so we hide in shame. We deeply fear being condemned and discarded. Due to the influence of the "father of lies" (Jn 8:44), we now have a distorted image of God. We perceive him as a demanding and distant tyrant, rather than a loving and merciful Father who seeks our good and desires communion with us.[1]

These distorted images of God deter us from bringing our sexual wounds to him for healing. Many of us wonder if our heavenly Father even knows or cares about what we are going through. Sometimes in the middle of our struggles we may perceive him as a disinterested bystander. Or worse yet, like Adam, we may blame him for causing our suffering. But the truth is exactly the opposite. God did not cause Adam and Eve's suffering, nor did he remain aloof from them. Rather, he lovingly pursued them. He has been pursuing each one of us ever since. The Church teaches this as a foundational truth: "God never ceases to draw man to himself" (*CCC*, 27).

God draws near to save us. The word "salvation" means to save, rescue, deliver, heal, restore, and make whole.[2] We all need salvation. We are enslaved by our sins and compulsions, disintegrated by our wounds and identity distortions, and bound by shame and fear. Even a casual reading of the scriptures demonstrates God's relentless pursuit of us, for our salvation. Think of Moses, the prophets, and Jesus' parables of the lost coin, the lost sheep, and the prodigal son (Lk 15). Yahweh's conversation with Moses is a perfect example of his compassion and pursuit of us in our suffering. "I have witnessed the affliction of my people . . . and have heard their cry . . . so I know well what they are suffering" (Ex 3:7).

God is not indifferent to our suffering. Quite the contrary, he is filled with "tender mercy" (Lk 1:78). He has a heart for our misery and moves toward us to free us. When we ask for his help, he acts decisively on our behalf (Ps 18:7). The scriptures are filled with stories of God's mercy in action. Throughout these accounts, he demonstrates his willingness to hear our cries, rescue us from danger, forgive us our wrongdoings, comfort us in our affliction, heal our wounded hearts, and restore us to wholeness. We see this most visibly in the gospels.

Jesus' compassion and decisive action is tangibly expressed in his healing encounters with wounded people (e.g., see John 4 and 8). On the Cross, he became one with every victim of abuse, showing that his suffering is intimately and irrevocably intertwined with ours.

He was stripped, humiliated, and violated. Yet his response was one of complete forgiveness for his abusers, betrayers, and all who abandoned and rejected him. He offers the same forgiveness to each of us, no matter what we have done to him, to ourselves, or to others.

God could not show his concern any more visibly than by coming among us as he did in the person and mission of Jesus Christ.

Jesus' Mission

Jesus' name literally means "God's salvation."[3] *His mission is restoration.* In case we have any doubt, he boldly proclaimed this mission in his hometown synagogue, as he began his ministry. With great authority he spoke the words from Isaiah as his own: "The spirit of the LORD God is upon me, because the Lord has anointed me . . . to bind up the brokenhearted, To proclaim liberty to the captives,   release to the prisoners," (Is 61:1). Then, "rolling up the scroll, he handed it back to the attendant and sat down, and the eyes of all in the synagogue looked intently at him. He said to them, '*Today this scripture passage is fulfilled in your hearing*'" (Lk 4:20–21; italics added).

Can you imagine participating in that gathering with his hometown folks? Many of the people who saw Jesus grow up were in attendance that day. These same people watched Jesus develop from a young boy into a mature man. They must have been dumbfounded as he publicly declared himself to be the long-awaited Messiah (i.e., "Anointed One"). While Luke's version is a shorthand summary of the passage, we can safely assume that Jesus proclaimed the entire passage in Isaiah 61. He was unequivocally letting everyone know that he had been sent by the Father and chosen for this unique mission. At his Baptism, the Holy Spirit poured out his anointing upon him. He was here to bring good news to the afflicted, to heal the brokenhearted, and to offer freedom to the oppressed. He promised a crown of beauty instead of ashes, the oil of joy instead of mourning, and a garment of praise instead of despair (Is 61:1–4).

Jesus did not merely read these words from Isaiah. He proclaimed them with the utmost authority and lived them with every fiber of

his being. His teachings, healings, crucifixion, and resurrection fulfilled his mission. Neither did his mission end when he ascended into
heaven. Before leaving, he commissioned his disciples to carry out
his mission and then poured out the anointing of the Spirit upon them
at Pentecost. His mission of restoration is ongoing, right up to our
present day. Jesus continues this work of redemption in unison with
his Spirit through his mystical Body the Church. The sacraments are
given to us for this purpose: to participate in his mission of restoration
through the anointing of the Holy Spirit. We are now his "anointed
ones" who carry out his mission in union with him.

This is the best possible news. But even for many of us who are
familiar with these gospel truths, we often remain disconnected from
their reality in our own lives. The Father's merciful love often fails to
penetrate our well-barricaded hearts. Our wounds and sins distort our
perception of him, even when our theological learning acknowledges
the objective truth of the gospel message. For many of us, there seems
to be a disconnect between our understanding of Jesus' mission as it is
revealed in the Bible and Church teaching and our personal experience
of it. We may feel drawn to the Jesus we read about in the gospels but
do not know how to relate to him in the here and now of our current
life circumstances, in the midst of our sexual wounds, compulsions,
and identity distortions.

I say this out of my own experience. Until my late twenties and
early thirties, I saw little connection between Jesus' mission of restoration and my own life experiences or personal mission. Though I was
already a family therapist, I could not assist others in experiencing
Jesus' mission of restoration until I knew it firsthand in my own life
and family.

Personal and Family Restoration

I grew up in a faithful Catholic family—at least that was my perception at the time. I attended Catholic grade school and high school and
took my faith seriously—up to a point. But when things in my world

began falling apart in my early teenage years, I did not turn to God for help. Like many others I tried to manage the circumstances myself.

At the age of fourteen, I was devastated by the events I mentioned in chapter 1, including my dad's unfaithfulness and my parents' subsequent separation and divorce. Within a week or two of my dad's leaving, my basketball coach attempted to sexually molest me. When I returned home, I told no one about the incident with my coach, as I dealt with still another traumatic betrayal from my first girlfriend while I was away. A few months later a second girlfriend betrayed my trust.

Though I was somewhat oblivious at the time, I can now look back and see how these events set my heart in a pattern of fear and self-protection. Without knowing it at the time, my heart shut down in pain, affecting nearly every area of my life. This was most evident in my loss of relationships with everyone I felt close to, as well as my declining performance in sports and school. Later that year, my uncle and I painted his room black, including his windows. Those black windows were an outward manifestation of how I felt inside. I couldn't see out, and people couldn't see in.

Soon after these events we moved from Pittsburgh to South Florida, leaving behind my older brother Dave, along with our extended family and all our friends. It was a rough year and a half, to say the least. We did not see or hear from my dad, until Dave went searching for him and discovered that he had started another family without us knowing anything about it. Soon after Dave dropped out of school, he became addicted to heroin. Our family survived on food stamps, as my mom went back to school. My mom and siblings were all struggling to survive in one way or another, emotionally and spiritually. I felt I was on my own and had to navigate the circumstances while taking care of my younger brothers and sisters. I had few friends, and I didn't feel close to anyone. Unwilling to risk rejection from girls, because of the earlier betrayals, I didn't engage in many social activities.

In the midst of all the spiritual darkness and disorientation, I was not aware of how God was actively working in my life and in our family. But looking back, I can now see his providential care and

guidance. I was invited by a new friend on my baseball team to trans-
fer to the Catholic high school he attended for my sophomore year.
My life changed dramatically—for the better. Almost immediately,
I made good friends and did well in sports and academics. I also
learned to love and trust God again, largely through the Catholic
school environment and the Fellowship of Christian Athletes (FCA).
God provided good male role models in my coaches and priests at
school and a professional football player who mentored me in faith
and invited me to an FCA summer camp. Most important, I met my
future wife, Margie, at my new high school.

It is sobering (and encouraging) to look back and see how God
worked through even those traumatic events from eighth grade and
my loneliness in ninth grade to accomplish his greater purposes in
my life. These formative events would continue to have ripple effects
throughout the years. This is his promise to each one of us who love
him: "We know that *all things work for good for those who love God,
who are called according to his purpose*" (Rom 8:28; italics added).
I do not believe God inflicted any of these painful events in my life
(or those in yours), but I believe he sovereignly redeems everything.
Without moving to Florida and then changing schools, I would not
have met Margie. We would not have our precious daughters, our
sons-in-law, or our grandchildren. I doubt I would have been drawn
to my life's work without those events. I can now see similar provi-
dences and redemption for all the members of our family. So many
things would have been completely different in my life and in our
family had God not been working through all these painful events to
bring joy out of our mourning.

From that point on in high school, I began to soar again. I went
to college, played football, got married, and went to graduate school,
where I prepared for my profession as a marriage and family therapist
and adjunct college professor. Margie and I delighted in the birth of
our children and loved parenting together. We each began our fulfilling careers helping people. (She was a labor and delivery nurse.) But
despite all these blessings, we were not wholeheartedly loving and
following God in our late teens to midtwenties in the decisions we

were making. Having been sexually involved with each other before marriage and having used contraception, we justified our choices. But there was a cost. We both slowly drifted away from God and brought a loss of grace into our relationship without any awareness of that reality. At the time, neither of us had been to Confession for years, and we were only infrequently attending Mass, though still (errantly) receiving Communion when we did. I had little awareness that my sins and wounds needed to be dealt with before God so I could be forgiven and more freely love him and those in my life.

Yet despite my spiritual apathy, God continued drawing me to himself. One day, a neighbor invited me to a Bible study that kick-started my deeper conversion. During our first meeting, one of the men read from two passages that exposed my apathy and self-sufficiency. The first came from the book of Revelation: "So, because you are lukewarm, neither hot nor cold, I will spit you out of my mouth. . . . Those whom I love, I reprove and chastise. Be earnest, therefore, and repent" (Rv 3:16, 19). The second was from Jesus' parable of the vine and the branches: "Whoever remains in me and I in him will bear much fruit, because without me you can do nothing" (Jn 15:5). Together these passages convicted me that I needed to make a wholehearted commitment to God and to rely on him more fully.

I left the Bible study that morning realizing I had been lukewarm in my relationship with Jesus. Until then I didn't realize my heart was still in a mode of self-protection. This confrontation with God's word seemed to open up a hornet's nest, stirring up my unhealed wounds and challenging the fortresses of self-protection I had built around my heart. I began to experience intense anxiety, which drove me to therapy. Once there, I slowly started uncovering my past wounds. I also started praying again, reading scripture, and attending Mass regularly.

Through it all, I could feel the spiritual tug-of-war going on within my mind and heart. The Holy Spirit was teaching me about the realities of the spiritual battle as I was going through it, but some days it felt as if I was losing the battle (whenever I tried to fight in my own strength). All hell seemed to be breaking loose within me and in our marriage; I started to understand how my childhood wounds were being projected into my current relationship.[4] During this same time, the Holy Spirit brought me through a process of acknowledging my sins, in light of God's holiness and mercy. It was liberating to acknowledge my sins, but the deeper freedom from sin and shame happened a few years later when I eventually made a whole-life Confession with a priest to address a lifetime of sexual wounds and sins, as well as the judgments and unforgiveness I held toward those who had sinned against me (see appendices 1–3).[5]

During this same time, the Lord also led me into spiritual community, much of it within my local parish. For the first time, I established intimate spiritual friendships with men and women of all ages. Yet the more I grew spiritually, the more it seemed Margie and I were drifting further apart. She did not share my newfound enthusiasm for our faith, and this led to a deeper divide between us. At one point in my early thirties, I became fearful that our emotional and spiritual disconnect might lead to divorce.

I was being confronted with my worst nightmare. I could not bear the thought of repeating the trauma of my childhood, hurting Margie and our daughters the way my mom and family were hurt by my dad's actions. And yet this intense fear and anxiety, which felt unbearable at the time, became the very instrument that opened my heart for deeper healing. Facing these fears in therapy led me to explore the hidden pain of betrayal and abandonment that I experienced as a young teenager.

Until this point, I had not cried since my dad left. But through a series of healing encounters, I was able to deeply grieve his leaving and face the other traumas from my early teenage years. Therapy was the first instrument God used to prepare me for heart surgery. It enabled me to feel and express my anger toward my dad's actions; from that I could finally uncover the pain buried beneath it. This in turn opened my heart to receive a powerful encounter with the Holy Spirit on a Christ Renews His Parish weekend retreat.

When I returned home from that weekend, my heart was open to love Margie unconditionally and with greater affection. A few months later I experienced another profound healing, this time in relation to my dad, through a process called Family Reconstruction.[6] I was able to release the trauma I had been carrying since my dad left. I forgave my father and felt a new level of trust and intimacy in my marriage as a result of that. This freedom enabled me to love Margie, my dad, and my heavenly Father with greater devotion.

These healing experiences made a major impact in all my relationships. I no longer feared divorce, trusting that the love between Margie and me would last a lifetime. This began a long process of restoration in our marriage and with my family of origin. It seemed as though my repentance and healing opened up a grace for the entire family. My brothers and sisters each began their own spiritual renewal process and found healing in the subsequent years. Each one repented of sexually immoral lifestyles during their teens and twenties. My mother and father also went through a similar process of spiritual renewal, healing, and repentance. I now look back and marvel at God's loving-kindness and tender mercy through all the events that transpired. I am amazed at how he answered our prayers through it all. At one point, soon after my deeper spiritual conversion and healing, my dad was going through a second divorce and my brother Dave was in jail for dealing drugs. During a prayer meeting one night, my brother Bart, my mom, and I prayed for them with bold faith. Within the next few weeks, we learned that both Dad and Dave had received dramatic answers to those prayers.

Over the next several years, God sovereignly arranged for my dad, brothers, and me to go on men's retreats together. We talked openly about our faith and the events from the past. My dad acknowledged how his actions hurt us and asked us for forgiveness. After sharing our pain with him, we assured him of our forgiveness and asked him to forgive us for our judgments and resentments toward him (see appendices 2 and 3). My sisters and mom had their own experiences of healing with my dad in subsequent years. We also had many powerful moments of healing as a whole family. Through it all, God was restoring my sexual integrity, while doing the same for all of our family members. I could go on with many other experiences of personal and family restoration, but this space does not provide enough room. Many of those stories can be found in my previously published books.[7]

Through all these events, I was amazed to see all the ways Jesus accomplished his mission of restoration in my personal life and in our family. He healed our broken hearts and set us free from our captivity; he glorified himself in the place of our shame and brought his beauty out of our ashes, joy instead of mourning. This process is ongoing. We are becoming oaks of righteousness, a planting of the Lord for his glory (see Isaiah 61, NRSV).

In the midst of our personal and family restoration, I realized he was preparing me (and others in my family) to participate in his mission of restoration. By the time I arrived at the Theology of the Body Institute (see introduction), I had witnessed Jesus' mission in action in the lives of numerous individuals, families, and whole assemblies of people. I knew, without a shadow of a doubt, that Jesus' mission of restoration was for today, just as powerfully as it was two thousand years ago. Yet I had no way of anticipating what he was about to do during the Sexual Healing and Redemption conference, or how our spiritual poverty would create an openness for him to demonstrate his powerful anointing.

Spiritual Poverty

For the six months leading up to the conference, our chaplain, Fr. Mark Toups, led our team and the staff of the Theology of the Body Institute in monthly prayer. At the end of every Skype meeting, Fr. Mark would end with these words: "Lord, lead us to embrace our spiritual poverty so we can rely totally on you." The prayer made me a bit uncomfortable. It reminded me of that initial Bible study, where Jesus told me, "Without me you can do nothing" (Jn 15:5). Fr. Mark's prayers for our spiritual poverty led me to reflect on how God often seems to work through our weaknesses and powerlessness (see 2 Corinthians 12:7–12). Over and over again this is evident in the scriptures. Nearly every story in the Bible involves someone in an untenable situation who has tried everything but God, and to no avail. When in their spiritual poverty they finally seek God, he intervenes in powerful ways. I also thought about God's powerful interventions in my life and family. They often happened when things seemed impossible and totally outside of our control. I thought of my dad and brother's spiritual conversion. Things seemed totally bleak that evening when we prayed for them, but God did the impossible.

When the course began at the Theology of the Body Institute, I was not thinking about spiritual poverty. But as the days passed, I discovered the wisdom of Fr. Mark's prayers. Each day it became more apparent that the students were becoming increasingly stirred as they listened to the teaching and examined their sexual sins, wounds, and compulsions through journaling and prayer. By the second day, the emotional pain in the room seemed palpable. I could tell that the majority of the participants were dealing with deep areas of shame and trauma. Their distress reached a climax on Wednesday afternoon. When I stood up to teach I saw a brick wall of resistance in the faces and body postures of the students. It seemed nearly everyone in the room had reached their limit.

After a moment of feeling helpless, I paused to pray and felt prompted to speak with Fr. Mark, who was interceding for all of us in the far back of the conference room. I told everyone I would be back in a few minutes. I then proceeded to discuss what I was sensing with Fr. Mark. After a brief conversation and prayer, we decided to dismiss the class and encouraged them to recreate on the retreat grounds for the rest of the day. Before sending them out, Fr. Mark coached them on how to prepare for the penance service that evening. This drastic change in plans seemed right, even though I knew we would be forfeiting vital teaching material to do this.

That night the atmosphere in the retreat center seemed much more relaxed, especially after all the students went to Confession. You could literally feel the release of shame and pain that evening. The students' peace continued the next morning as we gathered for meals and then assembled in the conference room. Everyone seemed lighter, *except me.*

Before teaching that morning, I went as usual to pray with Fr. Mark and to prepare a plan together for the day. I told him how much I was struggling. The incident the day before had left me feeling helpless and hopeless, and I didn't know how I could teach. I shared with him that I had nothing to offer the students. I will never forget his response. Rather than empathize with me, his face broke into a huge grin. "Great!" he said. "This is what we have been praying for." I looked at him with bewilderment. "What do you mean?" His comeback caught me off guard. "This is the spiritual poverty we have been praying for." With my heart sinking, I replied, "That's easy for you to say; you are going to be sitting in the back. I have to get up there and teach. What do I do? I have nothing to offer." He responded without skipping a beat, "If you knew what to do, it wouldn't be spiritual poverty." Not satisfied, I said again, "So I just go stand up there and do what?" Fr. Mark responded, "Wait until the Lord gives you something." Now it was my time to say, "Great!" But unlike Fr. Mark's exclamation, my "great" dripped with sarcasm. After confessing my self-reliance and lack of trust in the sacrament of Reconciliation, we proceeded to the conference hall.

Obviously, I had no way of knowing how or whether the Lord was going to meet us in our spiritual poverty. But he did not disappoint. What happened next has been dubbed by one of the seminarians in the class as "Pentecost Thursday."

Pentecost Thursday

Before I stood up to teach that Thursday morning, Fr. Mark exposed the Blessed Sacrament in front of the room. When it came time for me to teach, I could imagine how Peter must have felt getting out of the boat to walk on water. I don't remember ever feeling more vulnerable as a teacher, except perhaps during my first year teaching in graduate school. After overcoming my anxiety of public speaking that first year, I have always loved teaching. It comes naturally and freely, especially when I am passionate and deeply believe in what I am imparting. But this morning I felt unusually nervous. When I went to the front of the room and opened the workbook, I was tempted to run out of the room.

After an opening prayer and greeting of the participants, I stood frozen, staring at the workbook and waiting for the prompting of the Spirit. After what seemed like an eternity, I sensed these thoughts come to me: *Don't try to teach; just let me (Jesus) proclaim my mission.* I stared at the passage from Isaiah 61 that providentially headlined the lesson. Stepping out in faith, I yielded to the promptings of the Spirit. Turning off my microphone, I proclaimed the passage as though united with Jesus in the synagogue two thousand years ago. As soon as I began to proclaim the opening stanza, "The Spirit of the LORD God is upon me, the LORD has anointed me," I could feel a rush of the Holy Spirit's anointing. With an authority that seemed beyond me, I continued boldly proclaiming the rest of the passage. It was as though Jesus, in me, was reenacting his proclamation in the synagogue. The passage was being fulfilled in our midst (see Luke 4:21).

I find it nearly impossible to explain an experience like this in writing, but I'll do my best. I felt as if Jesus himself was proclaiming his words in and through me, even though I was speaking them. I soon realized it was not my imagination tricking me. Something powerful was happening throughout the room. One by one I heard the participants begin to cry. Within minutes some were sobbing, others wailing. This went on for some time. A few others came in late and must have been shocked by what they were seeing and hearing. Fr. Mark encouraged me to repeat the proclamation from Isaiah 61. As I did, a whole new wave of the Spirit seemed to be released into the room. Now more were crying. Everyone could feel the comforting presence of the Lord in the room and knew something supernatural was taking place.

Jesus was teaching all of us about his power in our spiritual poverty. After those initial proclamations, I did nothing, except stand there quietly and pray, silently praising Jesus for what he was doing. When the crying subsided, one of the participants stood and began to sing a song of praise. One by one, the other students/retreatants stood and sang, until everyone in the room joined in a chorus of heartfelt praise and thanksgiving to God. Fr. Mark and I entered in joyfully, thanking God for all he was doing.

After several songs of spontaneous praise, person after person began sharing testimonies describing how Jesus (or the Holy Spirit/ the Holy Family/angels, etc.) came to them personally and began to minister healing to their sexual wounds and to the deeper roots of their sexual sins and compulsions. We were all amazed at the uniqueness of each one's encounter with Jesus, but there was no doubt he had visited each one personally. That "Pentecost Thursday" morning, Jesus healed many broken hearts, set many captives free, and turned our collective mourning into joy. Some were miraculously healed of lifelong afflictions. For others, it marked the beginning of a longer process of restoration, which continues to this day.

Restoration Is a Process

I continue to be in touch with a few of the students that were present at that course. They each affirm that what happened on that Thursday morning was life changing for them. But some continue to undergo an intense journey of healing and restoration. One man in the room, Charlie, was separated from his wife and children at the time due to his sexual addiction. Prior to the course, he was beginning to face some of the root issues underlying his sexual compulsions, including early childhood parental abandonment and sexual abuse by a female babysitter. During the conference he received a lot of insight and understanding about his sexual compulsions and how the underlying traumas fueled these. On Wednesday evening, he was able to experience one of the best Confessions of his life. During that "Pentecost Thursday" morning, he had an interior vision of Jesus taking a huge sledgehammer and shattering the chains that kept him bound, after which he cried out, "Freedom!"

After the course he noticed a significant shift in freedom from his sexual compulsions and soon after was reconciled with his wife and children, but despite these significant breakthroughs, his healing journey continues to this day. Over the years, he has discovered progressive levels of sexual abuse and early childhood traumas that he continues to work through. I recently heard from him, and he is back in therapy with a gifted Catholic therapist, facing another traumatic sexual abuse experience, this time involving being sodomized by a man in early childhood. These incidences of abuse instilled confusion in his gender identity and perverted his sexual desires for many years to come.

Charlie now has a much greater sense of his identity as a beloved son, husband, and father. He now knows assuredly that Jesus is with him through everything he has suffered. Though his battle has been long and hard, he has a firm hope because he knows firsthand the reality of Jesus' mission of restoration. The words of that prophecy in Isaiah 61 remain very dear to his heart. Layer by layer, Jesus is transforming Charlie. He is being released from a lifetime of debilitating shame and crippling fear. He has been freed of his habitual patterns of sexual sin and compulsion. His masculine confidence is being restored, and his capacity to love has increased substantially.

For some of us, stories like Charlie's can be discouraging. We want a quick relief of our symptoms, not a long and drawn-out process of restoration that reaches the core wounds underlying our compulsions and identity distortions. But for those who have been working on these issues for a while, it is a great comfort to know that Jesus is the one who began the work and will surely bring it to completion (see Philippians 1:6). Jesus does not force his healing love upon us. He respects our free will and understands, better than we do, when we are ready to face deeper traumas. When it is time, he gently reveals the self-protective barriers around our hearts that can hinder our capacity to receive his healing love. He will not tear these barriers down without our consent. These must be released by our own free will (see appendices 1–4).

Be assured: the Holy Spirit is at work in you if you have offered your spiritual poverty to Jesus and asked him to restore you. If you haven't yet asked him, now is a good time to do so. Jesus promised he would respond to our request: "Ask and it will be given to you; seek and you will find; knock and the door will be opened to you. For everyone who asks, receives; and the one who seeks, finds; and to the one who knocks, the door will be opened" (Mt 7:7–8).

In chapter 8, we will discuss the process of liberation in the areas of our sexual sin and compulsions. Before turning there, however, I encourage you to take a moment to reflect on Jesus' mission of restoration and then apply this personally to your life circumstances in the personal activity and prayer.

Take a Moment

1. What in this chapter gives you hope that Jesus will restore you to sexual wholeness?

2. In what ways have you personally experienced spiritual poverty? How has Jesus met you?

3. What were your reactions while reading about "Pentecost Thursday"?

4. What encourages (or discourages) you when hearing my story and Charlie's healing process?

Personal Activity

The following activity is intended to help you prepare for the healing outlined in the next several chapters and to begin to integrate your understanding of the interrelationship between sexual wounding experiences and Jesus' promise of restoration.

1. Go back to chapter 1 and review the areas of sexual wounding you identified. Are there more that you have discovered as you have gone through this book? In which areas are you in need of restoration? Write them down.

2. Now go slowly through Isaiah 61. Write down each phrase and personalize it, as a way of reflecting on how Jesus desires to

restore you (e.g., "Jesus was sent and anointed to heal my broken heart that came from my experience of being sexually abused"; "He came to set me free from my sexual compulsion and sin"; "He will comfort me in my grief over my loss of sexual innocence").

3. Ask the Holy Spirit to show you the afflictions (in your sexuality) that need healing.

4. Where are you enslaved by sin, compulsions, and shame?

5. Specifically identify how your heart has been broken as a result of Type A or Type B traumas.

6. In what ways have these wounds and compulsions impacted your gender identity?

7. Write a prayer asking Jesus to restore you in each of these areas, and offer to him any shame, doubt, hopelessness, or spiritual poverty. Write out his response to your prayer.

8

BEAUTY INSTEAD OF ASHES: FINDING FREEDOM FROM OUR CAPTIVITY

The LORD has anointed me . . . to proclaim
liberty to the captives.
—Isaiah 61:1 (NABRE)

You may recall (from chapters 4 and 5) how Steve struggled with a sexual compulsion beginning soon after he found pornography in his father's room at the age of twelve. After experiencing the merciful love of Jesus in confession during a high school youth conference, Steve had the courage and support to push through his shame and genuinely engage in the process of restoration. After an intensive process of healing, over several years, he is now living in freedom from his sexual sins and compulsions. His journey into freedom has not been easy, but it has given him a greater confidence in Jesus' ability to restore all who seek him.

I offer Steve's journey into freedom as a guide for you and your loved ones, as you seek greater liberty in any area where you or they remain in captivity. Though the particulars are unique to Steve, the principles and practices are applicable to each one of us. As you read through this account of Steve's healing process, I invite you to reflect on how the steps he took trusting Jesus for his freedom apply to you.

The prayers for freedom mentioned in this chapter are included in the appendices (1–4) at the back of the book.

Steve's Path to Freedom

Steve's spiritual journey began many years before he found freedom from his sexual compulsions, sins, wounds, and identity lies. His life in Christ originated with his Baptism and grew through his participation in the sacraments during childhood. His spiritual life took a giant leap forward through his aforementioned high-school retreat experience. During that time of worship and communal adoration, he encountered Jesus' merciful love in a profound and life-changing way. This experience let Steve know that God loved him personally, and it enabled him to push past his shame and go to Confession. The darkness and shame that had been oppressing Steve for years lifted after his adoration and Confession, and he stayed free of temptation for several weeks.

However, within a month after the retreat, Steve fell back into the same habitual patterns of sexual compulsion, with pornography, fantasy, and masturbation. Deeply discouraged, he questioned the authenticity of his spiritual experience a month earlier. His subsequent "falls" only increased his sense of shame and his doubts about God. In daily life, he felt weak and powerless, due to his inability to resist temptation and engage in healthy relationships. His sexual fantasies allowed him a temporary escape from his self-loathing. But in the long run these fantasies only served to reinforce his underlying feelings of shame and inadequacy, which further drove his compulsions.

Through the next year or two, Steve continued indulging his sexual compulsions and concluded that it would be useless to go to Confession. His attitude changed, however, following another powerful retreat experience. After a cleansing Confession and another powerful encounter with Jesus during adoration, he sensed a call to the priesthood. In the subsequent months, Steve met with a vocations director and shared his perceived calling as well as his ongoing struggles with his sexual compulsion. The formation director encouraged him to enter into a more dedicated discipline of prayer and sacramental life before entering the seminary.

Once in seminary, regular spiritual direction, prayer, and sacramental life increased Steve's capacity to resist temptation for a period of time, but sooner or later he would fall back into sexual sin. Sensing Steve needed something more, his formation director recommended that Steve come to me for therapy. When I met Steve, I liked him immediately. I could see his goodness, as well as his genuine desire for healing. However, it was readily apparent that his sexual compulsion weighed heavily on him and caused him to doubt his self-worth as well as his vocation to the priesthood. It was around this time that many of the sex abuse scandals in the Church were being revealed publicly; Steve feared he could one day end up as one of those disgraced priests if he did not find freedom from his compulsions.

During our second meeting, Steve opened up about his past and current struggles with pornography. Throughout most of our discussion he kept his head down, obviously burdened by the weight of his shame. But I noticed a considerable shift in his countenance when he began to share some of the graces he had been receiving over the years and the progress he had been making in recent months. We spent the next few meetings exploring his family history and the painful experiences in his childhood, which involved his broken relationship with his father, his emotional enmeshment with his mother, and the humiliating experiences of ridicule and rejection by his peers in middle school.

At this point, I saw that Steve could benefit from prayer for inner healing. I sensed he would be a good candidate for it, given his spiritual experience and openness. I shared with him a few experiences of others who had found freedom from sexual compulsions and how this kind of prayer played a vital role in it. I asked him if he would be willing to pray in this way. Having engaged in a similar kind of meditative and contemplative prayer in seminary with his spiritual director, Steve seemed open to engage in the prayer for inner healing (see appendix 4 describing the basic prayer process and its foundation in Church teaching).

Praying for Inner Healing

Once Steve gave his general consent, I explained to him that the same faculty of imagination that he used for sexual fantasy could be sanctified by this kind of prayer. We would simply ask the Holy Spirit to reveal the disordered desires underlying his sexual fantasies so he could see how they were related to unhealed wounds in his psychosexual development and identity. Our goal was not to search for memories but to ask the Holy Spirit to guide the process. We would then invite Jesus to reveal his presence in these memories. Experiencing Jesus' love in his childhood memories would heal his wounds of rejection and abandonment. Receiving Jesus' truth in those same memories would overcome the identity lies that were keeping him bound.

As we were about to begin the prayer process, Steve expressed some apprehension about reexperiencing his past pain. He briefly protested, "The past is over, and I don't want to dig it up again." Reassuring him that we were not just going to dig up the past, I reminded him of his encounters with Jesus back in high school and how much freedom he experienced from those. He acknowledged that those were transformative but wondered why he was not able to gain freedom from his sexual compulsions after the first experience with Jesus on retreat.

After affirming his concerns, I explained that I believed his compulsions were more deeply rooted in his unmet needs and unhealed wounds from childhood. These core experiences of shame and the false beliefs about himself were still keeping him bound, even though his adult self was growing in grace and maturity. I reassured him that his freedom would come as those deeper wounds and identity lies were addressed. Encouraged that Jesus could bring healing to those painful memories and affirm the truth of his identity, Steve decided to enter into prayer.

One by one, as these memories from childhood came to Steve's awareness, we asked the Holy Spirit to reveal what he wanted Steve to know. Very gently, the Holy Spirit led him through each memory and showed him how he had internalized the rejections of his childhood and early adolescence into his self-image. We then asked Jesus to reveal what he wanted young Steve to know in those memories. Jesus showed him the insecurity and wounds of his father and peers that led them to treat him so cruelly. Jesus also reassured Steve of his love for him. We then stopped for a few minutes so that Steve could experience his hurt and anger before walking through the forgiveness process with his father and peers (see appendix 2).

We prayed in this way several times during our subsequent meetings. With each prayer experience, Steve shared what he was seeing, feeling, and sensing in his inspired imagination. I could see the genuineness of his encounters with Jesus, as his countenance lightened after each memory received Jesus' healing touch. Repeatedly, Steve moved from a state of intense anguish and fear to peace and joy. As these memory scenes unfolded, he was able to receive love and blessing from Jesus in ways he never had from his human father. With that, Steve's bitterness toward his father dissipated. In one prayer encounter, Jesus appeared as the age of one of his peers in middle school. As Steve received Jesus' love and acceptance in the areas where his peers had rejected and ostracized him, he felt peace. He was then able to let go of his anger toward his peers.

After these healing encounters, we returned to each of the memories to see if there was anything else unresolved. Steve reported that the images were no longer painful, but he was still wrestling with his perception of himself. He still doubted his masculinity and questioned his sexual orientation. Realizing he needed to hear from Jesus about those issues, we asked Jesus what he wanted Steve to know. Almost immediately, Steve heard Jesus speak words of affirmation to him as a preteen in the areas where his masculinity had been damaged. Jesus also revealed to him that these beliefs he internalized about himself were not true. At this point, I could see Steve experiencing internal conflict. He could tell that this process was being led by the Holy Spirit and that his inner images of Jesus were not of his own construction, but he was still having a hard time believing the truths he was receiving.

Seeing Steve's struggle, I invited him to talk about what he was experiencing. After a few minutes of quiet, he shared that he couldn't accept what Jesus was telling him about his masculine identity, especially with regard to his peers taunting him that he was "gay." He said, "Jesus is telling me, "It is not true.' My peers were picking up on my fear and awkwardness but were not capable of telling me who I am, or how God made me. Jesus said to me, 'Only the Father can affirm your true identity.' But then my mind raced to all the pornographic images I watched and focused on those sex acts. Don't those prove I am gay or at least bisexual?"

I responded to Steve, "I understand why that makes it hard for you to believe. But I don't sense that Jesus is lying to you or that you are making it up. Your past experiences, shame, and confusion are getting in the way of your ability to receive his love and truth. Would you be open if we brought those pornographic images to Jesus and let him show you what you are really looking for in those images?" Steve looked horrified at my suggestion. I then explained to him, "Our sexual desires and practices don't define us, but they do show us where we have been wounded." I told him that desires expressed in fantasies are expressions of unmet needs for affirmation and that they are often driven by shame, powerlessness, and other unhealed wounds.[1]

After my explanation, Steve visibly relaxed. He was still hesitant but willing to explore his fantasies and to face his deeper needs revealed in these pornographic images. I invited him to keep his focus on Jesus and not let the shame from the images discourage him (see Hebrews 12:1–2). With that reassurance, Steve took each fantasy image and shared it internally with Jesus in his imagination. One by one, Jesus spoke inwardly to Steve about each image, showing him what he was actually desiring and how his desires had been perverted by the "father of lies." He also showed Steve how these fantasies reinforced his childhood wounds and self-hatred, and that his fantasies were attempts to gain control over his pain and negative self-image.[2] After receiving these truths, Steve reported that he could finally believe what Jesus had said; neither his fantasies nor his memories defined his identity. I encouraged him to explore whether he was experiencing more interior freedom from his childhood wounds and shame. He said he felt his shame was dissolving.

I invited Steve to test the difference in his desires as he looked at those pornographic images in his imagination. He said he felt repulsed rather than sexually excited by these images. He was amazed they had lost so much of their power to entice him. He then went back to the memories from his childhood trauma and felt a new freedom from the wounds of rejection, abandonment, hopelessness, power-lessness, fear, confusion, and shame. He realized, with a new depth of understanding, that these long-standing wounds and identity lies were the driving force behind his sexual compulsions. Cumulatively these healing experiences brought about a major transformation in Steve's acceptance of himself. I noticed changes in his voice, body posture, and facial countenance, revealing his increased confidence in his masculine identity.

Afterward we joyously offered a prayer of thanksgiving to the Father and asked Jesus to seal these healed areas of Steve's mind and heart. I then encouraged Steve to pay attention to his daily experiences between sessions. I asked him to be aware of his thoughts and feelings, and to see if there were any compulsive desires or thoughts that emerged. In asking him to be aware, I was preparing him for the more active and ongoing work of engaging his will in the battle, through repentance.

Repenting: Changing Our Mind and Will

Genuine sexual freedom begins with *repenting from our sin and disordered beliefs*.[3] The word "repent" is mentioned often in Jesus' teaching and throughout the Bible. The Greek word for "repent" is *metanoia*. It means "to change your mind" or "change your direction."[4] Repentance begins with a change in our beliefs about God, our self, and others, acknowledging truth where we once believed identity lies. Repentance also involves a change in our direction. We move from a stance of ungodly self-reliance with our backs toward God, and we turn toward him in humble submission (see Ezekiel 18:21–22).[5]

Once we have fundamentally turned toward God (initial conversion), we enter into a lifelong process of deeper conversion, allowing God's truth and love to transform our minds and hearts. Even after his initial Confession in high school, Steve continued to engage in a spiritual tug-of-war that was constantly going on within his mind and heart. It is the epic battle we all have to engage in. It is the spiritual battle between the "flesh" and the Spirit (Gal 5:17). The flesh is our corrupted human nature ruled by concupiscence (the lust of the eyes, the lust of the flesh, and the pride of life). The Spirit is the Holy Spirit, who desires to bring us into holy communion with God and others, while leading us to greater personal integration.

In the words of St. Paul, repenting involves an ongoing transformation of our mind and will. "Do not conform yourselves to this age but be *transformed by the renewal of your mind*, that you may discern what is the will of God, what is good and pleasing and perfect" (Rom 12:2; italics added). Transformation is first and foremost the work of God's grace within us and around us, but our cooperation and surrender are essential.

Like the rest of us, Steve's personal choices (whether inspired by the Holy Spirit or seduced by demonic spirits) moved him each step of the way throughout his life. His own free will, influenced by the world, the flesh, and the devil, enslaved him to hold onto bitterness and judgments toward his father and peers, and later into the deadly traps of sexual compulsion. His acts of sexual sin were rooted in these underlying sins and compulsions. Similarly, his personal volition, infused by God's grace in the sacraments, prayer, and spiritual community, released the grip of these oppressive forces and led him to repent of his previous choices. Deep down, Steve always wanted to choose good, but there were parts of his body and mind still bound in deception, sin, and addiction. The lies he believed undergirded his sexual compulsions. Steve's mind and body had become habituated to seeking pleasure and relieving stress through fantasy and sexual orgasm. Even after his healing of the deeper wounds and shame, Steve had to actively choose to resist temptation and transform the physical and mental processes that had become a force of habit for him.

Russell Willingham, who has spent his career helping people overcome sexual addiction, notes, "As an addict seeks to redirect his thoughts and choices, new neural pathways will be created to facilitate this change in direction. The systems of his brain will literally regroup into a new configuration as he redirects his thoughts and attitudes of his heart. This is good news, but it doesn't happen overnight."[6]

For Steve, much of this work of repentance began with his conversion experience in high school, and then in seminary as he focused on his relationship with God in an intentional way, as a disciple of Christ. During that time he began to study the scriptures and was introduced to the Theology of the Body.[7] His growing understanding of God's design for sexuality inspired him. His repentance was greatly aided by centering his life on the sacraments. Every time Steve participated in the sacrament of Reconciliation and confessed his sins, he was actively choosing to practice repentance. Each time he prayed and worshipped at Mass and then received Jesus in the Eucharist, he was choosing to turn toward God to receive his grace.

These spiritual disciplines were given an added dimension during our prayer time together in therapy. Steve experienced a deeper repentance, one that touched the hidden recesses of his mind and heart where his sexual compulsions and identity distortions were most deeply rooted. In the healing contemplative prayer, his subconscious mind was being transformed as he consciously chose to bring his wounds and identity lies into the light. He needed to receive Jesus' love in place of his wounds, and Jesus' truth in the place of demonic lies. All of this is a form of repentance.

So it is with each of us. We cannot regain our sexual freedom without first turning our affections and will toward God. We must allow his truth and love to transform our minds and hearts, especially in the deeply held beliefs where our identity and desires are formed.

Once we have taken this first step of repenting, we are then ready to practice it in the specific areas of our captivity, through the practice of *renouncing*.

Renouncing Impediments to Freedom

Evil rarely gains a hold in our minds and hearts through force.[8] It usually enters through our human will, by deceiving us with something that seems good. Once we are deceived and seduced by temptations, we then make *agreements* with demonic lies and evil choices.[9] *Renouncing* is the way to free us from these unconscious agreements so we can embrace truth and actively choose good over evil. In renouncing, we verbally reject the lies, beliefs, and previous choices that have kept us bound. We thus break the mental agreements that prevent us from loving God and each other.

At our Baptism, we were given the spiritual authority and responsibility to renounce evil and choose good. If we were baptized as infants, our parents and godparents spoke on our behalf to renounce sin, evil, and deception, and to announce our allegiance to the Father, Son, and Holy Spirit. We formally renew these renouncements every Easter in the Catholic tradition, with the understanding that renouncing evil and choosing God's will should be a daily exercise of our human will.[10]

Baptized as an infant, Steve was brought up in a relatively faithful Christian environment where he learned to love and serve God according to the teachings of Christ, through the Catholic Church. But like many of us, Steve's environment contained a mixture of good and evil, and he too was beset by concupiscence. As a child no one taught him about his spiritual authority in Christ, though he knew about God's grace through the sacraments. He needed to be taught how to draw on this grace, to consciously choose to renounce evil and to embrace God's goodness and purity.

Even having experienced the grace of the sacraments, Steve didn't have the internal strength to resist temptation. He could not wholeheartedly choose freedom. A good part of him genuinely wanted to love God and follow his will, but there was another disintegrated part within him that remained demonically attached to his sin and compulsions. In order to renounce authentically, Steve, like each of us, had to overcome his *ambivalence*. As long as he was believing lies about his identity, he would continue being susceptible to living out these deceptions through pornography, fantasy, and masturbation.

After our prayer time together, Steve was much less divided in his mind and heart. Strengthened by Jesus' truth and love, he was now ready to engage the battle of his will to protect his newly found freedom. Seeing his readiness, I explained to Steve the importance of renouncing and then led him through a series of renouncing prayers to address the various areas where he had become bound by unholy attachments and agreements. Afterward, I gave him a collection of these prayers to continue practicing them at home. (These prayers are listed in appendix 3 for your benefit.) We began by renouncing Steve's unholy attachments.

Renouncing Unholy Attachments

First, I spoke to Steve about *unholy attachments* (also referred to as "unholy soul ties"). I explained to him how these unholy bonds are an impediment to our freedom. I began by showing him the passage in Corinthians about the "two . . . [becoming] one flesh" in sexual immorality (1 Cor 6:16). Then we discussed a second passage about how an unholy alliance can be formed by participating in acts of vice with others (see 2 Corinthians 6:14–16). In light of both passages, I explained how we can form mental, emotional, and spiritual soul ties through fantasy and pornography.

After explaining these realities, I asked Steve if he was willing to renounce his unholy attachments. When he consented, I invited him to mentally call to mind the various images from his fantasies with pornography (since he didn't know the names of the people) and then, if he was ready, to verbally renounce any unholy attachments between him and each person—mentally, emotionally, spiritually, and sexually. I also invited him to renounce (and later bring to Confession) the sins of lust and envy, which unconsciously motivated these fantasies.

Steve had not entered into any physical sexual relationships with anyone, but if he had, he would also have needed to walk through a prayer of renouncing those soul ties by naming the people individually and renouncing the unholy bonds with them. Steve acknowledged that some of his fantasies involved men and women he knew, so I invited him to make a list of their names and then renounce the unholy soul ties with them later, once he returned home.

We also talked about Steve's unhealthy emotional attachment with both his mother and his father, even though they were not sexual soul ties. His relationship with his mom was mostly positive, but through prayer and therapy Steve came to realize that his mom had transferred her affections onto him and away from her husband throughout his childhood. This created an unhealthy codependency between her and Steve. Steve participated in this unhealthy bond with his own willingness because he felt loved and special to his mom. Once Steve realized this, it made sense of the confusing feelings he was having in relation to his mother. He always wondered why he felt compelled to pull back from her emotionally, even though he loved her. With firm conviction, Steve then prayed the "renouncing unholy attachment" prayer to release him from being bound in an unhealthy way with his mother, while maintaining the good part of their relationship.

Steve's unholy attachment with his father was rooted in his unfor-giveness and judgments toward him. These kept Steve bound to his dad in an unhealthy way. After we renounced his unhealthy attach-ment with his dad, I spoke to Steve about renouncing his bitter-root judgments.

Renouncing Bitter-Root Judgments

Steve's bitter-root judgments toward his father formed over years of experiencing hurt and holding on to anger in the form of resentment and bitterness. I showed Steve, from the scriptures, how bitter-root judgments defile us and harm our relationships (see Hebrews 12:15). From there, I invited him to read the passage in Luke's gospel where Jesus warns against condemning others: "Stop judging and you will not be judged. Stop condemning and you will not be condemned. Forgive and you will be forgiven. . . . For the measure with which you measure will in return be measured out to you" (Lk 6:37–38).

After Steve read from the passage, I asked him if he understood what it meant for him personally. He was unsure. I explained that we all have a tendency to develop bitter-root judgments and barriers around our hearts when we have unresolved hurt. Jesus emphasized the necessity of releasing these judgments and forgiving as the necessary condition for our own freedom. Jesus said, "But if you do not forgive others, neither will your Father forgive your transgressions" (Mt 6:15). The *Catechism* shows how this dynamic of giving and receiving forgiveness and releasing bitter-root judgments brings us into freedom, and how neglecting to do so keeps us bound: "Now—and this is daunting—this outpouring of mercy cannot penetrate our hearts as long as we have not forgiven those who have trespassed against us. . . . In refusing to forgive our brothers and sisters, our hearts are closed and their hardness makes them impervious to the Father's merciful love; but in confessing our sins, our hearts are opened to his grace" (*CCC*, 2840).

Steve had already forgiven his dad in one of our earlier meetings, and much of his bitterness and judgments had dissolved and been replaced with compassion for his dad. But he realized as we spoke that he was still holding onto some judgments toward his father and that he was condemning himself in a similar way. With that awareness, Steve readily walked through the process of renouncing the specific bitter-root judgments he held toward his father as well as ones he held toward himself. His prayer went something like this: "In the name of Jesus Christ, I renounce my condemning judgments toward my father, specifically my judgments that he is selfish, cruel, and sexually perverted (because of his pornography). I ask you, Jesus, to forgive me for condemning my dad. Please release both of us from these judgments." We also renounced the judgments he held toward his peers and toward men in general. His experiences and judgments toward his dad and peers had given him a distorted perception of masculinity, which had been a driving force behind his sexual compulsions and identity confusion.

Renouncing Identity Lies and Wounds

Next, Steve and I addressed *identity lies*—those false beliefs we internalize as a result of our response to trauma. Steve's distorted beliefs about himself had been formed throughout his childhood in response to his wounds. These beliefs were reinforced through his pornography use and sexual fantasies. They contributed to his lack of masculine strength and his doubts about his sexual orientation. After the previous prayer experiences, Steve accepted the reality that he was a heterosexual man who was attracted to women. He also acknowledged that his need for male affection and affirmation was a healthy and holy desire. He realized he didn't receive enough of this because of the deficits in his development. He also realized that the condemnations and labeling from his peers (e.g., "you are gay"; "you are a puny weakling") originated from the "father of lies" and gained access to his heart because of his wounds and identity lies. He now understood that neither his father nor his peers were capable of telling Steve his true identity. Only God could do that accurately. With that confidence and clarity, Steve renounced the lies and announced the truth about his gender identity.

Steve did the same with each area of the *seven deadly wounds*. For example, with the wound of rejection, he renounced the lie that he was unloved and not wanted by his dad, and announced the truth that his dad loved him (though not always well) and that he was deeply loved, wanted, and chosen by his heavenly Father. These were not just empty words for Steve. After working through the wounds from his father and forgiving him, he began to have memories where his father demonstrated his love for him. He could finally believe that his dad loved him (however imperfectly) and more importantly that he was deeply loved by his heavenly Father. If he had any doubts before, his prayer encounters convinced him that he was a beloved son.

In renouncing the wound of shame, Steve also renounced many of the labels he had taken in as part of his identity from pornography. These included the lies that he was bad, dirty, perverted, gay, and weak. Having recently gone to Confession, he could say with added confidence that he was worthy of love, he was cleansed, and his core desires were good.

Renouncing Ungodly Vows

The next area of renouncing involved the *ungodly vows* that Steve made to protect his heart from past hurt and to save him from future pain. I shared with Steve the scripture passages about unholy vows (see Matthew 5:33–37 and James 4:13–15) and read him these comments from John and Paula Sandford's book *The Transformation of the Inner Man*: "We have all made many inner vows of varying intensity and tenacity. . . . There are good and helpful vows as well as destructive ones. Even the good ones need to be released, so that we are not impelled by the flesh, but by the Spirit in freedom."[11] I explained to Steve that our inner vows are resolutions impelled by ungodly self-reliance. We typically make these rash decisions out of powerlessness, fear, and judgments of others. These ungodly vows are very different from the holy vows impelled by the Spirit that we make when receiving the sacraments.

I showed Steve that his ungodly vow that led him to detach his heart from his father, though understandable, had actually caused him more suffering. In reality, though he did it to protect himself, it left him unprotected from the lies of the enemy, cut him off from the masculine love he needed, and set him up for more wounds from his peers. Other vows, such as "I will not be like my father" or "I will never let anyone hurt me," were well intended but also hindered his capacity to grow in his masculine identity. After understanding this, Steve gladly renounced these inner vows, one at a time, and invited the Holy Spirit to bring him into greater freedom in those areas. After all of these prayers, Steve seemed to have a greater capacity to receive the love he had always desired.

Receiving God's Love

Throughout his life, Steve was wounded by both *deprivations* of love (Type A traumas) and *distortions* of love (Type B traumas). In response he formed unhealthy attachments, bitter-root judgments, identity lies, and ungodly vows, which effectively hardened Steve's heart and closed him from receiving God's love. The same is true for each one of us. The challenging work of gaining freedom from sexual sins and compulsions and facing our wounds and bitterness is well worth all the struggle because it allows us to finally receive the genuine love we have always desired. When we are rooted and grounded in God's love and truth, we can mature in our capacity to give and receive. His truth enlightens our mind and his love softens and expands our hearts.

After our time together, Steve could see these realities much more clearly. Through the renouncing and healing prayer, Steve was able to receive God's love, joy, and peace. He also realized how much love he had been receiving throughout his entire life, without really being grateful for it. Freed from his bitterness and resentments, he could genuinely appreciate the love he received from his parents, sister, and grandparents from before he was born up through the present. Their love was never perfect, but it was real nonetheless. He was also more able to receive the blessings from God that had been continuously pouring out upon him throughout his life, especially through the sacraments.

Once Steve found substantial freedom from the tyranny of his sexual compulsions, and the sins that too easily proceeded from them, he was ready to invest himself wholeheartedly in his vocation to the priesthood. His final years in seminary were a source of delight for him, unshackled from the shame that had heretofore been his constant companion. In gratitude, he dedicated his life to being an instrument of God's love and truth, carrying out Jesus' mission of restoration as a priest. Today, he finds great satisfaction in offering God's mercy and forgiveness through the sacraments to all those who are struggling. His own experiences have allowed him to feel compassion for other sufferers in Confession and spiritual direction, and to feel confidence that they too can be set free.

Though not all of us are ordained priests like Steve, we are all part of the universal priesthood of believers. If we have been baptized and confirmed, we have been anointed and commissioned by Christ himself to participate in his liberating mission of restoration. But first we are called to live in the freedom of the Holy Spirit, receiving God's love and knowing our true identity as his beloved sons and daughters.

To live in the glorious liberty as children of God (Rom 8:21), we must continually practice *repentance, renouncing,* and *receiving.*

Practicing Spiritual Disciplines

Before Steve left to return to seminary, I encouraged him to practice these spiritual disciplines of repenting, renouncing, and receiving on a daily basis. I trusted that the support of the seminary would help him maintain these disciplines. We may not have the same external support system, but these spiritual disciplines of repenting, renouncing, and receiving are good daily practices for each one of us. They are especially necessary when we are in the moment of temptation and feel the force of our disordered desires.

As soon as we become aware of our thoughts and affections pulling us away from God, we can stop and ask him to help us become aware of his presence (repenting). Then we can recognize the lies lurking behind the temptation and renounce those immediately. When we experience bitter-root judgments, or become aware of ungodly vows or unhealthy attachments, we can also renounce them before they can become strongholds. Similarly, whenever we become aware of unforgiveness blocking our ability to give and receive love, we can practice giving and receiving forgiveness and ask the Holy Spirit to fill us with his truth, love, peace, and gratitude (receiving). Freed from all that enslaves us, we can know his *beauty instead of ashes.*

In the next chapter, we will continue drawing on these same spiritual tools (from appendices 1–4) as we focus on healing sexual trauma. Before turning there, however, I encourage you to take a moment to reflect on this chapter and then apply these insights to your own circumstances in the personal activity. I also invite you to read through the appendices before putting them into practice in the personal activity.

Take a Moment

1. In what ways do you relate to Steve's journey into freedom? In what ways have you already found freedom from sexual compulsions and sins? Where do you still desire more freedom?

2. How did Steve's sexual fantasies provide a window into his unhealed wounds and identity lies?

3. How did Steve experience Jesus' love and truth through contemplative prayer? What lies and wounds were confronted and transformed? What was the fruit of this prayer?

4. Describe how *repenting*, *renouncing*, and *receiving* are essential for gaining freedom from sexual sins and compulsions. How can these be practiced daily?

Personal Activity

As you enter into this personal activity, begin by reading through the appendices, which describe the foundational prayer processes that enable us to gain freedom. Pray through the various prayers in the specific areas you desire freedom. If you are not aware of any areas of sexual sin or compulsions in your daily life, you can apply these prayers to any aspect of your life where you desire more freedom. I encourage you to write your answers in a journal so you can bring these areas into the light.

1. *Repenting.* In what areas of your life have you turned your back from God? What sins or compulsions are kept hidden? Are you willing to change your mind and heart and to bring these areas to God?

2. *Renouncing.* Review the ways Steve renounced his unholy attachments, identity lies, bitter-root judgments, and ungodly vows. Then write down what you personally need to renounce in each

of these areas. Use the prayers in appendix 3 to pray through these issues:

a. Unhealthy attachments

b. Bitter-root judgments

c. Ungodly vows

d. Identity lies and wounds

3. *Receiving.* If you have not yet done so, receive God's tender mercy and forgiveness in any areas of sexual sin and compulsion throughout your life by making a whole-life confession (appendix 1). Either before or after your confession, forgive yourself by walking through the steps of the Forgiveness Prayer (appendix 2).

4. *Daily application.* Throughout your day today (and every day), practice repenting, renouncing, and receiving in an area of temptation where you become aware of a disordered desire.

9

JOY INSTEAD OF MOURNING: HEALING OUR SEXUAL TRAUMA

He has sent me . . . to bind up the broken-
hearted . . . to comfort all who mourn.
—Isaiah 61:1–2

Jesus' sacred heart is filled with the most tender compassion for us in the areas of our suffering. His kindness and gentleness are disarming. He longs to mend our broken hearts and comfort us in the deepest areas of our sexual trauma. Yet he understands more than anyone how difficult it is for us to trust, having firsthand knowledge of the devastating trauma resulting from betrayal, abandonment, and violation. He patiently waits for our readiness, respecting our freedom while restoring our shattered trust.

As I write these words, I envision the faces of men and women I know who are courageously working through the trauma of their sexual wounding. They are my heroes, because they have been willing to trust Jesus, the Good Shepherd, despite all the betrayals they have experienced throughout their lives. Though they have many doubts along the way, they trust him to lead them safely through this valley of the shadow of death and into the green pastures of his abundant life as he restores their souls (see Psalm 23 and John 10). This treacherous path through the dark valley is well known among survivors of sexual abuse.[1]

Sexual Abuse Trauma

I have mentioned several of these heroic men and women throughout this book. Remember Rita (from chapter 6). Though a lifelong
Catholic, she experienced considerable confusion about God due to
her brother's sexual torture. Even after she told her parents about
the abuse many years after it had ended, they did not comfort her.
She found the comforting compassion of Jesus in the person of a
faithful priest who helped restore her trust in Jesus. But several years
after that, another seemingly compassionate priest offered to help her
heal but instead sexually seduced her. His actions only compounded
her trauma and caused her to further lose trust in men, priests, and
ultimately in Jesus. Through these ongoing abuse experiences, Rita
eventually lost her capacity to trust her own perceptions. She hated
herself for being deceived. She blamed her body and her gender for
making her vulnerable.

Though her recovery process has been neither quick nor easy,
she is being restored in ways she never could have imagined. She
loves and trusts Jesus, though for a while when she envisioned him
in prayer, she feared he too would abuse her. Now, in her mind and
heart, she is able to separate her personal experiences with Jesus from
those who misrepresented him. She has also learned to trust men,
including faithful priests and bishops, who have played a crucial role
in her healing process. While still mourning over her many losses,
she is able to receive Jesus' comfort and healing for her broken heart.
She is beginning to enjoy life again. No longer wanting to die, she
has meaning and purpose in her life.

Similarly Charlie, whom I mentioned in chapter 7, has been
engaged in a long and difficult recovery process. He is learning to
be compassionate toward himself, realizing that his many years of
sexual compulsion were driven by his experiences of sexual abuse
by female babysitters and male neighbors during his first five years
of life. This abuse, along with his father's emotional detachment,
fueled considerable confusion in his masculine identity and resulted
in a lifelong pattern of sexual addiction. Over the years, Charlie has

experienced many powerful encounters with Jesus and has received deep comfort and restoration. But his healing has proceeded slowly, unfolding in layers as new painful memories are uncovered. In the beginning Charlie believed Jesus had abandoned him in his abuse, but now he has come to trust Jesus' presence, compassionately loving him and honoring his freedom (even when he cannot always sense his presence).

As difficult as the process has been, Charlie continues to be strengthened by the Holy Spirit working through prayer, sacraments, and community. He experiences Jesus' tenderness and compassion through his faithful wife and friends, some spiritually gifted therapists, a twelve-step support group, and several compassionate priests. With their help, he courageously works through layers of dissociation, uncovering each of the seven deadly wounds and identity lies that have taken root in his mind and heart as a result of his traumatic experiences and sexual compulsions.

As Charlie grows in sexual integrity, his relationships with his wife and children are also being restored. He is humbly acknowledging the ways he wounded each of them by acting out his sexual compulsions in previous years. Without desiring to hurt them, he has passed on his suffering in the form of betrayal trauma.

Betrayal Trauma

Before engaging in a healing process, sexually wounded people inevitably wound those closest to them, in one way or another. That was true for Charlie and his family, though he never desired to hurt them. Charlie did not sexually abuse them, but by acting out his sexual compulsions in other ways, he betrayed their trust. Charlic's wife especially experienced betrayal trauma as a result of his acting out his sexual compulsions. She is not alone. Many married and unmarried people are traumatized by the betrayal of their spouse or lover as a result of their unfaithfulness.

Remember Joyce (from chapter 1). She was severely traumatized by her husband's betrayal due to his adulterous relationship. Without adequately working through this trauma and addressing their under-lying wounds, they ended up divorcing, which only caused more suffering for each of them and their children. I could relate all too well. Some of my deepest wounds resulted from my dad's infidelity and the subsequent divorce of my parents. I know how deeply these *indirect* sexual wounds can shatter our hearts and leave us chronically discomforted. At the same time, I can testify to the hope and resto-ration that comes when we bring our broken hearts to Jesus and allow him to comfort us in our mourning.

Though restoring trust can be a long, exacting process, I have wit-nessed miraculous healings with many couples and families that have experienced betrayal trauma. Healing of sexual wounds, including betrayal trauma, begins when we face the reality of what happened and recognize our inability to heal ourselves. It is vitally important that the betraying partner acknowledges their sins and compulsions, accepts full responsibility for their actions, and addresses their effects on those they love, without losing hope. For the betrayed spouse/ partner/children, it is equally important that they acknowledge the betrayal and how it has wounded their trust. Charlie and his family are engaging in this process, and it is bringing healing to the entire family.

As Charlie knows, it is extremely difficult to face our traumas and to acknowledge how we have wounded those we love. We have to slowly learn to trust God and other people again, with these wounded areas of our hearts. We have to confront our self-justifications as well as the cultural lies and distortions telling us there is nothing wrong with certain sexual thoughts and behaviors. We have to face the reality that God never intended sexual intimacy to be experienced outside of a lifelong marital covenant. We have to acknowledge that there are always consequences when we violate God's protective boundaries for sexual intimacy.

When we give of ourselves, body, soul, and spirit, in sexual love and then later break the relationship, many hearts are inevitably broken. The consequences can be quite severe and challenging to overcome. I know many men and women who have been profound-ly traumatized by broken sexual relationships inside and outside of marriage. These include both heterosexual and homosexual experiences. Many times the trauma does not become fully evident until the person enters into another relationship and opens their hearts to love again. Trusting another person can stir intense fear and anxiety, revealing a previously broken heart. Many times the source of these fears goes even deeper than the teenage and adult betrayals. They are rooted in attachment and identity wounds from early childhood.

Attachment and Identity Trauma

Some of our deepest trauma is the result of psychosexual wounds from broken attachments and identity wounds. Jimmy (from the first chapter) is an example of someone who was traumatized without any overt sexual interactions. His Type A trauma (the lack of attachment with his father) was compounded by the Type B trauma (humiliation of his masculinity by the older boys in the locker room). As we have noted throughout the book, attachment loss with parents and same-sex peers can have severe consequences.[2] Steve, like Jimmy, experienced a broken attachment and identification with his father and then humiliation by his peers. He turned to same-sex fantasy and pornography as a way to medicate and reenact this trauma.

Attachment difficulties with mothers, especially early in life, can be even more debilitating.[3] In *Be Healed*, I mention the story of John, who experienced abandonment from his mother at two years old, when she left for six weeks to care for her dying mother. Her leaving caused a gaping wound of abandonment in John's heart that later manifested in his sexual compulsion. Cut off from his mother's love, he continued to both despise her and hunger for the nurturing of feminine love. His healing began with spiritual direction and through the sacraments. But it was not complete until he dealt with his deep unresolved abandonment trauma and identity wounds.

John detached his heart from his mother. This broken attachment fueled his compulsive hunger for feminine nurture. A critical step in John's healing came when he renounced the vow that he would never need anything from his mother. This opened his heart to experience his longing for his mother's nurture. It was only then in facing the pain of his unmet needs that he could grieve the loss of her love as a young child. A subsequent healing prayer experience several years later brought him the rest of the way into freedom from his sexual compulsion.[4]

Attachment problems with mothers early in life are often one of the main contributors to sexual compulsion in women as well. Leanne Payne, who dedicated her life to helping men and women find healing for same-sex compulsions, describes these dynamics as a way of understanding the process required for restoration: "The fact is that so often the one who falls into a lesbian relationship does so . . . in an unguarded moment, and out of a severe deprivation of a mother's loving arms in infancy and childhood."[5]

I have met with a number of women who, because of poor attachments with their mothers, were too easily seduced by older women into lesbian relationships. These relationships, which seemed superficially nurturing at first, later turned abusive. In the long run, the breakdown of the lesbian relationship only compounded the pain of attachment loss and added additional betrayal trauma and sexual abuse trauma. For many women caught in a lesbian lifestyle, this pattern of seduction, nurture, abuse, betrayal, and then abandonment becomes a hopeless treadmill of compounding pain and abuse.

As you can see from these accounts, and everything we have been discussing throughout this book, our early developmental experiences make a huge difference in our capacity to establish trust and form healthy attachments. These in turn have a significant impact on how we see ourselves (gender identity) and how we express our sexuality (sexual compulsions and sexual sin). Whether we are aware of it or not, our sexual wounds often involve a synergy of love deprivations (Type A traumas) and violations (Type B traumas). The source of wounding, violations, and identity distortions are unique in every situation, but in each case they leave a broken heart that needs to be healed by the tender love of Jesus.

Jesus' Heart Surgery

As we enter into the healing of our deepest traumas, keep in mind that a core part of Jesus' mission is to heal our broken hearts (Is 61:1). Bishop Robert Barron notes that all of us have a broken heart due to the rupture with God, known as original sin.[6] But those traumatized by sexual abuse, betrayal, and wounded attachments endure some of the deepest suffering. No matter how long or how much we have suffered, Jesus is unflinching in his dedication to restore us. Fr. Michael Scanlon underscores this point:

> The Lord intends us to know a new heart, a clean heart, a fleshly heart in place of a broken heart, a wounded heart, and a hardened heart. This is the Lord's work and in his time we know it. . . . In a moment of grace that appears to be a climax of memory healings—there is a crumbling of the hardened stony heart, or there is a washing clean and new wholeness to the wounded heart, or there is a replacement of the broken heart with the Lord's pastoral heart.[7]

In my years of accompanying those who have experienced sexual abuse, betrayal, and attachment loss, I have witnessed this miracle of a new heart many times. There is often a long process of building trust through the healing of memories. Then "in a moment of grace," as Fr. Scanlon so eloquently expresses it, the walls of the hardened heart crumble. Years of dissociation and defensive detachment give way to a new openness, trust, and hope. The person is finally able to experience Jesus' healing presence in the depths of their heart, where the seven deadly wounds had previously taken root. With his tender and compassionate love, he authoritatively speaks the truth where the identity lies have kept them bound (e.g., you are not alone; you are my beloved; you are safe; you are cleansed; you are free).

Having witnessed Jesus perform this heart surgery many, many times, I am convinced he desires to heal each of us in a similar way. He may minister to us directly in prayer, but he often works in and through his Body the Church. This combination of Christ and the Church is the surest remedy to our sexual healing. Those who have experienced sexual trauma need a combination of good Christ-centered therapy, solid preaching of the gospel, compassionate Christian pastoral support, and the graces available through the sacraments.

Through these various means, Jesus' merciful love reaches out to each person who has been wounded by sexual violations, including the survivors, the perpetrators, and family members. It is likely that each person has been deeply wounded by both Type A and Type B traumas. Therefore, healing needs to reach beyond the abuse and betrayal traumas to minister to the underlying attachment and identity wounds, including the places where our relationship with God has been ruptured. Restoration ordinarily begins with one motivated person, but it may eventually extend to each affected person, inside and outside the family.

Healing the Whole Family

Remember Hank (from chapter 5), who sexually abused his daughters. His healing, and that of his daughters, might never have happened had his wife, Danielle, not come seeking help first. And she only came because her brother and sister-in-law encouraged her, after their own healing. Though not directly affected by the abuse, they too suffered betrayal trauma when they heard about what happened to their nieces. After receiving substantial healing, they reached out to Danielle to encourage her to engage in therapy.

Danielle's Healing Process

When I first met Danielle, she looked shell-shocked, struggling to comprehend how her husband could have sexually abused their four daughters throughout the years without her awareness. Over the next many months, as she tried to come to grips with the reality and devastation resulting from the abuse, she progressed through the stages of the grieving process: denial, anger, bargaining, depression, and acceptance.[8]

Prior to therapy she remained stuck in the stage of shock and denial, finding it hard to comprehend what happened. As her denial broke down, she began to feel rage (intense anger, pain, and powerlessness). At one point she became afraid she would kill Hank if she saw him again. As she continued her grieving process, she relived the events and tried to figure out what she could have done to prevent it. This was her way of trying to regain control in the midst of feeling powerless (bargaining).

After coming to terms with her helplessness to change the past, she resigned to acknowledging the reality of what happened and then crumbled into a state of depletion and hopelessness (depression). Eventually she was able to express her anguish and sorrow and to accept the reality of what had happened with renewed hope (acceptance). She could finally mourn the overwhelming losses she, her husband, and their daughters had incurred. Her mourning, as you might imagine, was intense and exceedingly painful. It did not pass quickly or without struggle, but in the midst of it, she experienced Jesus' comforting presence consoling her.

A huge breakthrough occurred when Danielle confessed her sins (including her murderous rage and hatred for her husband) in the sacrament of Reconciliation (appendix 1). Another big turning point happened in the following weeks and months when she finally forgave herself for not being more aware of what was going on while the abuse was taking place (appendix 2). Through the entire process she felt Jesus' consoling presence in daily Mass and adoration.

Contemplative healing prayer was also a huge help for Danielle in her healing process (appendix 4). She faced her childhood wounds of abandonment, fear, and powerlessness, as well as the betrayal and powerlessness she experienced in her marriage. Encountering Jesus' presence in these memories consoled her considerably. She also renounced identity lies and her self-protective judgments and unhealthy attachments with Hank and her daughters (appendix 3). Each healing experience provided additional comfort and greater clarity. She eventually had the strength to forgive her husband, which was another huge breakthrough (appendix 2).

Slowly but surely Danielle began to feel a lightening in her spirit where the heaviness had once seemed suffocating. Her intense grieving process gave birth to intermittent sparks of supernatural joy. By learning to trust and abide in God's love and truth throughout each day, she began to hope that Jesus would heal and restore her family. With that hope in mind, she endeavored to face her husband again and to invite him to participate in the process of restoration.

When they found out about their mother's decision to reengage with their father, Danielle's daughters were outraged. But Danielle stood firm in her convictions, believing her choices would soon benefit her daughters as well, even if they couldn't yet see it. She felt confident she was following the path God prepared for her husband's salvation. Up till now she was haunted by the thoughts of her husband dying (whether through heart failure or suicide) before he could be reconciled with God. She couldn't bear the thought of him being lost forever in hell, even though a few months earlier she felt certain he deserved to go there.

Hank's Healing Process

At Danielle's request, I counseled with Hank for several months before I met with them together as a couple. Hank progressed through many of the same stages of grieving and healing as Danielle had, but according to his own inward progression and timing. Acknowledging the details of the sexual abuse and facing his intense shame and self-hatred proved to be the most difficult parts of the process. He felt a measure of freedom and peace after confessing his sins to a priest in the sacrament of Reconciliation (appendix 1).

Even after receiving God's forgiveness, Hank said he couldn't forgive himself until his family forgave him. But I encouraged him to keep his focus on Jesus' mercy, so he could face his wife and children without losing his strength and collapsing under the weight of his immense guilt. Hank also had to work through the identity lies associated with his personal sins, as well as those arising from his childhood wounds. He was beginning to understand how his underlying shame and abandonment wounds from childhood fueled his lifelong sexual compulsion. As we addressed these deeper heart issues in contemplative and renouncing prayer (appendices 3 and 4), Hank struggled to receive Jesus' love. Each time he envisioned (in contemplative prayer) Jesus reaching out to him with compassion, he could barely trust it was real. This made it especially difficult for him to receive the healing he needed. Yet over time he progressed in his healing and felt strengthened enough by God's grace to meet with Danielle in therapy.

Marital Healing

Hank realized that the meetings with his wife would be a real test for his growing trust in God. But he also knew that his healing would mean little if he could not listen to her pain and assume personal responsibility for his actions. The sessions between Hank and Danielle were extremely intense, but also surprisingly tender. Both remained humble and honest throughout many of the meetings. Hank received Danielle's anger, questioning, and tears with compassion and remorse. He was stunned by her forgiveness and overwhelmed with gratitude for God's mercy pouring through her.

Together, Hank and Danielle mourned over the immensity of losses in their marriage, their broken relationship with God, and especially the personal suffering of each of their daughters. Seeing his vulnerability and godly sorrow, Danielle could remember again the man she fell in love with, rather than the "monster" who had sexually abused their daughters. She didn't yet know if she could ever really trust him again. But she was soon to find out that he had truly changed, as she sat in on the meetings with Hank and their daughters.

Healing of Daughters

Two of the daughters had engaged therapists in other cities where they lived. This made it easier for them to enter into the process, having previously spoken about their abuse and dealt with some of their rage and trauma. One of the daughters had a serious drug addiction (to medicate her pain) and was currently engaged in a sexual relationship with another woman. A second had coped with her abuse by becoming an overachiever, masking her pain through perfectionism and success. They were both terrified to face issues with their father, as well as their mother with whom they had a love-hate relationship. Pushing past their fears and their intense feelings of hatred, shame, confusion, and betrayal, they entered valiantly into the process of confronting the suffering and degradation from their sexual abuse. The meetings were excruciatingly painful for all involved, but surprisingly beautiful and redemptive at the same time.

The daughters, each according to their own capacity, addressed their pain and rage with their father and mother. When they saw their parents' growth and humility, they were amazed and emboldened to share their pain with increasingly deeper levels of vulnerability. Soon the meetings turned into a time of communal grieving, acknowledging layers of heartbreaking pain and shame, and culminating in genuine repentance and forgiveness. I sat there amazed at God's goodness and mercy. He was turning their mourning into joy before our very eyes (see Psalm 30:12).

Family Restoration

Ten years after terminating therapy, Danielle contacted me to let me know that Hank had recently died. She was filled with gratitude for all the Lord had done in their lives. She told me that the family was grateful for those remaining years together, always mindful of the miracle God had worked in their midst. The healing was so complete that Danielle and their daughters and sons-in-law trusted Hank around his grandchildren. Danielle concluded, "Those last years with Hank were the happiest years of our marriage and family life. I firmly believe we will be reunited in heaven where we can love each other for all eternity and give endless praise to God for all he has done in our lives."

As you read about this family, what are your reactions? I encourage you to pay attention to how you are feeling and what you are thinking. Is there any experience in your life that mirrors this family's experience? Has your family experienced restoration in this way?

Or do you feel cheated because the one who violated your trust, or your family member's, has not responded with this kind of honesty and humility? Are you aware of feeling rage, sorrow, envy, doubt, or disbelief? Whatever you are experiencing, I encourage you to stop a minute and allow your thoughts and feelings to come to the surface. Then ask Jesus what he wants to show you. The same process of healing that Danielle's family experienced is available to you (see appendices 1–4). A major part of this healing process involves releasing our rage and pain.

Releasing Rage and Pain

Can you imagine sitting in front of the person who sexually violated you, betrayed you, or failed to protect you, as did Hank and Danielle's children? That took a tremendous amount of courage and a sense of safety to become that vulnerable. Yet facing our pain and rage is an essential part of the forgiveness process (see appendix 2). We need to be able to speak the truth of what happened and name what we have had stolen from us before we can wholeheartedly forgive. Otherwise our forgiveness remains shallow and does not heal the deeper recesses of our hearts that have been severely wounded.

Many of us are uncomfortable with intense feelings like these, especially rage. But these strong emotional reactions are not unusual with the kind of intense trauma that often accompanies sexual violations and other types of betrayal and attachment loss. If these feelings of pain and rage are not addressed, they will be internalized and manifest in various ways, including self-hatred, suicide, cutting, alcohol, drug addiction, shame, perfectionism, and sexual compulsion. Hank and Danielle's daughters exhibited many of these symptoms until they released their pain and rage and were able to forgive their mother and father.

Rage is an experience of intense anger, powerlessness, terror, and abandonment, mixed together in a swirl of confusion. It is a natural response to trauma. This rage may be directed toward the abuser/ betrayer, toward oneself (in self-destructive behavior), toward family members, or even toward God for allowing the abuse/betrayal to happen.

In his *Pursuing Sexual Wholeness*, Andrew Comiskey comments on the importance of facing our intense anger and pain as a critical part of the healing process. It is most beneficial when addressed directly to God, who is the only one who can fully receive and transform it. "He can handle her anger; He also wants her to release it to Him so that she can receive Him as advocate, not an ambivalent bystander."[9]

As I ponder this statement from Comiskey I am reminded of many situations accompanying others in the healing process. Many are furious at God, family members, or Church authorities who seemed like "ambivalent bystanders" rather than being advocates and protectors for them. Danielle's daughters expressed their rage toward their mother—perceiving her as an "ambivalent bystander." They also raged at Hank for stealing their innocence and ruining their life. If Danielle and Hank could take their daughters' anger (with God's grace) and respond with love, how much more can God the Father, who received Jesus' pain from the Cross, receive our pain and respond with merciful love?

As I have personally meditated on Jesus' passion in light of sexual abuse, betrayal, and abandonment trauma, I realize that he too was violated and experienced the full force of betrayal and abandonment. Betrayed by at least two disciples in his intimate circle, he was then stripped naked and publicly humiliated. Afterward his body was forcefully pierced and penetrated. In all of this, I believe Jesus was fully absorbing every survivor's experience of violation and betrayal and expressing the pain inherent to this experience. His words from the Cross echo down through the centuries: "My God, my God, why have you abandoned me?" (Ps 22:2).

In uttering these words from the depths of his soul, Jesus gives each of us permission (and an example) to release our anguish to the Father. Can you envision yourself expressing your pain to God? As Comiskey notes, these are legitimate feelings: "She can then release the torrent of hurt and anger within her. These feelings are absolutely legitimate—Christ grieves as she does. . . . Her need to get in touch with the emotion bottled up inside her is vital. Without that release, an emotional impasse develops that will help prevent healthy relating in the present."[10]

Christ grieving and feeling our pain with us is a glorious idea. But what happens when we don't really believe he is present in our traumas, let alone sympathetic to our suffering? This is the situation with many of those who have been sexually violated. In the depths of their hearts they desperately wonder, "Where was God?"

Where Was God?

Do you find it hard to believe that Jesus grieves as you do, especially in the tender areas of your sexual violations, betrayal trauma, and attachment wounds? Do you trust that he is with you at your most vulnerable and needy points? If you doubt this, you are not alone. It is quite common for victims of sexual violation, abandonment, and betrayal, as well as their family members, to entertain serious doubts about Jesus' presence in the midst of these horrific events. Many ask, "How could he be there and allow this happen?" Because of dissociation, there is often an emotional and spiritual block to our capacity to know his presence in this way. Behind these dissociative walls lurks a whirlpool of abandonment pain and rage. Until these areas are addressed honestly in prayer, the healing process can only go so far.

Rita's Experience

I mentioned Rita earlier in this chapter. Releasing pain and rage was a major stumbling block for her. From the time she was a young girl, her faith in God was important to her. Even as an adult, she would spend hours in adoration. But she couldn't reconcile her love for God with the intense abandonment she felt from him during her sexual abuse experiences. From her earliest childhood memories, she felt alone and unprotected by her parents, but she could always turn to God and be comforted. But something shifted once her brother began to abuse her. In the silence of her heart, she asked, "Where are you God? How could you let this happen to me?" Rita's question is a universal one. "How could a good and loving God allow us to be harmed and continue to suffer?"

Rita's feelings of being alone and unprotected only intensified after she told her parents about her brother sexually abusing her. Instead of believing her and offering comfort, her parents resolutely denied anything happened and blamed her for trying to destroy their family. Many years later, when she publicly revealed that a priest had sexually violated her, her parents were vicious in their attacks against her character. This abandonment pain felt too overwhelming for Rita to face, so she kept these feelings buried for many years. Her rage and pain didn't come to the surface until she began to face the gory details of her sexual abuse with her brother and the abandonment she experienced in her relationship with God.

Though I was not involved with most of Rita's healing process, her bishop asked me to walk through this most intense part with her. For the first time in her life she had finally spoken about the cruel and sadistic details of how her brother sexually abused her. As she entered into these memories, her terror felt palpable. I encouraged her to ask the Holy Spirit to reveal anything he wanted her to know about the abuse. After he revealed some important details she had forgotten, we asked the Holy Spirit to let her know where Jesus was in the midst of these memories. At this, Rita began to protest, stammering as though she was speaking from the heart of her nine-year-old traumatized self: "He wasn't there. He couldn't have been there. If he were there, how could he let this happen?"

Encountering this young, traumatized part of Rita, I realized we were standing on sacred ground. So I proceeded even more tenderly. After several minutes of silence, I queried, "Rita, can you tell me what you are experiencing?" With that question, Rita erupted with rage, like a volcano spews hot lava in fits and bursts. Screaming from the depths of her being, she released decades of suppressed pain. Her shrieking defied words. Even now I find it impossible to adequately describe the experience. All I can say is that I felt her terror viscerally, and her rage felt as if it contained the force of Niagara Falls. After releasing her intense anger, Rita began to wail. With the deepest heart-wrenching sorrow, she spoke to Jesus again in her nine-year-old voice: "How could you say you love me and let this happen to me?" As she addressed her questions to Jesus, I softly prayed, "Jesus, please reveal your presence to Rita in this memory."

Rita quieted. Within minutes, her torturous mourning turned into the most beautiful heartfelt nine-year-old little girl laughter. Relief seemed to permeate her entire being. She exulted: "I can't believe it. *He's here. Jesus really is here.* He never left me. He has been here the whole time. He is kneeling next to my bed praying for me. He is crying. I can see his pain and his love for me. His eyes are so full of love and his face is so kind. . . . Now I see him on the Cross, and all those cruel things my brother is doing to me, Jesus is taking them on himself. Is this really true? Can this really be happening? . . . It has to be real. I can feel his love and presence, and I don't feel alone anymore. He's completely taken my hurt. I don't have any more fear. Oh, Jesus, I love you. Thank you, Jesus. Thank you, so much. Thank you for being here."

Next, in her inner vision, Rita saw Jesus still on the Cross and heard him speak these words directly to her brother: "Father, forgive him, for he doesn't know what he is doing" (see Luke 23:34). At this Rita fell silent again. After a few minutes, she spoke directly to Jesus. "Jesus, how could you forgive Dan? You know what he did to me. Don't you care about me? Doesn't he need to be punished for this?" In the silence of her heart, Rita heard Jesus respond, "Rita, you know how much I care about you. I also care about Dan. I have forgiven him, and I know how much he is hurting too. I ask you to forgive him and to pray for his salvation. He is hurting more than you will ever know."

After experiencing Jesus' love and hearing his explanation, Rita was ready to forgive her brother. I encouraged her to pray through the forgiveness process (appendix 2) so she could also work through any remaining hurts, judgments, unhealthy attachments, or identity lies that might hinder her freedom in forgiving him (appendix 3).

After these prayers, she felt free in a way she couldn't ever remember. Together, we ardently expressed our gratitude to Jesus, marveled at his love and kindness, and asked him to seal Rita's healing with his precious blood when she received him in the Eucharist again.

After this breakthrough, Rita still needed to walk through many areas of her healing process, including the abandonment she felt from her parents, but there was a notable shift in her trust in God. Over the years, she has found compassionate priests and bishops to assist her. Through them, she is restoring her relationship with God and the Church, realizing that the priest who abused her (Fr. Tony) was not truly representing Jesus or the Church but was listening to the "father of lies." Rita has since been able to forgive Fr. Tony. But she continues to work through areas where she blamed her body and hated her gender for what happened.

Restoring Gender Identity

Whether gender distortions are the result of sexual abuse or deprivations in psychosexual development, it is fairly common for survivors to despise their God-given sexual nature and feel deeply ambivalent about their feelings of sexual arousal. These distortions can manifest in either same-sex or opposite-sex compulsions. This depends on a number of factors, including the degree of wounding and how much gender distortion has taken place. For healing to be complete, the survivor's gender identity needs to be restored according to God's design.

The restoration of gender identity follows a similar pattern to the healing process we have been discussing throughout part II. All of the spiritual tools in appendices 1–4 are both necessary and exceedingly beneficial in this process, as we saw with Steve in the last chapter. The following steps are essential:

- Acknowledging the goodness of God's design for sexuality (Theology of the Body)

- Acknowledging sexual sins and compulsions and their consequences (appendix 1)

- Facing and releasing the trauma from sexual abuse or betrayal traumas; forgiving self, others, and God for what happened (appendix 2)

- Renouncing identity lies and reaffirming core identity beliefs; renouncing unholy attachments, ungodly vows, and bitter-root judgments (appendix 3)

- Healing the wounds that occurred in psychosexual development, with regard to attachment and identification; experiencing God's love and truth in all the areas where attachment and gender identity have been wounded (appendix 4)

- Growing in sexual integrity and establishing healthy boundaries (appendix 5)

We will focus on the process of restoring sexual integrity in the next chapter. Beforehand, I encourage you to take a moment to reflect on the insights from this chapter and apply them to your own circumstances in the personal activity. Whether or not you have been sexually violated, or experienced betrayal wounds, you most likely have some Type A and Type B traumas that have affected your gender identity and sexual integration to some degree.

Take a Moment

1. What do you think sexual abuse trauma, betrayal trauma, and attachment wounds have in common?

2. How can Jesus heal our broken hearts and comfort us in our grief? How could the prayers in appendices 1–4 come into play in your healing process?

3. Why do you think the question "Where was God?" is essential to address? What role does rage play in the healing process?

4. What aspect of your gender identity needs restoration? How can it be restored?

Personal Activity

1. Ask the Holy Spirit to reveal any areas of sexual trauma, betrayal trauma, or attachment wounds in your life history.

2. Walk through the steps of the healing prayer in appendix 4. Let the Holy Spirit lead you.

3. If you have questions about Jesus' presence, express your doubts, pain, and anger to him.

4. Ask him to reveal his presence in the memory and to reveal what he wants you to know.

5. Keep coming back to the process until you experience his presence and receive his truth in the areas where you have internalized wounds and identity lies.

6. If you encounter barriers, apply the other spiritual tools. You may need to give or receive forgiveness (appendix 1 and 2). Or you may need to renounce ungodly vows, bitter-root judgments, unhealthy attachments, or identity lies associated with wounds (appendix 3). Pray through those areas and then return to the inner healing process.

7   If you find the process overwhelming or you get stuck, you may benefit from engaging a therapist, a priest, or a trained prayer minister to help you. You may also find some of the resources at the John Paul II Healing Center to be helpful.

8. Thank Jesus for his love and presence in your suffering, and for his desire to heal your broken heart, to comfort you in your grief, and to turn your mourning into joy.

10

OAKS OF RIGHTEOUSNESS: RESTORING OUR SEXUAL INTEGRITY

You will be called oaks of righteousness,
a planting of the LORD for the display of
his splendor.

—Isaiah 61:3

Throughout this book we have been exploring the various causes and manifestations of our disintegration. Our sexual sins, wounds, compulsions, and identity distortions are sirens alerting us to our sexual brokenness and beckoning us to sexual wholeness. We all naturally desire relief from suffering, but our healing must go beyond mere symptom relief. Deep down, we yearn for communion with God, integration within ourselves, and restoration in all of our relationships. This communion restores our sexual integrity and enables us to become "oaks of righteousness, a planting of the LORD for the display of his splendor" (Isa 61:3).

Each of the people mentioned throughout this book (including my family and myself) experienced some measure of disintegration in our sexuality as a result of our sexual sins and psychosexual wounds. To one degree or another these sins and wounds left us mired in shame, conflicted in our sexual thoughts and feelings, and largely disconnected from our hearts and cut off from authentic love. But then we encountered the merciful love of Jesus touching the precise areas of our sexual shame. As Fr. John Riccardo testifies: "Shame, especially sexual shame, is [ultimately] not a barrier to God's love. Indeed, when we finally tire of it enough that we are willing to bring the truth of our chains of shame to the light, we find they become a bridge to personal transformation."[1]

Throughout part II, we have witnessed the miraculous healing power of God's love and truth as the antidotes to our sin and shame. Our sexual brokenness and our inability to heal ourselves are not obstacles to Jesus. Our spiritual poverty is actually the precondition for experiencing his restoration in our lives. Healing occurs when we humbly acknowledge our sexual wounds and sins and bring our broken hearts to Jesus, depending on him (often working through his representatives in the Body of Christ) to restore us to sexual integrity.

Sexual Integrity

Sexual integrity entails thinking, feeling, and acting according to the truth of who we are, in full conformity with God's design for our sexuality. Dr. Janet Smith elaborates: "St. John Paul II used the term 'sexual integrity' to mean that *a person knows the truth about the meaning of sexuality, can abide in that truth, and joyfully acts in accord with that truth*."[2]

Acting in accordance with the truth of our sexuality requires a continuous and ongoing renunciation of the lies we believe. We renounce the world's idolatry of the body, in favor of what St. John Paul II refers to as the "Theology of the Body." This begins with an understanding that God is at the center of our sexuality. We are created male and female to represent God's image, in whatever state of life we find ourselves. Our bodies are his sacred temple, and we are called to worship him with our bodies (1 Cor 6:19; Rom 12:1). We worship him by self-giving love and generativity.

Sexual integrity is not an easy virtue to acquire, especially in a world beset by idolatry, confusion, self-centeredness, and a myriad of other sexual distortions. We have to first acknowledge the many ways we are currently disintegrated due to our personal and family sexual history, as well as the pervasive cultural influences that distort our understanding of sexuality. Each of the people we followed throughout this book has been immersed in a culture that worships at the altars of Baal and Ashtoreth (demonic powers associated with sexual immorality), offers our children in sacrifice to Molech and Lilith (demonic powers behind abortion and contraception), and embraces the sexual distortions evidenced by the infamous Ahab and Jezebel (archetypes of gender distortion).[3]

In this sexually perverted culture, it is often difficult to find exemplary witnesses who are *living the truth in love*. We have all had personal role models in our families, in our culture, and sometimes even in our church communities who lack sexual integrity in one way or another. Under these influences, we ourselves have made numerous choices that have compromised our own integrity. Yet we still need inspiring role models and community to show us the meaning and purpose of our sexuality and how to live joyfully in the fullness that God intends.

As we have emphasized throughout the book, the members of the Holy Family are the ultimate role models and community revealing the beauty and fulfillment of sexual integrity. Having lived fully in obedience to God's design, they *lived the truth in love* each moment of their lives. Their joyful witness and intercession prepares the way for each one of us to find sexual freedom and wholeness. Whether we are celibate, single, or married, we can all learn sexual integrity by modeling after them. They reveal to us the fullness of the masculine and feminine genius as God intended from creation.

Jesus is more than a role model. He is the source and summit of our integrity. We are each called to abide in his love, through the power of the Holy Spirit working in and through the sacraments. "In all of his life Jesus presents himself as *our model.* . . . Christ enables us to *live in him* all that he himself lived, and *he lives it in us*" (*CCC*, 520–521). Jesus exemplifies the three essential qualities inherent in sexual integrity: *security, maturity,* and *purity.* And he enables us to live these ourselves, in the security of the Father's love.

Security: Rooted in Love

Our ultimate security comes from being rooted and grounded in the Father's love (see Ephesians 3:17). Jesus grew up knowing he was securely loved by Mary and Joseph. Yet his parents understood perhaps more than anyone else who ever lived that they were not and could never be the ultimate source of Jesus' security. They faithfully and humbly conveyed the Father's love to their son throughout his childhood and adolescent years, while continually directing him to find his identity and security in his heavenly Father. As Jesus continued to grow and develop, his allegiance to the Father became fully evident to his parents (Lk 2:49). Later at his Baptism, he publicly received the blessing of the Father in his identity as *beloved Son* (Lk 3:22). He remained grounded in this primary identity throughout his life, enabling him to abide constantly in the Father's love and to be strengthened by his perpetual blessing (Jn 15:9).

Recapitulating Jesus' pattern of development, we come into our families dependent and vulnerable and remain that way for many years. During childhood and throughout our life we need to be consistently nurtured and affirmed in our identity in order to grow in trust and security. Our parents, made in the image and likeness of God, are called to imitate Joseph and Mary as the primary representatives and conduits of the Father's love for us. To the extent that our caregivers humbly and faithfully love us well, we can experience security. But even with good nurturing parents, we need more than their human love to be fortified.

Like Jesus, our ultimate security is in the Father. We also need to be affirmed in our true identity as beloved sons and daughters of the Father. We first received this blessing at our Baptism and need to continue to live it daily. Our identity and security are strengthened as we participate actively and faithfully in the sacraments and enter wholeheartedly in prayer and community life. However, unlike Jesus, we and the people in our life have a proclivity to sin—to separate ourselves from the love of God and to forget who we are and to whom we belong. We end up vainly acting according to our own designs and faulty conceptions, rather than trusting in his love and truth. The more we find our identity outside of the Father, the more lies we are prone to believe about ourselves and the more distorted our identity becomes. Separation from God ultimately threatens our security, leaving us brokenhearted and deceived. Until we experience restoration, our growth into sexual wholeness is impeded.

As we have seen throughout this book, the process of disintegration begins early in life to the degree that our parents, family, and community are not able to humbly mediate the Father's love. Many of our deepest wounds are rooted in our early childhood development, where we failed to develop a secure attachment and receive tender affirmation from our mother, father, and other caregivers in our life. These early traumas, as well as the traumas incurred throughout our life, instill fear and create barriers around our hearts, thus blocking our capacity to give and receive love.

The authors of *The Life Model* describe how these trauma-based attachments differ from secure love bonds: "There are two essentially different and incompatible types of bonds—one based in fear and the other based on love. . . . Fear bonds energize people to avoid pain-like rejection, fear, shame, humiliation, abandonment, guilt or even physical abuse. Love bonds motivate people to live in truth, closeness, joy, peace, perseverance, kindness and authentic giving."[4]

Simply stated, *love bonds* are the source of our *security*, whereas *fear bonds* are the basis for our *insecurity*. Deriving from our traumas and the resultant seven deadly wounds (i.e., fear, shame, rejection, abandonment, powerlessness, hopelessness, and confusion), these fear bonds are reinforced through the *identity lies* we internalize. *FEAR* stands for "*False Evidence Appearing Real*." Our wounds and identity lies appear real to us, with lots of experiential evidence to support them. But they hinder our capacity to trust in the Father's love and thus distort our identity as beloved sons and daughters of the Father.

Fear bonds and the insecurity they engender are the driving forces behind our sexual compulsions and the soil in which our gender identity becomes distorted. We see examples of this in each of the stories throughout this book. Those who were deprived of genuine love, to any degree, experienced a corresponding loss of security; they subsequently formed fear bonds with those who wounded them. Conversely, in their healing encounters with Jesus, these fear bonds were transformed into love bonds, which in turn fostered greater security in the Father and in all their relationships.

Steve's story (chapters 4, 5, and 8) demonstrates the process of transformation from fear bonds into love bonds. Due to his childhood wounds, he formed fear bonds with his father and his male peers. These unhealed wounds, along with his self-protective responses, deeply impacted the way he saw himself, kept him insecure in his relationships, and fueled his sexual fantasies. These fear bonds severely limited his capacity to give and receive love, which manifested in his distorted masculine identity and sexual compulsions.

Steve experienced a major breakthrough in his security after encountering the Father's merciful and tender love while on retreat in high school. Subsequent healing experiences later in life enabled him to develop greater confidence in his masculine identity and enabled him to establish secure love bonds with trustworthy men and women. Steve's story highlights for each of us the benefits of contemplative prayer for strengthening the bonds of security and healing emotional wounds (appendix 4). By bringing the areas of our insecurity (fear, shame, and disintegration) into the light of Christ's presence, we can encounter the Father's love even in the darkened and most damaged areas of our wounded heart.

Dominican sister Sara Fairbanks affirms our need for healing these emotional wounds as the foundation for forming strong love bonds with God. She asserts, "Falling in love and staying in love with God and all that God loves is at the heart of healthy, integrated sexuality. Perhaps the single most crucial skill for promoting lifelong intimacy with God, self, and others is attending to emotional wounds—a skill for sexual integrity."[5] From this firm foundation of the Father's love, we become capable of growing in *maturity*.

Maturity: Growing in Virtue

Maturity is the process of growing in Christlike virtue. All authentic virtues are expressions of love originating out of our union with Christ (Eph 4:13–14; 1 Pt 1:3–9).[6] Pope Benedict XVI elaborates: "It is characteristic of mature love that it calls into play all of man's potentialities; it engages the whole man, so to speak . . . this process is always open-ended; love is never 'finished' and complete; throughout life it changes and matures, and thus remains faithful to itself."[7]

When we are rooted and grounded in love, we naturally mature through the developmental stages previously described in chapter 2. We move through the following successive stages of life: we begin life receiving love as a child; we learn to share this love in our relationships with peers (friends and siblings); and we then mature into spouses and parents who are able to embody sexual integrity. Throughout the stages of our psychosexual development, we progressively mature in our capacity for authentic love through *attachment, identification, belonging, self-giving,* and *generativity* (see table 10.1).

Table 10.1. Relational identities and psychosexual maturity

RELATIONAL IDENTITIES	PSYCHOSEXUAL MATURATION
Child: Daughters and sons	Attachment and identity
Peer: Siblings/friends	Boundaries and belonging
Spouse: Brides and bridegrooms	Self-mastery and self-giving

RELATIONAL IDENTITIES	PSYCHOSEXUAL MATURATION
Parent: *Mothers and fathers*	Blessing and generativity

We all begin life in our identity as *daughter or son* (even those who grow up as orphans, in foster care, or in broken families). From the earliest experiences in life, beginning in the womb, we learn how to trust, receive, enjoy, and imitate. When we experience healthy attachments and are affirmed in our gender identity, we form love bonds and come to know our fundamental identity as a beloved son or daughter. Without healthy attachments, we form fear bonds. These foundational experiences formed early in life continue to have a tremendous impact on our capacity for sexual integrity throughout our days.

During childhood, we are also called to mature into another kind of relational identity as a *sister or brother*. Whether with siblings, friends, peers, cousins, or with humanity in general, we learn how to share, challenge, support, and belong. We also need to learn to respect our own dignity and that of others by establishing healthy boundaries. During this stage we begin to develop the capacity for caring friendships. The ability to treat others our age with respect is critical for developing sexual integrity later in life. Conversely, deficits in this formation handicap our capacity to love chastely in the next phase of life in our spousal identity.

Whether we are single, celibate, or married, we all need to develop in our identity as *bride or bridegroom*. This identity begins to form in our teenage years, and it often takes several years for us to develop a capacity for chaste, intimate, faithful love. Within this stage of life, we learn self-mastery and self-giving, which are two essential virtues for developing sexual integrity inside and outside of marriage (whether we are single, married, or celibate). Without learning these vital skills our relationships become self-centered and we fail to mature to the fourth and final phase of relationship—in our identity as parent.

We are each called to the pinnacle of sexual maturity as a *mother or father*, whether or not we have our own (biological) children. During this phase of life, which includes parents, mentors, spiritual parents, aunts, uncles, and grandparents, we learn how to be generative, through nurturing, blessing, providing, and protecting. These are the virtues necessary to live in the fullness of our psychosexual maturity. In this phase we assist children, adolescents, and other adults to become sexually mature and integrated. These qualities are needed for all men and women.

These four primary relational identities spanning our lifetime are markers of sexual maturation. The members of the Holy Family exhibit these relational identities in fullness. Jesus is the son of the Father (Lk 3:22) and the son of Joseph and Mary (Lk 2:16). He is our brother in humanity (Heb 2:17), the bridegroom of the Church (Eph 5:25), and the revelation of the Father to his disciples and to all of us (Jn 14:7).

Joseph likewise fully matured in his masculine identity from son to brother, bridegroom, and finally father, revealing the love of the Father to Jesus. In a similar way, Mary embodies the most exemplary virtues of the feminine genius. She is first the beloved daughter of the Father; then she is the humble sister to us in humanity; as she matured she became the spotless bride of the Holy Spirit and the virginal bride of Joseph (Mt 1:18–20); and finally Mary becomes the loving mother of Jesus (Lk 1:31) and all of us (Jn 19:26; Rv 12:17).

Each member of the Holy Family inspires us to live the fullness of maturity, regardless of our state in life. They are much more than an ideal for us to imitate, however. We are intimately and eternally united with them in Christ. They are *our spiritual family*. The entire Communion of Saints finds its identity and belonging in the Holy Family as the center. We cannot overestimate the impact of their love and intercession in our sexual integration. They provide the intimate loving family we each need so we can mature through the various stages of our psychosexual development. Since the members of the Holy Family were without any apparent identity lies, they provide us the blueprint of what God intended from the beginning.

Conversely, many of the saints had to overcome severe sexual wounding, sexual compulsion, and sexual sin. Their biographies show us that restoring maturity does not happen quickly or easily. It is a lifelong endeavor. They are also our role models and support, providing both the example and the assistance we need to be restored in sexual integrity.[8] Like them, we too may have been wounded in any or all of the four stages of development. Our capacity in each stage of development has likewise been hindered by the traumas that have blocked our maturity. We remain fragmented and find it exceedingly difficult to integrate our sexual desires and gender identity into a cohesive whole. That is why we constantly need God's help and the assistance of the whole community of believers, in heaven and on earth, to grow in maturity.

Our spiritual family on earth also plays an essential role in our maturation, helping us to overcome the areas we lack maturity due to our psychosexual wounds. We can be honest and vulnerable with people who love us well.[9] In this kind of nurturing, healing community, "people can overcome shortcomings that result from faulty training, they can receive repair for traumas. . . . That is good news. People can help one another get unstuck, and begin to mature again. No wonder the Bible is so emphatic about loving one another, bearing each other's burdens, and being an active participant in the family of God!"[10]

In a particular way mature Christian therapists, pastors, and prayer ministers are called to minister to our brokenness in the power of the Holy Spirit: "The godly counselor, just like all mature believers, participates with God helping others put their lives right again. . . . Christian counseling must address these evils but not in human strength, not by human wisdom, and not by human plans. This is the work of God's redemption and He alone is worthy to direct and achieve His divine purpose in our salvation. This work can only be accomplished in the life of the Spirit through hearts that are alive in God."[11]

It takes the entire family of God, in heaven and on earth, to help us grow in maturity. The saints in heaven, and especially the Holy Family, are the ones who love us most purely and show us it is humanly possible to become sexually integrated persons. The community of believers on earth is called to mediate God's love, drawing on the life of the Spirit, to help us grow in purity.

Purity: Life in the Spirit

Purity is the fullest expression of love, without any distortions or perversions (Eph 5:1–2; 1 Jn 3:3). Once again, the members of the Holy Family are our models for purity. As we mature in Christ, we are called to emulate the immaculate heart of Mary and the chaste heart of Joseph. Jesus also calls each of us to participate in his Sacred Heart—the source of our purity. On the sermon of the mount he taught that the "pure in heart" are blessed to see God (Mt 5:8). When we are pure in heart, we see God in everyone and everything and are thus prepared to meet him face-to-face in the beatific vision at the end of our lives.

Conversely, St. Paul warns that we cannot enter the kingdom of heaven without being purified (Eph 5:5; 1 Cor 13–15; 1 Cor 6:9). It seems clear from these passages (and many more) that purity is a necessary precondition for heaven.[12] This realization could leave many of us discouraged as we reflect upon all the ways we lack and have lacked purity in our lives. But the apostle Paul goes on to say that all of us, once impure, have been washed by the blood of Christ (in Baptism) and are being made pure again by his mercy and grace (see 1 Corinthians 6:11). In those areas where we continue to have impure thoughts, desires, and actions, we are invited to bathe constantly in Christ's redeeming blood through prayer and adoration, as well as through the sacraments of Reconciliation and Eucharist (see 1 John 1:7). Purification in Christ, for ourselves and others, is also one of the main purposes of the sacraments of Confirmation, Matrimony, and Holy Orders. Finally, the sacrament of Anointing of the Sick purifies us for our ultimate hope. "Everyone who has this hope based on him makes himself pure, as he is pure" (1 Jn 3:3), recognizing that it is ultimately Jesus who completes this work of purification in us through his Spirit (Philippians 1:6, 10).

Purity is progressively manifested in our lives as we yield to the Holy Spirit and bear the "fruit of the Spirit" (Gal 5:22–23). The tradition of the Church lists twelve fruits of the Spirit: charity, joy, peace, patience, kindness, goodness, generosity, gentleness, faithfulness, modesty, self-control, and chastity. I find it interesting that these fruits of the Spirit begin with charity (the foundation of purity) and end with chastity (the full flowering of purity). The other fruits of the Spirit accompany chastity: "Chastity is the joyous affirmation of someone who knows how to live self-giving, free from any form of self-centered slavery. . . . Chastity makes the personality harmonious. It matures it and fills it with inner peace."[13]

Whether we are consciously aware of it or not, we each have an insatiable desire for chaste love. We yearn to be loved purely and to become capable of loving others in the same way. Deep down, no one really wants to be used by another for their momentary pleasure. No one wants to feel like an object of another's lust or to be bound by their own sexual compulsions. Addictions counselor Jeff Jay underscores this reality:

> Human beings like pleasure, and we are naturally
> drawn to pleasurable experiences [but] . . . humans
> want more than transient sexual gratification; we want
> real love, connection, and intimacy. We want fami-
> lies and communities. Unbridled sex can destroy all
> these things. We may veer off from the sexual integrity
> we desire because of adverse childhood experiences,
> early exposure to pornography, or traumatic sexual
> encounters. Whatever the challenge we are left with
> the reality of our brokenness, and we can only regain
> control by facing the issue.[14]

Many of us have experienced the kinds of sexual brokenness that Jay mentions. When we bring this brokenness to Jesus, we grow in purity. This growth takes place within a loving Christian community, through honest prayer, and with openhearted participation in the sacraments. But this is the road less traveled. Few of us, even in the Church, actively pursue this path. Purity eludes us as long as we conceal our wounds and compulsions and pretend, out of pride, that we are better than others. If we pursue sexual purity in our own strength and aren't willing to face our sexual brokenness, we will become puritanical, which is a counterfeit for purity.

When we are puritanical, we dutifully repress our sexual desires and live with a sense of shame and fear about anything related to sexuality. This counterfeit path to purity leaves us largely disintegrated in our sexual thoughts and desires. We then put on a facade and end up leading a double life, acting religious on the outside but lacking true purity of heart. Denying both our sexual brokenness and our need for a redeemer, we then look down on others and condemn them for their lack of purity.[15] We may run and hide for a while, but eventually our lack of integration will catch up with us. As a result many in our culture hear the words "purity" and "chastity" and immediately associate these words with joyless sexual repression, prudishness, hypocrisy, and self-righteousness. This is the antithesis of sexual integrity.

By contrast, purity that is the fruit of the Holy Spirit leads to our sexual integration. We grow in purity when we humbly face our sexual brokenness and seek out other honest and compassionate people whom we can trust with our vulnerability. Brother Daniel Keating, from the Sword of the Spirit community, comments on the importance of honest sharing in community:

> It is a sign of mature freedom when a man can speak directly about sexual challenges that he has faced in the past and that he faces in the present, and gain the help and encouragement from others to press on and not give up. Most men experience the same (or similar) challenges in their sexuality, and yet most men naturally do not want to speak about these challenges! The result is that they remain hidden and unattended, and block the path to mature sexual health and peace. But when men find a context in which they can speak of sexual issues openly and yet with modesty, knowing that what they say will be held in confidence, healing and transformation are much more likely to occur.[16]

What Keating describes here is true for both men and women, whether single, consecrated, or married. To grow in purity, we need to courageously bring the areas of our impurity into the light of Christ's truth and compassion. Sacramental Confession is indispensable in this process (see appendix 1), but it is not sufficient by itself to remediate shame and completely restore our sexual integrity. We need to align our lives with the Word of God and enter into a process of vulnerable sharing with a few others whom we can trust. Every person we have journeyed with throughout this book can attest to the futility of trying to achieve purity on their own. They also know of the grace that comes when we look to Jesus and his Body to accompany us.

In addition to sharing in community, we grow in purity through honest, searching prayer. It is in contemplation that we meet Jesus face-to-face and allow his own purity to penetrate the depths of our hearts. "All of us, gazing with unveiled face on the glory of the Lord, are being transformed into the same image from glory to glory, as from the Lord who is the Spirit" (2 Cor 3:18). Notice that restoration occurs when we take our eyes off ourselves and fix our gaze on the Lord *with unveiled faces.* Leanne Payne explains: "Only the real 'I,' shedding its illusory selves, can draw near to God. In His Presence, my masks fall off, my false selves are revealed. I stand stripped and naked before Him. To continually abide in His Presence is to have one face only—the true one. To draw near to Him, therefore, is to find the real 'I' as well as the true home, my true Center."[17] This nakedness before God is purity.

Pope Benedict XVI underscores that it is only Jesus' penetrating gaze that enables us to come before him without pretense:

> Before [Jesus'] gaze all falsehood melts away. This encounter with him, as it burns us, transforms and frees us, allowing us to become truly ourselves. . . . His gaze, the touch of his heart heals us through an undeniably painful transformation "as through fire." But it is a blessed pain, in which the holy power of

his love sears through us like a flame, enabling us to
become totally ourselves and thus totally of God.[18]

Deep down, don't we all desire "to become totally ourselves and thus
totally of God"? Why then do we so often resist Jesus' gaze? "His
gaze, the touch of his heart" heals us. But our shame and fear put up
barriers to avoid intimacy with him in the deepest areas of our sexual
brokenness. When we avoid this "blessed pain" we too easily become
hopeless about ever becoming pure, disdaining even the notion of
chastity. But as we gaze upon Jesus in the sacraments, in community,
and in contemplative prayer, we become ever more like him. Eventually we discover that we have graciously acquired his security, his
maturity, and his purity.

This process of transformation is expressed in a poem I wrote
several years ago for priests and seminarians. Though it was written
for celibate men, I believe it is applicable for each one of us—as we
seek to be restored in our sexual integrity:

> What does it take to be a chaste, celibate man?
> To know in your heart that you certainly can
> In the face of temptation, continue to stand
>
> What does it mean to stand in Christ's shoes?
> To withstand the assault and pay all your dues
> To wait on the Spirit, as your heart he renews
>
> Grace is the means to a chaste celibate life
> Strengthened by Christ and loving his "wife"
> With the Church as your Bride, despite all her strife
>
> How can a man become pure in his heart?
> Without secure love, right from the start
> Becoming a mature man, is truly an art
>
> Chastity is none other than Jesus' own purity
> He is the rock of all our security
> He is the One who brings us maturity

Most often he works along with His Bride
Wherever is Jesus, She's there by His side
Both Bridegroom and Church with arms open wide

There's been many a man who's sexually bent
Off to some treatment, he's often been sent
Sorely aware of his great need to repent

This treatment while needed is doomed to fail
Unless, Father's love, ultimately prevail
We mustn't see therapy as some Holy Grail

The only real healing comes from the Source
He alone can restore a man's sexual course
Anything less will leave that man worse

But thanks be to God, who sets our heart free
To be the true man, he made us to be
To love with His heart, through His eyes we may see

He gives us His love and restores our security
He gives us His Church, to bring our maturity
He gives us His heart, to bless us in purity.[19]

Whether this is the beginning of your healing journey or you have
been pursuing sexual wholeness for some time, I pray that you will
know in the depths of your heart that healing and restoration are not
only possible but also the very reason Jesus came and continues to
come to set us free and heal our broken hearts. Keep your gaze on
him. May the courageous witness of those whose stories were shared
throughout the book be an inspiration to you, as they are to me. They
show me that Jesus is present and powerful, even in the most hopeless
and difficult circumstances, as we turn to him with unveiled faces.

I pray for you now: may you know deeply and profoundly the
security of the Father's love and your identity as his beloved. May you
continue to grow in Christlike *maturity*, through his school of love,
surrounded by the Holy Family and with the community of believers

in heaven and on earth. And may the Holy Spirit continue to restore you in *purity*, so you can experience his joy, peace, and fulfillment.

Your lifelong quest for *sexual integrity* will not end until you are safely in the presence of our heavenly Father, but I pray that every step you take toward him now will bring you greater peace and joy and profoundly bless everyone you encounter. May you become a sturdy oak of righteousness, a planting of the Lord for his glory.

Before reading the afterword by Fr. Mark Toups (the chaplain at the Theology of the Body Institute course), I encourage you to take a moment to reflect on this chapter and then participate in the personal activity by applying the material in the appendices.

Take a Moment

1. What is sexual integrity, and what can you do to cultivate it?

2. Describe any experiences you've had with the fruits of purity and how they contrast with being "puritanical."

3. In which of the four relational identities do you believe you need the most healing? (See page 185.)

4. How have you grown in security, maturity, and purity? In what ways are you currently experiencing the fruits of purity in your life?

Personal Activity

1. Read through the material in appendix 1 and prepare for a whole-life confession.

2. Using the format in appendix 2, work through the process of forgiveness, forgiving God, yourself, and those who have contributed to your psychosexual wounds.

3. Drawing on the prayers in appendix 3, pray through the barriers that prevent healing.

4. Identify areas where you have internalized identity lies from your psychosexual wounds. Walk through the healing prayer process in appendix 4 to heal these wounds and identity lies.

AFTERWORD

The *Catechism of the Catholic Church* paragraph 2706 states: "To meditate on what we read helps us to make it our own by confronting it with ourselves. Here, another book is opened: the book of life." Thus, when we read words of wisdom, light shines on the "book" of our heart. This is where the more personal story is: the story of our lives. As I read *Be Restored,* I found myself reading not one, but two, books. The text of *Be Restored* was a light shining on my heart. As I read, I found myself pausing more frequently, putting the book aside, and paying attention to what was stirring in my heart. Admittedly, the reading of this book took longer than expected, for I wasn't merely reading a book; I was encountering the Lord anew in my heart as I read the book.

There are three aspects of this book that I would like to comment on. First, in chapter 7, Dr. Bob states that "restoration is a process." There is a difference between being fixed and experiencing authentic healing. My experience personally, as well as my journey with others, has taught me that the gift of time often reveals the fullness of the gift. In other words, there is usually more that needs to be healed than what I can initially see. Oftentimes, in the *process* of healing, God's intentional timeline of healing is slower than what I or others want in a "one and done" prayer period. However, time has a way of revealing more than what I could see at the moment. I encourage all of us to be patient. Trust the process. And, more importantly, trust the One who is the process—namely, Jesus Christ.

Second, in appendix 4, Dr. Bob writes: "Don't try to figure out where Jesus is or what he might say or do. Allow him to reveal himself." God wants our freedom infinitely more than we do. Again, to quote the *Catechism of the Catholic Church* paragraph 2567: "God calls man first. Man may forget his Creator or hide far from his face;

he may run after idols or accuse the deity of having abandoned him; yet the living and true God tirelessly calls each person to that mysterious encounter known as prayer. In prayer, the faithful God's initiative of love always comes first; our own first step is always a response." As Christians, we believe that God is always taking the initiative – always. The aforementioned process of healing is what God does, not what we do, per se. God does the leading. We are simply called to give Him permission and follow His lead. As mentioned in the paragraph above, I can trust the process because I can trust the One who is the process—namely, Jesus Christ. And I can trust that Jesus is always doing something to lead me to deeper freedom.

Third, in chapter 8, Dr. Bob urges us to "practice spiritual disciplines." If healing is a process, that means that learning to live in freedom is also a process. We can become so familiar with the landscape of woundedness that living in freedom is actually sometimes an "uncomfortable" place of the unknown. This is when we need to stay still and resist the urge to return to the familiar self-imposed prison of isolation. This is when we need to engage our will and "practice spiritual disciplines" such as the cardinal virtues, accountability, and relentless self-reflection. Living in freedom requires the same courage as receiving freedom.

I pray that those of you who read *Be Restored* had the courage to read your heart as much as the words from Dr. Bob. Be not afraid. Trust the process. And, more importantly, trust the One who is the process—namely, Jesus Christ.

Fr. Mark Toups

ACKNOWLEDGMENTS

There are many people who have shaped my life, influenced my development, and helped me to know the reality of Jesus' merciful love. I couldn't possibly name all of them, but I am grateful for each one, beginning with my family, parish priests, and friends, and our team at the John Paul II Healing Center. I have mentioned many of you in my previously published books, so here I simply say thank you for loving me and being such a vital part of my journey.

Many people played a role in the development of this book. I want to express my gratitude for the courageous men and women whose stories of sexual wounding and restoration are described in these pages. Your courage in walking through trauma and your faith in trusting Jesus have been an inspiration for me and many others.

I also want to thank each of you who reviewed earlier copies of this manuscript and provided valuable input: Fr. John Burns, Fr. John Riccardo, Andrew Comiskey, Marco Casanova, Sr. Mary Peter Joost, Sr. Miriam James Heidland, Lisa Lively, David Costanzo, Michael Sullivan, Mary Bielski, Peggy Schuchts, Wayne Schuchts, Anna Daunt, Carrie Daunt, Duane Daunt, Kristen Blake, Stephen Blake, Alan Hebert, Elza Spaedy, Dr. Tom Nelson, Fr. Burke Masters, Sr. Janelle Buettner, Megan Murphy, Carrie Gress, and Jeannie Hannemann. I can't imagine a more qualified group of advisors. You each live with integrity, have demonstrated a deep love for Jesus, and have an intimate knowledge of his merciful love.

I would also like to express my appreciation to those of you who reviewed the manuscript to offer endorsements: Scott Hahn, Fr. John Burns, Fr. John Ricardo, Jake Khym, Heather Khym, Carrie Gress, Bruce and Jeannie Hannemann, Matt Fradd, Andrew Comiskey, and Christopher West. I honor each of you for your valuable contributions to Christian anthropology related to sexuality and your tireless proclamation of the gospel of Jesus' merciful love and participation in his mission of restoration.

Through the past fifteen years, I have had the privilege of teaching much of this material alongside Sr. Miriam James Heidland and Fr. Mark Toups. You have each influenced my life and touched thousands of people through your faithful witness and teaching. I am grateful to you for writing the foreword and afterword for this book.

Next, I want to thank all of the faithful staff at Ave Maria Press. It has been a privilege to work with you these past many years. Thank you for your contributions to *Be Restored*. I want to especially thank my editor Kristi McDonald. Kristi, it's been a joy sharing in this process. Thank you for your enthusiasm for this project and your patience as it took me a while to get started. Thank you as always for your wise editorial comments and suggestions.

Finally, and most importantly, I want to thank you, Jesus, for your merciful love exhibited over and over again in my life, within our family, and to the many people I have accompanied in the process of restoration. I am continually in awe of the way you love and touch the deepest recesses of our broken hearts and disordered desires. Thank you for showing us the Father's love and for guiding us into authentic identity through the Holy Spirit. I also thank you, Joseph and Mary, for giving Jesus and all of us the most beautiful image of chaste love and authentic masculinity and femininity in God's image. St. John Paul II, thank you for highlighting these realities through your teaching on the Theology of the Body.

APPENDIX 1

WHOLE-LIFE CONFESSION

God's commandments and precepts governing our sexuality are motivated by his love and desire to protect us, both personally and collectively. When we violate these sexual boundaries, we inevitably experience disgrace and disintegration, and hurt others in a similar way. Until we humbly acknowledge these and receive God's mercy and healing, we can remain bound in guilt and shame. Or we may remain in denial, failing to see how we have wounded ourselves, others, and God.

It took King David some time before he acknowledged his adultery with Bathsheba (see [Psalm 51), and this occurred only after the prophet Nathan confronted him. Psalm 32 expresses his great relief after confessing his sin and his intense suffering while it remained unconfessed:

> Blessed is the one whose fault is removed, whose sin
>   is forgiven.
> Blessed is the man to whom the LORD imputes no guilt,
>   in whose spirit is no deceit.
> Because I kept silent, my bones wasted away; I
>   groaned all day long.
> For day and night your hand was heavy upon me; my
>   strength withered as in dry summer heat.
> Then I declared my sin to you; my guilt I did not hide.

> I said, "I confess my transgression to the LORD," and
> you took away the guilt of my sin. (Ps 32:1–5)

When we hold on to our sins, they cause us continual suffering, physically, emotionally, and spiritually. We also remain perpetually bound in shame, which fosters deceit and internal disintegration. When we face and confess our sins, we release their heavy burden. This is true whether our sins are recent or well in the past. Time does not heal. Only Christ's precious blood and merciful forgiveness can fully heal these self-inflicted wounds.

A whole-life confession is an opportunity to cleanse your body and soul from guilt and release you from the shroud of shame. It also enhances your sexual integrity and will restore your joy. If you desire this freedom, I encourage you to reread chapter 5 ("Crushed by Iniquities: Acknowledging Our Sexual Sins") as part of your preparation for making this whole-life confession. Specifically, review the list of sexual sins and their consequences. After reviewing chapter 5, I encourage you to follow these steps, slowly and prayerfully. Don't rush. It may take some time to prepare yourself for this healing experience.

- **Purpose:** The purpose of the whole-life confession is first to restore your relationship with God. But in the process it will bring healing and freedom in areas where your personal sins have hurt you, wounded others, and kept you bound in shame. Every sin that is not confessed and forgiven will continue to bring harm to yourself and others, while creating a barrier in your relationship with God. Releasing these sins in confession and receiving God's mercy will not only bring freedom but also further integrate you and foster healing in all your relationships, including in your relationship with God. "God is light, and in him there is no darkness at all. If we say, 'We have fellowship with him,' while we continue to walk in darkness, we lie and do not act in truth. But if we walk in the light as he is in the light, then we have fellowship with one another, and the blood of his Son Jesus cleanses us from all sin. If we say, 'We are without sin,' we deceive ourselves, and the truth is not in us. If we acknowledge our sins, he is faithful and just and will forgive our sins and cleanse us from every wrongdoing" (1 Jn 1:5–9).

- **Process:** A whole-life confession begins with a review of your entire life to examine any areas where you have acted in ways that have violated God's design for your sexual health. This may include grievous and obvious sins, as well as more subtle or hidden areas of sin, including your thoughts and fantasies. Go back through the list (in chapter 5) and identify which sins have already been confessed and which have not been. If you are making a sacramental Confession with a priest, you only need to name those sins that have not been confessed before. If, however, you are confessing with a friend, a spiritual director, a sponsor in a twelve-step program, or someone else you trust, I encourage you to go through the entire list of sins. In this case you might also include the sexual wounds that you received or inflicted on others, so you can see how all these are interconnected. Remember your goal is to grow in freedom and to experience healing, while also enhancing your communion with God and loved ones.

- **Examination of Conscience:** As you begin, ask the Holy Spirit to guide you in this process. Then review chapter 5 to help prompt your awareness. You may want to read through Leviticus 18, Matthew 5, 1 Corinthians 6 and 7, and similar passages in the Bible to educate yourself on God's moral law regarding sexuality. The following sections of the *Catechism* are a summation of various ways we can violate the sixth commandment (*CCC*, 2351–2359, 2380, 2384, 2388, 2399–2400). These are all offenses against sexual integrity and the gift of sexuality.

- **Writing:** Many of us are uncomfortable writing down our sexual sins. We may not want to look at them objectively, or may fear that others might find our list. While these are understandable reasons, I encourage you to push past these fears. It is important for you to see your sins objectively—and to have a memory guide for your confession. Write them on a piece of paper that you can keep to yourself. After confession, as a symbol of your sins being wiped away, go through a private ceremony of burning the paper with your sins on it. (For this and other reasons I would recommend you not write your list on your computer.)

- **Identifying the Consequences:** As you write down each area of sin, be as specific as possible: what you thought, what you did, when, and with whom. Then acknowledge how it affected you and your relationship with God, and everybody you hurt, directly or indirectly, by your actions. What wounds did your actions cause? What identity lies did you internalize? (See appendix 3.) This section can be especially healing (and challenging), facing the reality of how our actions have caused harm. This is deep heart surgery—and surgery can be painful before it brings healing. I encourage you to draw on the Holy Spirit for comfort and strength. As you go through this, avoid self-condemnation or blaming others. Simply pray and ask the Holy Spirit to guide you, while remembering the promises of redemption in Isaiah 61. As you persevere through this activity, Jesus will turn your mourning into joy and your shame into his glory.

- **Preparing for Confession:** I strongly encourage you to pray about the person you will share your list with during your time of confession. Whether it is a priest or someone else, discern someone you can trust and who will have the time, patience, and mercy to walk through it with you. Call them in advance to set up an appointment. Let them know what your desire is. If it is a nonsacramental confession, let them know you are not asking anything of them except to listen and pray for you while you share. If it is a sacramental confession, ask them if they want you to share your whole list or just those sins that have not been confessed before.

- **Confession and Thanksgiving:** When it is time for the confession, begin with prayer and invite the Holy Spirit to guide you. Don't be surprised if you have insights you didn't have until that moment. Regardless of how you feel, recognize that Christ is with you as you confess. Keep your focus on his love and mercy. If you confess in humility, he will forgive and cleanse you. Recognize the tremendous price he paid for your sin, and thank him. "Give thanks to the LORD, for he is good; his mercy endures forever" (Ps 118:1).

- **Healing of Shame:** In my experience, some people are liberated from the shame surrounding the sins once they are confessed, but others are not. If your shame and guilt are not completely released after confession, there are usually beliefs (identity lies and judgments) that are keeping you bound in shame. Ask the Holy Spirit to reveal the identity lies and judgments you are holding on to and where these are rooted. Appendices 2–4 may help uproot these remaining areas of shame and the identity lies surrounding them.

APPENDIX 2

GIVING AND RECEIVING FORGIVENESS

Healing occurs in our lives largely to the extent that we give and receive forgiveness. Forgiving and being forgiven go hand in hand. Jesus made it abundantly clear that our receiving forgiveness is contingent upon our offering others forgiveness when they offend us. In the Sermon on the Plain he said, "Be merciful just as your heavenly Father is merciful. Stop judging and you will not be judged. Stop condemning and you will not be condemned. Forgive and you will be forgiven. Give and gifts will be given to you; a good measure, packed together, shaken down, and overflowing, will be poured into your lap. For the measure with which you measure will in return be measured out to you" (Lk 6:36–38). Notice the last line. The measure we use in offering mercy and forgiveness is the measure with which we will receive God's mercy and forgiveness.

How do we understand this contingency in light of Jesus' forgiveness on the Cross, which was unconditional? The story of the unforgiving servant helps us understand. The servant was forgiven a large amount but refused to forgive his fellow servant a small amount (Mt 18:21–35). He was free when he was forgiven but then became imprisoned again by his unforgiveness. The *Catechism of the Catholic Church* explains: "Now—and this is daunting—this outpouring of mercy cannot penetrate our hearts as long as we have not forgiven those who have trespassed against us. . . . In refusing to forgive our brothers and sisters, our hearts are closed and their hardness makes them impervious to the Father's merciful love; but in confessing our sins, our hearts are opened to his grace" (*CCC*, 2840).

Continuing on, the *Catechism* explains: "It is there, in fact, 'in the depths of the heart,' that everything is bound and loosed. It is not in our power not to feel or to forget an offense; but the heart that offers itself to the Holy Spirit turns injury into compassion and purifies the memory in transforming the hurt into intercession" (*CCC*, 2843).

There are several key points in these passages that help us understand Jesus' teaching and our need to give and receive forgiveness.

1. Jesus fully reveals the Father's love and mercy. He has already forgiven us unconditionally on the Cross.

2. We receive his forgiveness when we acknowledge and confess our sins (see appendix 1). But we can't stop there.

3. We need to pass on the mercy we have received because, if we don't, we inevitably block our own capacity to receive God's mercy and compassion. This is sobering, isn't it? When we don't forgive ourselves or others, our hearts become hardened and we hinder our capacity to give and receive love.

Forgiving is not easy, or even fully possible, when we try to do it in our own strength. It requires God's mercy, grace, and truth working in and through us. But sometimes we can't even release our anger at God because of our perception of what he allowed to happen to us. Sometimes we can't forgive ourselves for the pain we have caused ourselves and others. And sometimes we can't forgive the people who have hurt us. This is especially true with our sexual wounds, such as in situations of sexual abuse, because these wounds are deeply personal and often affect us to the core of our being. It is not possible to forget these offenses, even if we have completely dissociated from the memory, because the effects of the trauma are held in our bodies and souls until we release them. The pain may be beyond our capacity to fully express it, and the impacts of the trauma can scar us for a lifetime. But even in horrible circumstances of abuse like Rita's and

Hank's stories (in chapters 6, 8, and 9), it is still necessary that we ask God for the grace to forgive him, ourselves, and our offenders. We also need to forgive anyone who didn't protect us from the violations we experienced.

The following prayer is one we have found to be extremely helpful (at John Paul II Healing Center) in working through the process of forgiveness, especially in areas we have been wounded deeply. It acknowledges the offense against us, as well as our pain, fear, and anger that we experience as a result of the offense. It also addresses the judgments that we hold, the unhealthy attachments that keep us bound, and the identity lies that bind us to our pain. After finding release and healing in those areas of our hearts, we become more capable of allowing the Holy Spirit to release our hearts in offering and receiving forgiveness. Spend as much time as you need in each step of the process.

Step-by-Step Forgiveness Prayer

1. Ask the Holy Spirit to show you who you need to forgive (could be family, friend, abuser, God, spouse, girlfriend, boyfriend, or yourself).

2. Picture the person in front of you, and pay attention to what you think and feel in their presence.

3. Think about what they did and how it affected you. How do you feel about it? Make note of what you are feeling and allow it to surface.

4. In your imagination tell them everything they did to hurt you and how it affected you.

5. Ask the Holy Spirit to reveal to you what you believe about yourself based on that incident. (It may be helpful to review the various *identity lies* in chapter 6.)

6. Renounce the identity lies (see appendix 3, "Renouncing Barriers to Healing").

7. Ask Jesus to reveal the truth about your identity (see appendix 4, "Healing Identity Wounds").

8. Ask the Holy Spirit to reveal to you the condemning judgments you hold toward yourself and the person who hurt you.

9. Renounce these judgments (see appendix 3, "Renouncing Barriers to Healing").

10. Renounce any unhealthy attachments between you and that person (see appendix 3, "Renouncing Barriers to Healing").

11. Bring that person to the foot of the Cross, and ask Jesus to forgive them (and you).

12. As you stand with the person at the foot of the Cross, turn to them and forgive them.

13. Pray blessing over the person and ask God to bless them in the opposite way they hurt you. Ask Jesus to heal both of you.

14. Thank Jesus for his forgiveness and healing.

APPENDIX 3

RENOUNCING BARRIERS TO HEALING

In chapter 8, we addressed various kinds of barriers to healing and then walked through specific prayers to release these barriers (in Steve's story). These barriers may include any of the following: unhealthy attachments (related to unholy soul ties), bitter-root judgments (related to unforgiveness), ungodly vows (related to self-protection); and identity lies (related to unhealed wounds). The following are short prayers that you can employ to release these barriers that bind you. They will enable you to receive God's love and healing graces.

Unhealthy Attachments (Unholy Soul Ties)

First pray and ask the Holy Spirit to reveal any unhealthy or unholy attachments in your life. These may involve sexual relationships outside of marriage (past or present) or images from pornography/and or fantasy. These may also involve emotional affairs. Consider too any unhealthy relationships where control, manipulation, or codependency replace genuine love with family members, friends, or community members. Additionally, any relationship where you have transgressed God's moral boundaries with another person (such as occult involvement or taking drugs together) can result in an unholy soul tie. Ask the Holy Spirit to give you the strength to release these attachments. If there are good aspects of your relationship, past or present, you will be renouncing not the person or relationship (say with a parent, spouse, or friend) but only the parts of the relationship that are unhealthy and against God's will. Pray:

> In the name of Jesus Christ, I renounce all unholy attachments with [name of person]. I take the sword of the Spirit, which is the word of God, and break and cut all unhealthy mental, emotional, physical, sexual, or spiritual ties with [name of person]. Lord, I ask you to forgive us both for sinning against you and each other. Please release us each to live in the freedom of the Holy Spirit.

Bitter-Root Judgments

Bitter-root judgments are the perceptions we form about others, ourselves, and God based on our past or present woundedness. These judgments are usually associated with unforgiveness and lead us to condemn ourselves or others. They are different from healthy judgments (discernments of right and wrong). When we hold bitter judgment toward a person or groups of people, ourselves, or even God, we develop a distorted image of them and lose sight of their inherent goodness. The following prayer can be used to release these judgments. You may pray it in relation to God, yourself, and others.

> Lord, I acknowledge my perceptions of [name of person] are not loving. [Name the specific judgments— and be real with the way you view this person in a negative light]. In the name of Jesus Christ, and by the power of his precious blood, I now renounce these judgments [name each judgment] toward [name of person]. I ask you now to free me to see [name of person] the way you see them and to bless them now. Please forgive me for holding this person in contempt and losing sight of their dignity.

Ungodly Vows

Ungodly vows are inner resolutions to protect and save ourselves out of fear and woundedness. These ungodly vows are very different from the holy vows we make in receiving the sacraments. They set our wills in a way that blocks the flow of God's grace. When we renounce them, we then invite the Holy Spirit to bring us into freedom to receive God's grace in that area of our life. The prayer is simple. The more challenging part is asking the Holy Spirit to show you where you have made ungodly vows. They are usually areas of repetitive struggle where you have tried to handle situations in your own strength. Start by praying to ask the Holy Spirit to reveal where you are bound by an ungodly vow. (These vows are often accompanied by a wound and bitter-root judgment.) When you become aware of a vow, ask for the strength and grace to release it. Pray:

> In the name of Jesus Christ, I renounce the vow that [name the vow, e.g., I will never be like my mother or father, I will protect myself, I will never trust a man or woman again, or I will please people so that I won't be rejected]. I ask you, Lord, to forgive me for relying on myself, and I now ask you to bring me into new freedom in the Holy Spirit.

Identity Lies and Wounds

In chapter 6 we identified a number of *identity lies* associated with the wounds of sexual abuse. These identity lies are prevalent in all kinds of psychosexual wounds. Ask the Holy Spirit to show you the specific wounds you have experienced (abandonment, rejection, fear, shame, powerlessness, hopelessness, and confusion) and the specific beliefs you have internalized as a result of those wounds. Appendix 4 will allow you to pray more deeply addressing the roots of these wounds and identity lies. But renouncing prayers can be helpful as an ongoing tool to gain freedom from the lies that continually plague us. The following is a general form of the prayer. Underneath are renouncing prayers for each wound and their identity lies.

> In the name of Jesus Christ, I renounce the lie that [e.g., I am alone, I'm not loved, I am not safe, I'm bad, I am trapped, things will never change, or I have to figure it out]. I announce the truth that [e.g., you (God) are with me, you love me unconditionally, you are my protector, you have made me good, you set me free, you are my hope, or you give me understanding].

- **Rejection:** In the name of Jesus Christ, I renounce the lie that I am unloved and unlovable. I renounce the lie that I am not wanted, desired, or good enough. In Jesus' name, I announce the truth that I am the Father's beloved (1 Jn 3:1). I am loved, valued, wanted, and cherished by God and others (Rom 8:31–39).

- **Abandonment:** In the name of Jesus Christ, I renounce the lie that I am alone, that no one understands me or cares for me. I renounce the lie that God has abandoned me. In Jesus' name, I announce the truth that Jesus is always with me (Mt 28:20). He will never leave or forsake me (Heb 13:5). I announce the truth that I am surrounded by a great cloud of witnesses (Heb 12:1).

- **Fear:** In the name of Jesus Christ, I renounce the lie that I am not safe, that I am unprotected, and that if I trust, I will be hurt, let down, or die. In Jesus' name I announce the truth that God is my rock, my fortress, my deliver, and my protector (Ps 23, 27, 91). I announce the truth that God's perfect love casts out all fear (1 Jn 4:18).

- **Shame:** In the name of Jesus Christ, I renounce the lie that I am bad, dirty, ugly, stupid, worthless, perverted . . . [fill in other beliefs based on shame]. In Jesus' name, I announce the truth that I am accepted, cherished, washed, cleansed, and restored in Christ (1 Cor 6). I announce the truth that Jesus does not come to condemn me (Jn 3:17–21).

- **Powerlessness:** In the name of Jesus Christ, I renounce the lie that I am powerless, weak, stuck, trapped, a victim, helpless, and so forth. In Jesus' name, I announce the truth that God's grace is made powerful in my weakness, so when I am weak, I am strong (2 Cor 12:8–10). I announce the truth that I can do all things through Christ who strengthens me (Phil 4:13).

- **Hopelessness:** In the name of Jesus Christ, I renounce the lie that nothing will ever change and I will never have what I want or need. I renounce the lie that life is meaningless and that I have nothing to live for. In Jesus' name, I announce the truth that my hope is steadfast and that he makes all things new (Rv 21:5). I announce the truth that God is at work in me and he will bring it to completion (Phil 1:6).

- **Confusion:** In the name of Jesus Christ, I renounce the lie that I have to figure everything out by myself and that nothing makes sense and everything is confusing. In Jesus' name, I announce the truth that I have the mind of Christ (1 Cor 2:16) and that the Holy Spirit will give me wisdom, understanding, and enlightenment when I ask (1 Cor 1:7; Jas 1:5).

APPENDIX 4

HEALING IDENTITY WOUNDS

Sexual violations and psychosexual deprivations impact us long after the traumatic events have passed. As we have discussed throughout this book, these wounds impact our identity and color our perceptions of life, ourselves, others, and God. Thus, they hinder our capacity to enjoy healthy and holy relationships. Time does not heal. Only God's merciful love and truth can heal us. We need psychological and spiritual healing in order to become integrated in our sexuality. Without seeking healing, we will allow our unresolved suffering to affect our lives and influence our relationships.

I have found the following prayer process to be invaluable for healing wounds and restoring sexual wholeness. The foundations for this type of prayer are explained in the *Catechism of the Catholic Church* in the section on meditative and contemplative prayer. Here are some key phrases that will help you prepare for this prayer experience:

- "According to Scripture, it is the *heart* that prays" (*CCC*, 2562).

- "Only the Spirit of God can fathom the human heart and know it fully" (*CCC*, 2563).

- "[The heart] is the place of encounter" (*CCC*, 2563).

- "[Jesus'] name is the only one that contains the presence it signifies" (*CCC*, 2666).

- "Meditation engages thought, imagination, emotion, and desire . . . but Christian prayer should go further: to the knowledge of the love of the Lord Jesus, to union with him" (*CCC*, 2708).

- "Contemplation is a *gaze* of faith, fixed on Jesus. . . . His gaze purifies our heart" (*CCC*, 2715).

- "Contemplative prayer is also the pre-eminently intense time of prayer. In it the Father strengthens our inner being with power through his Spirit 'that Christ may dwell in [our] hearts through faith' and we may be 'grounded in love'" (*CCC*, 2714).

As you enter into this prayer process, engage your thought, imagination, emotion, and desires. Keep your internal gaze fixed on Jesus. As you speak his name, you are invoking his presence. The goal is to invite his love and truth into the depths of your wounds and identity lies.[1]

1. Identify the area of sexual wounding where you desire healing. Ask the Holy Spirit to show you the specific experience of sexual wounding that needs to be healed (could be an area of sexual violation or psychosexual deprivation).

2. Don't try to figure out which memory or experience to focus on. Allow the Holy Spirit to reveal it to you. If there are multiple experiences that come to mind, see what they have in common.

3. Ask the Holy Spirit to reveal what you thought and felt before, during, and after the wounding experience. Ask him to reveal anything he wants you to know in the memory/experience.

4. Allow yourself to feel the emotions in the memory/experience, and as you do, ask the Holy Spirit to show you what you believe about yourself (identity lie) as a result of this experience. (Do you feel alone, rejected, afraid, unprotected, helpless, hopeless, confused, dirty, or ashamed?) What do you believe about yourself as you experience those feelings (see the identity lies in chapter 6)?

5. Ask Jesus to reveal his presence in the wounding experience. Wait on his response. Don't try to figure out where Jesus is or what he

might say or do. Allow him to reveal himself (his love and truth) to you in your inspired imagination. His revelation may come as an image, in words, or in feelings. You will know whether it is from him by the fruit of the Spirit and by the freedom he brings.

6. Stay in the memory until you experience everything he wants to reveal to you.

7. If you are not able to experience Jesus in the memory of the wounding experience, ask the Holy Spirit to show you whether there are any barriers. If barriers are identified, you may need to work through the prayers in appendices 2–3 (forgiving and renouncing).

8. Once you experience Jesus' presence, test the fruit in the memory/experience. See if you feel differently. Do you see yourself or the situation differently? Have your identity lies lost their power? Jesus won't change the objective reality, but his presence will change your subjective experience of the event (including your beliefs).

9. Test the healing in the wounding memory/experience by the following:

   • Do you feel connected and understood instead of alone?

   • Do you feel safe and protected instead of unprotected and afraid?

   • Do you feel loved and cared for rather than unloved?

   • Do you feel pure and worthy instead of dirty or ashamed?

   • Do you feel liberated and empowered rather than powerless?

   • Do you feel encouraged and hopeful rather than hopeless?

   • Do you feel enlightened and understanding rather than confused?

10. If you still have an experience of any of the unpleasant feelings/beliefs, apply the renouncing prayer in appendix 3 by renouncing the identity lies and announcing the truth.

11. Do you experience peace, joy, love, and compassion for yourself and anyone involved?

12. If you do not yet feel peace, revisit this prayer experience again.

13. Thank God for his love for you and his promise of healing. Ask him to seal it in Jesus' precious blood.

Once you have prayed through this process, it may be helpful to revisit Steve's healing experiences in chapter 8. I encourage you to incorporate this prayer process into your prayer routines.

APPENDIX 5

ADDITIONAL RESOURCES

The following resources are recommended for continuing your journey of sexual restoration.

John Paul II Healing Center (jpiihealingcenter.org)

Healing the Whole Person: conference and workbook
Holy Desire: conference and workbook
Restoring the Glory: conference and workbook
Undone: conference and workbook
Unveiled: conference and workbook

Daunt, Carrie Schuchts, ed. *Undone: Freeing Your Feminine Heart from the Knots of Fear and Shame*. Notre Dame, IN: Ave Maria Press, 2020. On authentic femininity (modeled after Blessed Mother Mary).

Daunt, Carrie, and Duane Daunt, eds. *Man Your Post: Learning to Live Like St. Joseph*. Charlotte, NC: St. Benedict Press, 2021. On authentic masculinity (modeled after St. Joseph).

Heidland, Miriam James. *Loved as I Am: An Invitation to Conversion, Healing, and Freedom through Jesus*. Notre Dame, IN: Ave Maria Press, 2014. On healing through Theology of the Body.

Schuchts, Bob. *Be Devoted: Restoring Friendship, Passion, and Communion in Your Marriage*. Notre Dame, IN: Ave Maria Press, 2020. On healing in marriage.

————. *Be Healed: A Guide to Encountering the Powerful Love of Jesus in Your Life*. Notre Dame, IN: Ave Maria Press, 2014.
On Jesus as our healer.
————. *Be Transformed: The Healing Power of the Sacraments*.
Notre Dame, IN: Ave Maria Press, 2017.
On healing power of sacraments.

Christ-Centered Therapy Organizations

American Association of Christian Counselors
Association of Christian Therapists
Catholic Psychotherapy Association

Christ-Centered Ministries Addressing Sexual Brokenness and Wholeness

The Allender Center
Celebrate Recovery
Courage and Encourage
Covenant Eyes
Desert Streams and Living Waters
Eden Invitation
Grief to Grace through Rachel's Vineyard
Heart of the Father
Integrity Restored
Reclaim Sexual Heath
Theology of the Body Institute

Recommended Books

Allender, Dan B. *Wounded Heart*. Colorado Springs: NavPress, 1995.
Dalbey, Gordon. *Healing the Masculine Soul: How God Restores Men to Real Manhood*. Nashville, TN: W Publishing Group, 2003.

Eldredge, John. *Wild at Heart: Discovering the Secret of a Man's Soul*. Nashville, TN: Thomas Nelson, 2010.

Eldredge, John, and Stasi Eldredge. *Captivating: Unveiling the Mystery of a Woman's Soul*. Nashville, TN: Nelson Books, 2005.

Fradd, Matt, and Jason Evert. *Forged: 33 Days toward Freedom*. Scottsdale, AZ: Totus Tuus Press, 2020.

Gress, Carrie. *The Anti-Mary Exposed: Rescuing the Culture from Toxic Femininity*. Charlotte, NC: Tan Books, 2019.

Hahn, Scott. *A Father Who Keeps His Promises: God's Covenant Love in Scripture*. Ann Arbor, MI: Charis, 1998.

Hathaway, Patricia Cooney, ed. *Sex and the Spiritual Life: Reclaiming Integrity, Wholeness, and Intimacy*. Notre Dame, IN: Ave Maria Press, 2020.

Healy, Mary. *Men and Women Are from Eden: A Study Guide to John Paul II's Theology of the Body*. Cincinnati: Servant Books, 2005.

Hébert, Alan A., ed. *Abuse of Trust: Healing from Clerical Sexual Abuse*. Round Rock, TX: Broussard Press, 2019.

John Paul II. *Man and Woman He Created Them: A Theology of the Body*. Boston: Pauline Books & Media, 2006.

Lozano, Neal. *Unbound: A Practical Guide to Deliverance*. Grand Rapids, MI: Chosen, 2010.

Payne, Leanne. *The Broken Image: Restoring Personal Wholeness through Healing Prayer*. Grand Rapids, MI: Hamewith Books, 1996.

———. *Crisis in Masculinity*. Grand Rapids, MI: Baker Books, 1995.

Spaedy, Elza. *Freedom through Christ: A Memoir of Healing in the Aftermath of Sexual Abuse*. Gastonia, NC: TAN Books, 2020.

Stringer, Jay. *Unwanted: How Sexual Brokenness Reveals Our Way to Healing*. Colorado Springs: NavPress, 2018.

Watson, William M. *Whole-Life Confession: Four Weeks of Awakening to Mercy, Healing and Peace*. Seattle: Sacred Story Press, 2016.

Weiss, Douglas. *The Final Freedom: Pioneering Sexual Addiction Recovery*. Fort Worth, TX: Discovery Press, 1998.

West, Christopher. *Theology of the Body Explained: A Commentary on John Paul II's Man and Woman He Created Them*. Boston: Pauline Books & Media, 2007.

Willingham, Russell. *Breaking Free: Understanding Sexual Addiction and the Healing Power of Jesus*. Downers Grove, IL: InterVarsity Press, 1999.

Podcasts

Abiding Together with Sr. Miriam James Heidland, Heather Khym, and Michelle Benzinger

FM with Fr. Mark Toups

Lust Is Boring with Jason Evert

Restore the Glory with Jake Khym and Bob Schuchts

Documentary Movie

Eric Esau, dir. *The Heart of Man*. Produced by Jason Pamer and Jens Jacob. Written by Eric Esau and Jason Pamer. Granite Bay, CA: Ocean Avenue Entertainment, 2019.

NOTES

Introduction

1. Curt Thompson, *The Soul of Shame* (Downers Grove, IL: InterVarsity Press, 2015), 177.

2. Thompson, *Soul of Shame*, 171.

1. Shining Light in the Darkness

1. Throughout the book I have changed the names and some particular descriptions to maintain the confidentiality of the people mentioned.

2. Juli Slattery, *Rethinking Sexuality: God's Design and Why It Matters* (Colorado Springs: Multnomah, 2018), 6.

3. Slattery, *Rethinking Sexuality*, 79.

4. Christopher McCluskey and Rachel McCluskey, *When Two Become One: Enhancing Sexual Intimacy in Marriage* (Grand Rapids, MI: Baker, 2006), 27.

5. Mauro Piacenza, "Priestly Chastity," *Clerus*, November 26, 2011, 1.

6. See Kenneth M. Adams, *Silently Seduced: When Parents Make Their Children Partners* (Deerfield Beach, FL: Health Communications, 2011).

7. Dan B. Allender, *The Wounded Heart* (Colorado Springs: NavPress, 1995), 34.

8. See Jay Stringer, *Unwanted: How Sexual Brokenness Reveals Our Way to Healing* (Colorado Springs: NavPress, 2018), 23–24.

2. Living the Truth in Love

1. James G. Friesen, E. James Wilder, Anne M. Bierling, Rick Koepcke, and Maribeth Poole, *The Life Model: Living from the Heart Jesus Gave You* (Pasadena, CA: Shepherd's House, 2010).

2. Friesen et al., *Life Model*, 69.

3. Second Vatican Council, *Gaudium et Spes* (On the Church in the Modern World), 22, Holy See, December 7, 1965, http://www.vatican.va.

4. John Paul II, *Letter to Families*, 79–81, Holy See, February 2, 1994, http://www.vatican.va.

5. For more on security, maturity, and purity, see my book *Be Healed: A Guide to Encountering the Powerful Love of Jesus in Your Life* (Notre Dame, IN: Ave Maria Press, 2014), 89–91, and chapter 10 of this book.

6. This table has developed over many years of teaching classes and giving conferences on human development, family relations, sexuality, and healing,

as well as years of working as a therapist and seeing how it naturally unfolds in the lives of individual people. There are many contributors over the years, including several textbooks on child, adolescent, and life-span development. Notable influences include Erik Erikson, *Identity and the Life Cycle*; Friesen et al., *Life Model*; John Paul II, *Man and Woman He Created Them*; Mary Healy, *Men and Woman Are from Eden*; Christopher West, *Created and Redeemed* (CD set); Leanne Payne, *The Broken Image* and *Crisis in Masculinity*; Andrew Comiskey, *Pursuing Sexual Wholeness*; Gordon Dalbey, *Sons of the Father* and *Healing the Masculine Soul*; Alan Medinger, *Growth into Manhood*; John Eldredge, *Wild at Heart*; John and Stasi Eldredge, *Captivating*; and Jack Frost, *Experiencing the Father's Embrace*.

7. Friesen et al., *Life Model*, 22.

8. Dennis Linn, Sheila Fabricant Linn, and Matthew Linn, *Belonging: Bonds of Healing and Recovery* (New York: Paulist Press, 1993), 89–90.

9. John Bowlby, *A Secure Base* (New York: Basic Books, 1988); Amy Van Buren and Eileen L. Cooley, "Attachment Styles, View of Self and Negative Affect," *North American Journal of Psychology* 4, no. 3 (December 2002): 417–30.

10. See the story of John in Schuchts, *Be Healed*, chap. 7; and Andrew Comiskey, *Pursuing Sexual Wholeness* (Santa Monica, CA: Desert Stream Ministries, 1988).

11. Comiskey, *Pursuing Sexual Wholeness*, 47.

12. Leanne Payne, *The Broken Image: Restoring Personal Wholeness through Healing Prayer* (Grand Rapids, MI: Hamewith Books, 1996), 39.

13. Comiskey, *Pursuing Sexual Wholeness*, 47.

14. See Rick Fitzgibbons, "Appendix I: The Origins and Healing of Homosexual Attractions and Behaviors," in *The Truth About Homosexuality: The Cry of the Faithful*, by John F. Harvey, 307–44 (San Francisco: Ignatius Press, 1996).

15. Comiskey, *Pursuing Sexual Wholeness*, 213.

16. Payne, *Broken Image*, 39–40.

17. John Paul II, *Man and Woman He Created Them: A Theology of the Body* (Boston: Pauline Books & Media, 2006), 57:3.

18. John Paul II, *Man and Woman He Created Them*, 43:2.

19. Paul IV, *Humanae Vitae* (On the Regulation of Birth), 9, Holy See, July 25, 1968, http://www.vatican.va.

20. Christopher McCluskey and Rachel McCluskey, *When Two Become One: Enhancing Sexual Intimacy in Marriage* (Grand Rapids, MI: Baker, 2006),

21. See my book *Be Devoted: Restoring Friendship, Passion, and Communion in Your Marriage* (Notre Dame, IN: Ave Maria Press, 2020) for an extensive treatment of marital love and healing.

22. Daniel Keating, "Growing in Sexual Integrity as a Consecrated Man," in *Sex and the Spiritual Life: Reclaiming Integrity, Wholeness, and Intimacy*, ed. Patricia Cooney Hathaway, (Notre Dame, IN: Ave Maria Press, 2020), 106, 108.

23. Susan Muto, "Sexuality, Spirituality, and the Single Life," in Hathaway, *Sex and the Spiritual Life*, 69–82, 73.

24. Sara Fairbanks, "Love and Intimacy as a Religious Sister," in Hathaway, *Sex and the Spiritual Life*, 119–32, 121.

25. Adela Galindo, "Manifestations of God's Love to the World," 8, Servants of the Pierced Hearts of Jesus and Mary, February 2003, https://pierced-hearts.org.

3. Reflecting God's Image

1. Alan P. Medinger, *Growth into Manhood: Resuming the Journey* (Colorado Springs: Waterbrook Press, 2000); John Eldredge, *Wild at Heart: Discovering the Secret of a Man's Soul* (Nashville, TN: Thomas Nelson, 2010).

2. Andrew Comiskey, *Pursuing Sexual Wholeness* (Santa Monica, CA: Desert Stream Ministries, 1988), 47–48; George Alan Rekers, *Shaping Your Child's Sexual Identity* (Grand Rapids, MI: Baker Book House, 1982), 39.

3. See Ryan T. Anderson, *When Harry Became Sally: Responding to the Transgender Moment* (New York: Encounter Books, 2018); Kristen Rogers, "Gender Identity: The Difference between Gender, Sex and Other Need-to-Knows," CNN, June 10, 2020, https://www.cnn.com/2020/06/10/health/gender-identity-explainer-wellness/index.html.

4. Lawrence S. Mayer and Paul R. McHugh, "Part One: Sexual Orientation," in "Sexuality and Gender: Findings from the Biological, Psychological, and Social Sciences," *New Atlantis: A Journal of Technology and Science* 50 (Fall 2016): 13–58; Anderson, *When Harry Became Sally*.

5. "What Is Gender Dysphoria?" American Psychiatric Association, accessed March 11, 2021, https://www.psychiatry.org/patients-families/gender-dysphoria/what-is-gender-dysphoria.

6. See Walt Heyer, "Hormones, Surgery, Regret: I Was a Transgender Woman for 8 Years—Time I Can't Get Back," *USA Today*, February 11, 2019. See also Walt's website: https://waltheyer.com.

7. Dan Kogut, "Pastoral Letter to Parents regarding Gender Theory," Renewal Ministries, November 2, 2019, https://www.renewalministries.net/wordpress/author/fr-dan-kogut/.

8. See James Keating, "Christ Is the Sure Foundation: Priestly Human Formation Completed in and by Spiritual Formation," *Nova et Vetera* (English ed.) 8, no. 4 (2010): 883–89. https://priestlyformation.org/site_files/PDFs/Faculty%20Articles/Deacon%20Keating/Keating-Christ-is-the-Sure-Foundation-Nova-et-Vetera.pdf

9. See Gordon Dalbey, *Healing the Masculine Soul: How God Restores Men to Real Manhood* (Nashville, TN: W Publishing Group, 2003); Leanne Payne, *Crisis in Masculinity* (Grand Rapids, MI: Baker Books, 1995).

10. John Eldredge and Stasi Eldredge, *Captivating: Unveiling the Mystery of a Woman's Soul* (Nashville, TN: Nelson Books, 2005); Leanne Payne, *The*

Broken Image: Restoring Personal Wholeness through Healing Prayer (Grand Rapids, MI: Hamewith Books, 1996).

11. See Congregation for Catholic Education for Educational Institutions, *Male and Female He Created Them: Toward a Path of Dialogue on the Question of Gender Theory in Education* (London: Catholic Truth Society, 2019).

12. Walter Schu, *The Splendor of Love: John Paul II's Vision for Marriage and Family* (New Hope, KY: New Hope Publications, 2003), 40.

13. Mayer and McHugh, "Part One."

14. Schu, *Splendor of Love*, 40.

15. Mayer and McHugh, "Part One."

16. Anderson, *When Harry Became Sally*, 2.

17. John Paul II, *Man and Woman He Created Them: A Theology of the Body* (Boston: Pauline Books & Media, 2006).

18. Jonathan Merritt, "Moving beyond Gender Stereotypes: An Interview with Larry Crabb," Religious News Service, July 24, 2013, https://religionnews.com/2013/07/24/moving-beyond-gender-stereotypes-an-interview-with-larry-crabb/.

19. See Donald Calloway, *Consecration to St. Joseph: The Wonders of Our Spiritual Father*, (Stockbridge, MA: Marian Press, 2020); and Carrie Daunt and Duane Daunt, eds., *Man Your Post: Learning to Live Like St. Joseph* (Charlotte, NC: St. Benedict Press, 2021).

20. See Colossians 1, John 15, Ephesians 5, and Luke 22:18–20.

21. Craig S. Hill, *The Power of a Parent's Blessing* (Lake Mary, FL: Charisma House, 2013).

22. Jason Evert, *Theology of His Body: Discovering the Strength and Mission of Masculinity* (West Chester, PA: Ascension Press, 2009); Dalbey, *Healing the Masculine Soul*.

23. Eldredge, *Wild at Heart*, 67.

24. John Paul II, *Mulieris Dignitatem* (On the Dignity and Vocation of Women), 10, Holy See, August 15, 1988, http://www.vatican.va.

25. John Paul II, *Mulieris Dignitatem*, 10.

26. Merritt, "Moving beyond Gender Stereotypes."

27. Jason Evert, *Theology of Her Body: Discovering the Beauty and Mystery of Femininity* (West Chester, PA: Ascension Press, 2009).

28. John Paul II, *Letter to Families*, 79–81, Holy See, February 2, 1994, http://www.vatican.va.

29. Leanne Payne, *The Healing Presence: Curing the Soul through Union with Christ* (Grand Rapids, MI: Baker Books, 1995), 233; Bob Schuchts, *Restoring the Glory: Workbook and Journal* 3rd edition (Tallahassee, FL: John Paul II Healing Center, 2020), 76–77.

30. See Carrie Gress, *The Anti-Mary Exposed: Rescuing the Culture from Toxic Femininity* (Charlotte, NC: Tan Books, 2019), 29–44.

31. Eldredge and Eldredge, *Captivating*, 53.

32. Edith Stein, *Essays on Woman*, (Washington D.C., ICS Publishing, 2nd Ed. Rev. 1996), 48, 198.

4. Lured by Desires

1. Jay Stringer, *Unwanted: How Sexual Brokenness Reveals Our Way to Healing* (Colorado Springs: NavPress, 2018), 44.

2. Stringer, *Unwanted*, 35.

3. John Paul II, *Man and Woman He Created Them: A Theology of the Body* (Boston: Pauline Books & Media, 2006), 28:5.

4. Karol Wojtyla, *Love and Responsibility*, trans. Grzegorz Ignatik (Boston: Pauline Books, 2013); Christopher West, *A Crash Course in the Theology of the Body: Naked without Shame*, 2nd ed. study guide (Milwaukee, WI: Ascension Press, 2009), 25.

5. See Patrick Carnes, *Out of the Shadows: Understanding Sexual Addiction*, 3rd ed. (Center City, MN: Hazelden Information and Education, 2001); Douglas Weiss, *The Final Freedom: Pioneering Sexual Addiction Recovery* (Fort Worth, TX: Discovery Press, 1998); and Dean Byrd, "Obsessive Thoughts and Compulsive Behaviors," presentation at the 2002 NARTH Conference; see also Bruce Hannemann and Jeannie Hannemann, Reclaim Sexual Health, accessed March 15, 2021, http://www.reclaimsexualhealth.com.

6. See Hannemann and Hannemann, Reclaim Sexual Health; and Pascal-Emmanuel Gobry, "A Science-Based Case for Ending the Porn Epidemic," American Greatness, December 15, 2019, https://amgreatness.com/2019/12/15/a-science-based-case-for-ending-the-porn-epidemic/.

7. See Carnes, *Out of the Shadows*; Stringer, *Unwanted*; Weiss, *Final Freedom*; Leanne Payne, *The Broken Image: Restoring Personal Wholeness through Healing Prayer* (Grand Rapids, MI: Hamewith Books, 1996),; Mark R. Laaser, *Healing the Wounds of Sexual Addiction* (Grand Rapids, MI: Zondervan, 2004); Russell Willingham, *Breaking Free: Understanding Sexual Addiction and the Healing Power of Jesus* (Downers Grove, IL: InterVarsity Press, 1999); Matt Fradd, *Delivered: True Stories of Men and Women Who Turned from Porn to Purity* (San Diego: Catholic Answers Press, 2013); Karin Cooke, *Dangerous Honesty* (Bowburn, UK: Naked Truth Resources, 2015); Andrew Comiskey, *Pursuing Sexual Wholeness* (Santa Monica, CA: Desert Stream Ministries, 1988)

8. Steve's story is drawn from my *Holy Desire: The Path to Freedom* workbook (Tallahassee, FL: John Paul II Healing Center), www.jpiihealingcenter.org. Steve's name and some details of his story have been changed to ensure anonymity.

9. Andrew Comiskey, Desert Streams Ministry, http://www.desertstream.org.

10. Andrew Comiskey, *Pursuing Sexual Wholeness: Workbook* (Lake Mary, Florida: Siloam Charisma Media, 1989), 47–48.

11. C. S. Lewis, quoted in Payne, *Broken Image*, 81–82.

12. See Rick Fitzgibbons, "Appendix I: The Origins and Healing of Homosexual Attractions and Behaviors," in The Truth About Homosexuality: The Cry of the Faithful, by John F. Harvey, 307–44 (San Francisco: Ignatius Press, 1996)

13. Medinger, *Growth into Manhood: Resuming the Journey* (Colorado Springs: Waterbrook Press, 2000), 17–18.

14. David Kyle Foster, *Sexual Healing* (Ventura, CA: Regal Books, 2005), 90.

15. Cooke, *Dangerous Honesty*, 19–20.

16. Cooke, *Dangerous Honesty*, 19–20.

17. Cooke, *Dangerous Honesty*, 18.

18. Stringer, *Unwanted*, 121.

19. Comiskey, *Pursuing Sexual Wholeness*, 49.

20. Fradd, *Delivered*, 104.

21. Suzana Rose, "Lesbian Violence Fact Sheet," National Violence against Women Prevention Research Center, 2000, accessed March 12, 2021, https://mainweb-v.musc.edu/vawprevention/lesbianrx/factsheet.shtml; Luca Rollè et al., "When Intimate Partner Violence Meets Same Sex Couples: A Review of Same Sex Intimate Partner Violence," *Frontiers in Psychology*, August 21, 2018, https://www.frontiersin.org.

22. Payne, *Broken Image*, 25–26, 89–96.

5. Crushed by Iniquities

1. This material is from a talk that Dr. Fraser gave at the Catholic Virtual Conference in October 2020.

2. For scripture sources, see Leviticus 18, Matthew 5, Romans 1, 1 Corinthians 6 and 7, and Revelation 21:8.

3. C. S. Lewis, *Mere Christianity*, 92.

4. Andy Reese, *Sozo Training Manual*, 26.

5. Bob Schuchts, *Be Transformed: The Healing Power of the Sacraments* (Notre Dame, IN: Ave Maria Press, 2017), chap. 8.

6. David Kyle Foster, *Sexual Healing* (Ventura, CA: Regal Books, 2005), 164.

7. Raniero Cantalamessa, *The Fire of Christ's Love: Meditations on the Cross* (Frederick, MD: Word Among Us Press, 2013), 104.

8. Christopher McCluskey and Rachel McCluskey, *When Two Become One: Enhancing Sexual Intimacy in Marriage* (Grand Rapids, MI: Baker, 2006),

9. McCluskey and McCluskey, *When Two Become One*, 50.

6. Mourning Broken Hearts

1. I introduce the "seven deadly wounds" in my earlier books, *Be Healed* and *Be Transformed*. They are derived from a list of eight wounds identified by

Dr. Edward M. Smith, in *Beyond Tolerable Recovery: Moving beyond Tolerable Existence into Biblical Maintenance Free Victory*, 4th ed. (Campbellsville, KY: Family Care, 2000). Smith identifies an eighth wound: "tarnished," which is a variant of shame inherent in sexual violation.

2. See Bob Schuchts, *Be Healed: A Guide to Encountering the Powerful Love of Jesus in Your Life* (Notre Dame, IN: Ave Maria Press, 2014),, chap. 7; Smith, *Beyond Tolerable Recovery*, appendix.

3. See Bob Schuchts *Be Transformed: The Healing Power of the Sacraments* (Notre Dame, IN: Ave Maria Press, 2017), chaps. 3–9.

4. Cynthia Kubetin and James Mallory, *Shelter from the Storm: Hope for Survivors of Sexual Abuse* (Nashville, TN: Lifeway, 1995), 26–27.

5. Dan B. Allender, *The Wounded Heart* (Colorado Springs: NavPress, 1995),

6. See Allen A. Hébert, *Abuse of Trust: Healing from Clerical Sexual Abuse* (Round Rock, TX: Broussard Press, 2019), 60.

7. Allender, *Wounded Heart*, 75.

8. Hébert, *Abuse of Trust*, 15.

9. Bessel A. van der Kolk, *The Body Keeps the Score: Brain, Mind, and Body in the Healing of Trauma* (New York: Viking, 2014), 123.

10. Van der Kolk, *Body Keeps the Score*, 123.

11. Van der Kolk, *Body Keeps the Score*, 66.

12. Allender, *Wounded Heart*, 74.

13. Van der Kolk, *Body Keeps the Score*, 1–2.

14. See Elza Spaedy, *Freedom through Christ: A Memoir of Healing in the Aftermath of Sexual Abuse* (Gastonia, NC: TAN Books, 2020), 14–16.

15. See Hank's story in Schuchts, *Be Transformed*, chap. 8.

Part II. Restoring Sexual Wholeness

1. This prayer is a modified version of one written by Allen Hébert after he read the manuscript for this book prior to publication. He is the author of *Abuse of Trust*, a book of testimonies by those traumatized as a result clergy sexual abuse.

7. Anointed by the Spirit

1. See John Paul II, *Crossing the Threshold of Hope*, ed. Vittorio Messori, trans. Jenny McPhee and Martha McPhee (New York: Knopf, 1994), 228; Dain Scherber, *The Primordial Father Wound: And the Glorious Freedom of the Children of God* (self-pub., 2019); and Mark C. Priessner, *Will the Real Father Please Stand Up* (self-pub., Createspace, 2017).

2. See Bob Schuchts, *Healing the Whole Person: Workbook and Journal* 3rd edition (Tallahassee, FL: John Paul II Healing Center 2021), 4; Dictionary.com, s.v. "salvation," accessed March 15, 2021, https://www.dictionary.com; Thesaurus.com, s.v. "salvation," accessed March 15, 2021, https://www.thesaurus.com.

3. Emiliano Tardif, with José H. Prado Flores, *Jesus Lives Today!* (South Bend, IN: Greenlawn Press, 1989), 56.

4. I address these issues more expansively in *Be Healed* and *Be Devoted.*

5. To learn more about whole-life Confessions, see William M. Watson, *The Whole-Life Confession: Four Weeks of Awakening to Mercy, Healing and Peace* (Seattle: Sacred Story Press, 2016). You may also want to approach it as a fourth-step activity in the twelve-step recovery process for addictions.

6. For more about Christ Renews His Parish, contact the national organization through Dynamic Catholic. For more about Family Reconstruction, see "What Is Family Reconstruction?," Life Story Healing, accessed March 15, 2021, https://www.lifestoryhealing.com.

7. See my books *Be Healed: A Guide to Encountering the Powerful Love of Jesus in Your Life* (Notre Dame, IN: Ave Maria Press, 2014); *Real Suffering: Finding Hope and Healing in the Trials of Life* (Charlotte, NC: St. Benedict Press, 2018); and *Be Devoted: Restoring Friendship, Passion, and Communion in Your Marriage* (Notre Dame, IN: Ave Maria Press, 2020).

8. Beauty Instead of Ashes

1. See Jay Stringer, *Unwanted: How Sexual Brokenness Reveals Our Way to Healing* (Colorado Springs: NavPress, 2018), for a more detailed discussion of how pornographic images reveal our wounds.

2. See Stringer, *Unwanted*, 44.

3. Repenting is the first step in a three-step process—repent, renounce, and receive—discussed by Catholic therapist Jake Khym on our *Restore the Glory* podcast ("Episode 11: Faith or Fear: Part 3," September 2, 2020, https://www.restoretheglorypodcast.com). It is also presented in a slightly different form in the work of Bruce and Jeannie Hannemann on the Reclaim Sexual Health website as a way to combat sexual compulsions; in William M. Watson, *Forty Weeks: A Journey of Healing and Transformation for Priests* (Seattle: Sacred Story Press, 2018); and in Neal Lozano, *Unbound: A Practical Guide to Deliverance* (Grand Rapids, MI: Chosen, 2010).

4. Jack Wellman, "What Is Repentance? Bible Definition of Repent and Repentance," *Christian Crier* (blog), May 29, 2014, https://www.patheos.com/blogs/christiancrier/2014/05/29/what-is-repentance-bible-definition-of-repent-and-repentance.

5. See Robert Cardinal Sarah, with Nicolas Diat, *The Day Is Now Far Spent*, trans. Michael Miller (San Francisco: Ignatius Press, 2019), 51.

6. Russell Willingham, *Breaking Free: Understanding Sexual Addiction and the Healing Power of Jesus* (Downers Grove, IL: InterVarsity Press, 1999),

7. John Paul II, *Man and Woman He Created Them: A Theology of the Body* (Boston: Pauline Books & Media, 2006).

8. For more on renouncing the "Seven Deadly Wounds" and "Identity Lies," see appendix 3.

9. See John Eldredge, *Waking the Dead: The Secret to a Heart Fully Alive* (Nashville, TN: Nelson Books, 2016), 152, for a discussion on how our agreements keep us bound.

10. See Lozano, *Unbound*, 49–54.

11. John Sandford and Paula Sandford, *The Transformation of the Inner Man* (South Plainfield, NJ: Bridge Publications, 1982), 193.

9. Joy Instead of Mourning

1. See Dan B. Allender, *The Wounded Heart* (Colorado Springs: NavPress, 1995), 20.

2. See Michael Scanlan, *Inner Healing: Ministering to the Human Spirit through the Power of Prayer* (New York: Paulist Press, 1974), 50.

3. Bessel A. van der Kolk, *The Body Keeps the Score: Brain, Mind, and Body in the Healing of Trauma* (New York: Viking, 2014), 121–22.

4. See Schuchts, *Be Healed: A Guide to Encountering the Powerful Love of Jesus in Your Life* (Notre Dame, IN: Ave Maria Press, 2014),, chaps. 8 and 10.

5. Payne, *Broken Image*, 89–91.

6. Robert Barron, "Joy for the Brokenhearted" (Sunday sermon), Word on Fire, December 12, 2020, https://www.wofdigital.org.

7. Leanne Payne, *The Broken Image: Restoring Personal Wholeness through Healing Prayer* (Grand Rapids, MI: Hamewith Books, 1996), 54.

8. Elisabeth Kübler-Ross, *On Death and Dying* (New York: Collier Books, 1993).

9. Andrew Comiskey, *Pursuing Sexual Wholeness* (Santa Monica, CA: Desert Stream Ministries, 1989 ed.), 120.

10. Comiskey, *Pursuing Sexual Wholeness*, 120.

10. Oaks of Righteousness

1. John Riccardo, "Foreword: Sexual Integrity Is for Everyone," in *Sex and the Spiritual Life: Reclaiming Integrity, Wholeness, and Intimacy*, ed. Patricia Cooney Hathaway (Notre Dame, IN: Ave Maria Press, 2020), ix–xx, xi.

2. Janet E. Smith, "What Is Sexual Integrity?" in Hathaway, *Sex and the Spiritual Life*, 1–16, 3, 5.

3. See Bob Schuchts, *Restoring the Glory: Workbook and Journal* (Tallahassee, FL: John Paul II Healing Center),, 75–76; Carrie Gress, *The Anti-Mary Exposed: Rescuing the Culture from Toxic Femininity* (Charlotte, NC: Tan Books, 2019), 29–44; Leanne Payne, *The Healing Presence: Curing the Soul through Union with Christ* (Grand Rapids, MI: Baker Books, 1995), 231–36.

4. James G. Friesen, E. James Wilder, Anne M. Bierling, Rick Koepcke, and Maribeth Poole, *The Life Model: Living from the Heart Jesus Gave You* (Pasadena, CA: Shepherd's House, 2010), 31.

5. Sara Fairbanks, "Love and Intimacy as a Religious Sister," in Hathaway, *Sex and the Spiritual Life*, 129–30.

6. Friesen et al., *Life Model*, 29.

7. Benedict XVI, *Deus Caritas Est* (God Is Love), 17, Holy See, December 25, 2005, http://www.vatican.va.

8. Dawn Eden, *My Peace I Give You: Healing Sexual Wounds with the Help of the Saints* (Notre Dame, IN: Ave Maria Press, 2012).

9. Larry Crabb and Dwight Edwards, "The Power of Connecting Conference Workbook" (Dallas, TX, 1998), 2.

10. Friesen et al., *Life Model*, 47.

11. Friesen et al., *Life Model*, 6.

12. Many people have not become fully sexually integrated and pure before death. This is the reason the Church teaches the necessity for purgatory for believers; we need to be cleansed of all impurity to share in the purest love of heaven.

13. Pontifical Council for the Family, "The Truth and Meaning of Human Sexuality," 17, Holy See, December 8, 1995, http://www.vatican.va.

14. Jeff Jay, "Sexual Integrity and the Challenge of Addiction," in Hathaway, *Sex and the Spiritual Life*, 31–50, 33.

15. Russell Willingham, *Breaking Free: Understanding Sexual Addiction and the Healing Power of Jesus* (Downers Grove, IL: InterVarsity Press, 1999), 126.

16. Daniel Keating, "Growing in Sexual Integrity as a Consecrated Man," in Hathaway, *Sex and the Spiritual Life*, 111.

17. Payne, *Healing Presence*, 82.

18. Benedict XVI, *Spe Salvi* (On Christian Hope), 47, Holy See, November 30, 2007, http://www.vatican.va.

19. Robert A. Schuchts, "Security, Maturity, and Purity: Foundations for Chaste Celibacy," in *Chaste Celibacy: Living Christ's Own Spousal Love*, ed. Edward G. Mathews Jr. (Omaha, NE: Institute for Priestly Formation, 2007), 71–81.

Appendix 4. Healing Identity Wounds

1. For more on this, see Bob Schuchts, *Healing the Whole Person: Workbook and Journal* (Tallahassee, FL: John Paul II Healing Center), and talks at jpiihealingcenter.org.

Bob Schuchts is the bestselling author of *Be Healed*, *Be Transformed*, and *Be Devoted*. He is the founder of the John Paul II Healing Center in Tallahassee, Florida, and cohost of the *Restore the Glory* podcast with Jake Khym.

After receiving his doctorate in family relations from Florida State University in 1981, Schuchts became a teacher and counselor. While in private practice, he also taught graduate and undergraduate courses at Florida State and Tallahassee Community College. Schuchts later served on faculty at the Theology of the Body Institute and at the Center for Biblical Studies—where he taught courses on healing, sexuality, and marriage—and was a guest instructor for the Augustine Institute. He volunteered in parish ministry for more than thirty years.

He retired as a marriage and family therapist in December 2014.

Schuchts has two daughters and eight grandchildren. His wife, Margie, died in 2017.

jpiihealingcenter.org
www.restoretheglorypodcast.com
Twitter: @JPIIHealing
Facebook: JP2HealingCenter

Sr. Miriam James Heidland, S.O.L.T., is a Catholic speaker, podcaster, and the author of *Loved as I Am*.

Very Rev. Mark Toups, V.G., is vicar general of the Diocese of Houma-Thibodaux and pastor of Our Lady of the Isle Catholic Church in Grand Isle, Louisiana.

MORE BOOKS BY
BOB SCHUCHTS

Be Healed
A Guide to Encountering the Powerful Love
of Jesus in Your Life

Do you suffer from spiritual or emotional wounds that are keeping you from reaching that goal? The bestselling book *Be Healed* is based on Bob Schuchts's popular program for spiritual, emotional, and physical healing. Incorporating elements of charismatic spirituality and steeped in scripture and the wisdom of the Church, this book offers hope in the healing power of God through the Holy Spirit and the sacraments.

ALSO AVAILABLE IN SPANISH!

Be Transformed
The Healing Power of the Sacraments

Whether it is the wounds of past hurts, the strains in our relationships, or the stresses of daily life, we all need to be comforted and made whole by Christ. Bob Schuchts guides you to tap into the power of Christ present in the sacraments and to experience the ongoing effects of their graces in every aspect of your life.

Be Devoted
Restoring Friendship, Passion, and Communion
in Your Marriage

In *Be Devoted*, Bob Schuchts presents his first resource for married and engaged couples and those who desire true love in their relationships. This guide delivers sound Catholic teaching, rich storytelling, and practical tools for healing, along with psychological insights and expertise to help couples create a relationship that is rich in trust, passion, and unity.